HOW TO LOOK AT ART

SUSIE HODGE

First published 2014 by order of the Tate Trustees
by Tate Publishing, a division of Tate Enterprises Ltd,
Millbank, London SW1P 4RG
www.tate.org.uk/publishing

A catalogue record for this book is available from the British Library
ISBN 978 1 84976 223 6
Distributed in the United States and Canada by ABRAMS, New York
Library of Congress Control Number: 2013949980

Designed by Untitled
Colour reproduction by Evergreen Colour Management Ltd. Hong Kong
Printed in China by Toppan Leefung

Front cover, top to bottom: Pablo Picasso, *Weeping Woman* 1937 (see p.43); Cerith Wyn Evans, *Inverse Reverse Perverse* 1996 (see p.113); William Blake, *Pity* c.1795 (see p.7); Auguste Rodin, *The Kiss* 1901–4 (see p.57)
Back cover, clockwise from top left: Edgar Degas, *Little Dancer Aged Fourteen* 1880–1 (see p.56); George Stubbs, *Mares and Foals in a River Landscape* c.1763–8 (see p.90); David Bomberg, *In the Hold* c.1913–14 (see p.115); Giorgio de Chirico, *The Uncertainty of the Poet* 1913 (see p.114); Jacob Epstein, *Torso in Metal from 'The Rock Drill'* 1913–14 (see p.58)

Measurements of artworks are given in centimetres, height before width and depth

Photo credits
All photograhs of the works © Tate Photography unless stated otherwise
Museo Archeologico Nazionale, Naples, Italy / Giraudon / The Bridgeman Art Library p.30

CONTENTS

Introduction	4
Ways of looking at art	8
Visual thinking	18
Subjects	28
Portraits	32
Figures	46
Scapes	60
Still life	74
Animals	90
Abstraction	98
Themes	110
Motivation and inspiration	120
Art vocabulary	124
Checklist	126
Index	127

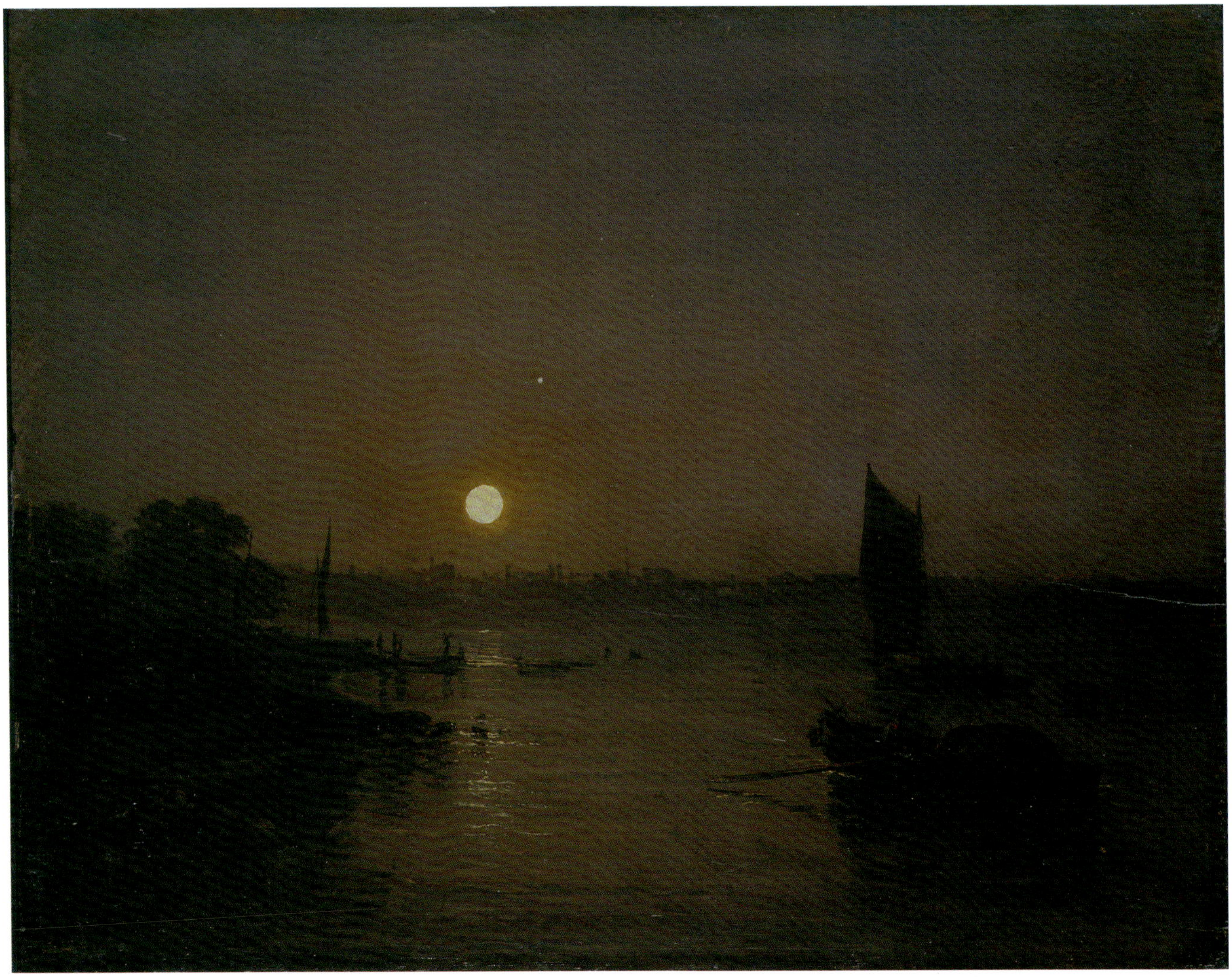

J.M.W. Turner, *Moonlight, a Study at Millbank* exhibited 1797, oil on wood, 31.4 x 40.3, Tate
One of Turner's early oil paintings, this atmospheric scene was inspired by Dutch 17th-century paintings that were popular with the artist's contemporaries. Turner (1775–1851) saw the River Thames every day, but the way he has painted it shows his innovative ideas about capturing a fleeting moment rather than creating the kind of static, idealised and detailed image that was customary at the time. Turner's unconventional ideas became hugely influential in the development of art.

INTRODUCTION

'You use a mirror to see your face;
you use works of art to see your soul.'
George Bernard Shaw

Art can be unlike any subject you've ever studied, or it can have similarities with them all. It can resemble familiar items, complex equations or the simple doodles of children. It can be two-dimensional or three-dimensional, made of traditional art materials, industrial materials or of objects we might have chosen to discard.

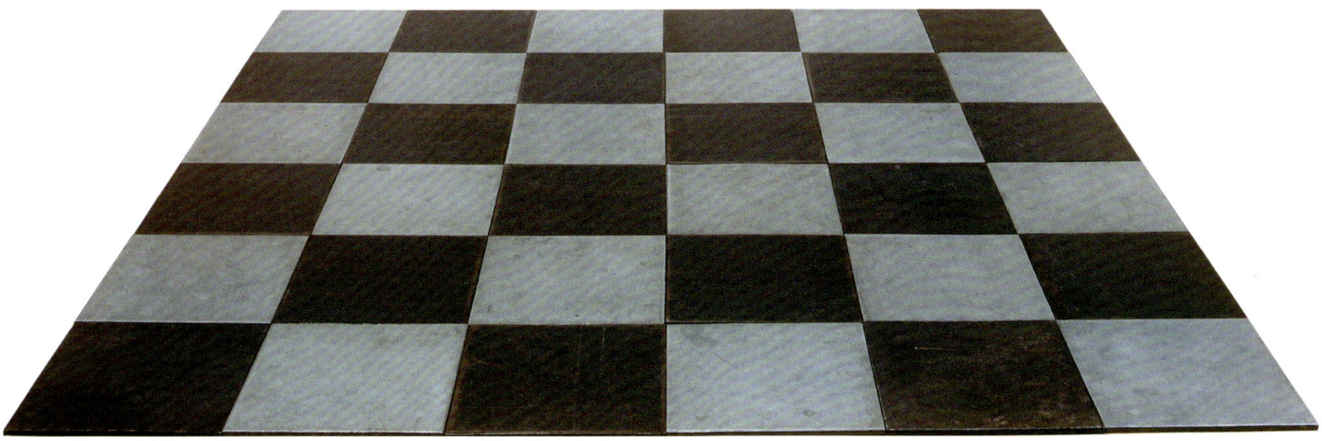

Carl Andre, *Steel Zinc Plain* 1969, steel and zinc, 0.9 x 184 x 184, Tate
Focusing on simply-formed objects that have been made for other purposes, Andre (born 1935) separates sculpture from traditional artists' methods to create art that only involves choice and placement, not skill or technique. Using unremarkable, often mass-produced, industrial materials, he organises them in regular, uncomplicated arrangements, challenging viewers to reconsider artists' roles and the nature of sculpture. By placing this work on the floor rather than on a plinth, Andre also invites viewers to walk across it, altering the expectations of visitors to art galleries.

A window on society

With the power to affect us all, art can be enjoyed in many different ways. Its impact can be both straightforward and unexpected. It can change our minds or our attitudes, provoke anger or shock, or make us laugh or cry. It can intimidate, disconcert, pose conundrums or puzzles, or instruct or enlighten. Ultimately, it offers a window on society's values and ideals, and every work of art expresses the perceptions and memories of the artist who created it.

Because of its diversity, art can sometimes be bewildering or difficult to understand. Most people make up their minds instantly whether they like what they see, basing their decisions on cursory glances that do not necessarily involve any prior knowledge about a work, or about the artist who made it. Although this is a common way of judging art, with a more informed understanding of intentions and processes and some knowledge of how to 'read', observe and analyse a work of art, all art can be appreciated – and enjoyed – in far greater depth. When considered in this way, art can be understood for its place in history or society, for any hidden meanings, messages and cultural significances, recognised for its styles or techniques, and also used to stimulate your own ideas and creative responses.

Creative looking

Like reading and writing, art is a means of communication, and is one of the things that distinguishes humans from all other living species on earth. Evaluating, interpreting and appreciating it has been a topic of philosophical interest since ancient times, while artists and designers have always studied the work of others to develop their understanding and to assist the formulation of new ideas. Influences can come from the ancient past or from recent developments. For instance, after photography had been invented in 1839, artists such as the Impressionists and the Cubists began producing art that offered new ways of portraying the world.

Many art courses require students to analyse and respond to artworks, to engage with and form links between their own and others' work, and to inspire the

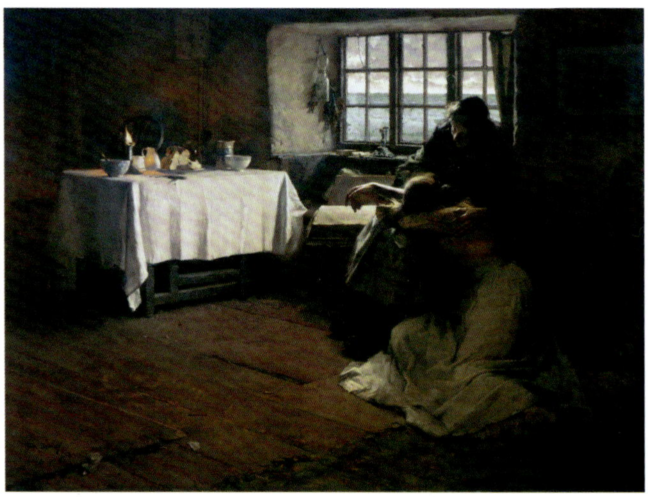

Frank Bramley, *A Hopeless Dawn* 1888, oil on canvas, 122.6 x 167.6, Tate
The two women are the wife and mother of a fisherman. They have just realised he is lost at sea. They have waited all night, but as dawn rises they have to accept he will not return. The dying flame of the candle on the table is evidence of their night vigil and it symbolises the fisherman's death and the end of their hope. How else, do you think, has Bramley (1857–1915) shown the women's feelings? Is there anything positive in the picture? How would you describe the light and colours? This work was greatly admired when it was first shown in 1888. Bramley was a leading member of the Newlyn School, a colony of painters based in or near the Cornish fishing village of Newlyn in the late 19th and early 20th centuries.

William Blake, *Pity* c.1795, colour print finished in ink and watercolour on paper, 42.5 x 53.9, Tate
This is an illustration of 'pity' from Act I, Scene VII of Shakespeare's play *Macbeth*. Distorting his figures, Blake (1757–1827) drew on the 18th- (and 19th-) century notion that beautiful young blonde women were all pure and innocent and so naturally elicited our pity if they faced adversity. Pity is also embodied in the baby (held high safely, or being snatched?). Like the young woman, a baby is innocent and blameless. The cherub holding the baby is believed to have been based on one of Raphael's (1483–1520) representations of God in the Vatican in Rome. What do you think of this work? What do the lines and colours tell you about the emotions Blake wanted to evoke in viewers? How does the image affect you now? How might it have affected original viewers? What elements stand out as important to you and how has Blake shown this?

development of new, personal creative solutions. This book will help you to do all of that, giving you starting points to help you think visually, critically and originally, to analyse, interpret and understand art, and to develop ideas, opinions and imaginative solutions. A range of vocabulary will help you to describe and evaluate what you see. In clarifying and demystifying art, the book can be used as a self-help guide, a textbook, a guidebook to be carried with you in art galleries and museums, a personal instruction book or a motivational manual. It will help you through your art course or even if you simply want to reconsider art in an informed and creative way. Ultimately, you will gain more from the experience of looking at art.

The structure of the book

Each chapter focuses on different subjects, such as portraits, figures and landscapes, and themes such as conflict or identity. In every chapter, there are suggestions and explanations of ways of approaching art, what to look for, how to develop your own ideas, and methods to help you understand the processes and intentions of artists. You will learn how to extract ideas from others' work and how to write about artwork you have observed. Much of the advice and information in each chapter is transferable across styles, subjects and themes, so the book will be effective whether you read through it chronologically, or dip in and out of it as you please. Every chapter shows you methods of thinking visually, creatively and critically by looking and exploring, asking questions and making notes, sketches and mind maps, and using various other types of investigation that will help you to increase your understanding, awareness and creativity.

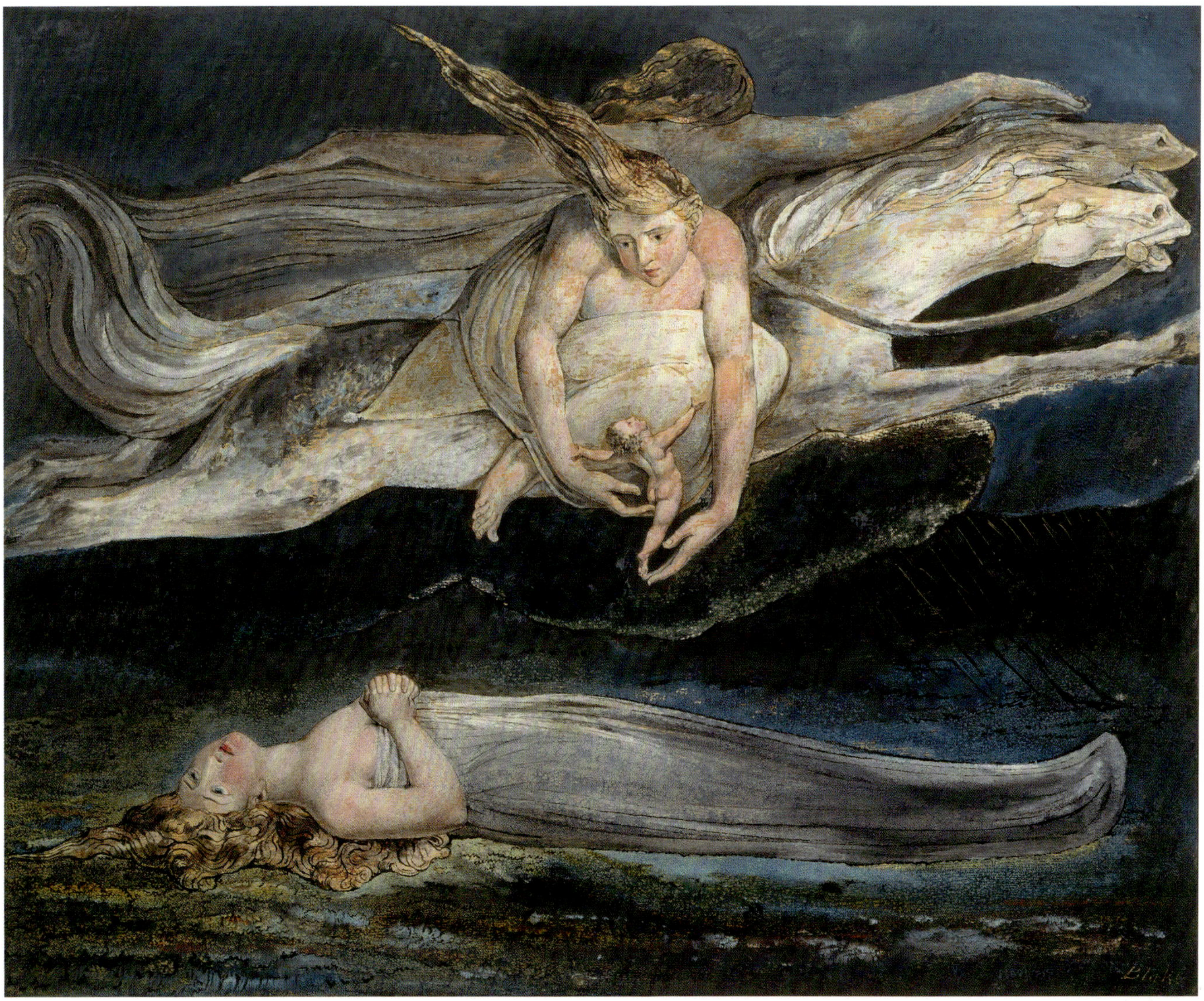

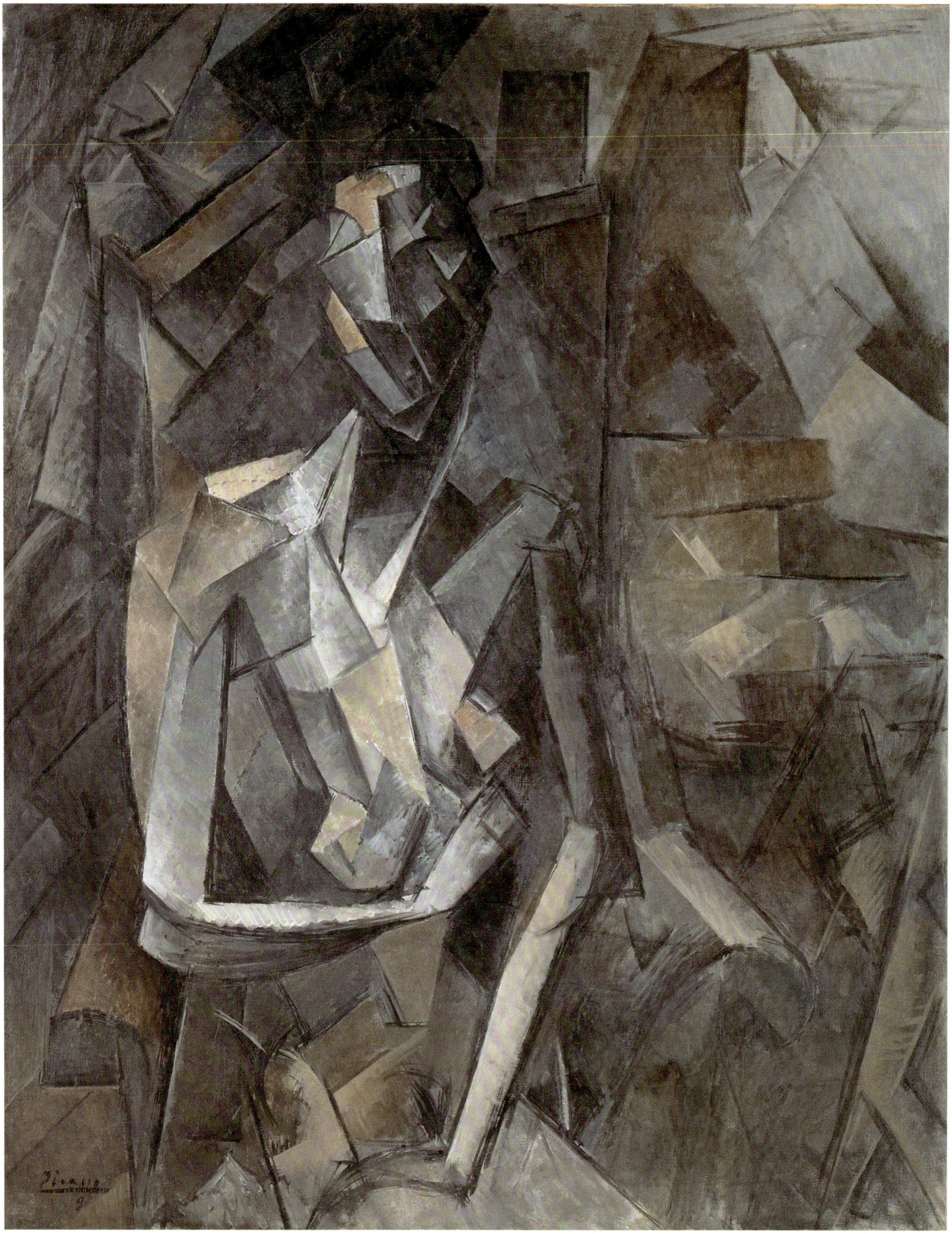

WAYS OF LOOKING AT ART

'It's not what you look at that matters, it's what you see.'
Henry David Thoreau

Everyone has different ideas about art. These are usually influenced by personal experiences, such as beliefs, tastes and the opinions of others around us. In general, our judgements are unconscious or instinctive, and a lot of the time we base them on second-hand images – without ever seeing the real thing.

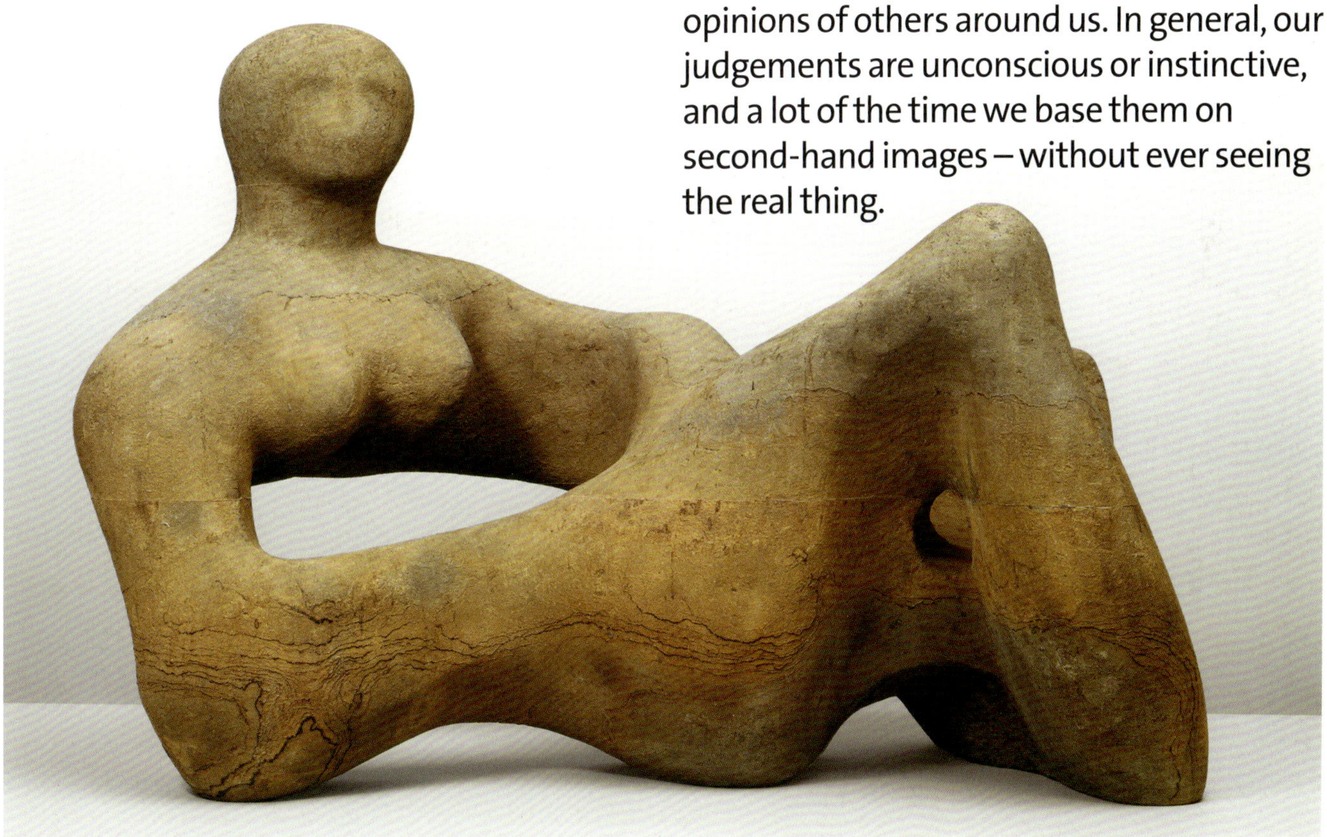

Pablo Picasso, *Seated Nude* 1909–10, oil on canvas, 92.1 x 73, Tate
Look carefully and pick out a woman with her right arm bent across her body, her left hanging down. Picasso (1881–1973) used neutral colours so that he could focus on the shapes, showing them from more than one viewpoint. The lines and geometric shapes show how he was aiming to portray the woman from several angles at once, representing reality in a way that had not been attempted before on a flat, two-dimensional canvas. This painting was produced in the early years of Cubism, and although it was a completely new concept, Picasso hints at traditional art through the woman's pose and the play of light on the image.

Henry Moore, *Recumbent Figure* 1938, green Hornton stone, 89 x 132.7 x 73.7, Tate
Is this a landscape, a female figure or an uncarved block of stone? What words would you use to describe it? Bulky? Gritty? Heavy? Solid? Rounded? Weathered? The title implies that Moore (1898–1986) intended it to be a figure, but did he mean an ordinary woman or a goddess? Commissioned by the architect Serge Chermayeff (1900–96) to stand on the terrace of his modern home, Moore made the figure appear stable and permanent. No hands, feet or features mean she has no expression and no legs to walk away! She represents a mother figure, a human and a celestial being, a creator and an essential part of nature.

Getting personal

There are many different ways of looking at, analysing, engaging with and recording art, and none of them is 'wrong', but it is always best to try to see any artwork at first hand: the primary source. Then you'll get the full impact the artist intended and you'll see the dimensions, colours and textures that photographs can rarely portray.

All art starts with an idea but sometimes an artist's original concept can be difficult to discern, while sometimes it's glaringly obvious. Your first, personal reaction to a work of art is a good place to begin. Before you know anything about it, you will respond to it from your own emotional connections and experiences. It may remind you of something, prompting memories, comparisons or associations. It might appeal to you, you might take an instant dislike to it, or you may think it has nothing worthwhile to offer. Most of us also instinctively judge art on the level of the artist's skill, on how well he or she has replicated the world around us: depending on the actual work of art, that might be irrelevant, but we all tend to do it anyway.

The four Ss

Continue just using your eyes to gather information. Consider the four Ss: setting, size, subject and substance. If the work is in a gallery, think about where it is, what's around it and how it's displayed. Is it on its own, taking up an entire room, on a small part of one wall, or even out in the open air? Think about its dimensions. Is it huge, much bigger than you, or so small you almost missed it? What about the subject? Does the work have an obvious topic or theme? Even if this seems elusive, what do you think it is about? What about the work's mood? Does it seem to you to be serious, sad, funny or uplifting, for instance? Then consider substance, or what it is made of. Are traditional materials involved, or materials that you would not normally associate with art? Does this seem relevant?

Mark Rothko, *Light Red over Black* 1957, oil on canvas, 232.7 x 152.7, Tate
Note the size of this canvas. It's large enough to cover a wall; what does that make you think of the work? What does that make you think Rothko (1903–70) thought of it? What about the content? The theme does not seem to represent anything from life. Even the title describes only the colours. Does the work convey a mood? Does the darkness seem sombre, thoughtful or calming? Perhaps it suggests an opening, a tunnel to another world? Can you imagine stepping through the space or does it seem solid? Why do you think the shapes are blurred? Even though the subject is not traditional, the materials used are – does that make a difference to your ideas about the painting? Rothko wanted this to be shown with others in a series he produced, and gave the gallery instructions about their display.

Ford Madox Brown, *Mauvais Sujet* 1863, watercolour on paper, 23.2 x 21, Tate
How would you describe this work? Consider words such as powerful, sensuous, or even surprising. What about subdued, soft or sketchy? Do these words make you look at aspects of the work in more detail? Unlike Rothko's work opposite, this is a tiny watercolour, also known as *The Writing Lesson*. Madox Brown (1821–93) gave all the proceeds from the sale of the picture to the Lancashire Relief Fund, to help those affected by the Lancashire cotton famine, a depression in the textile industry of north-west England in the 1860s caused by an interruption in cotton imports during the American Civil War. The region plummeted from prosperous to impoverished and many people lost their jobs. Does your knowledge of Madox Brown's social conscience affect your opinion of the painting?

Before you begin to analyse art using a conventional or rational method, consider your feelings. You will need to write them down. Does the work provoke your emotions or remind you of something? Do you like it or not? Why? Has the artist exploited new ideas that you had not considered before? The artist may have accomplished what he or she intended, but you may still dislike it. Try not to judge it solely on whether or not it represents the real world effectively as this might not be relevant.

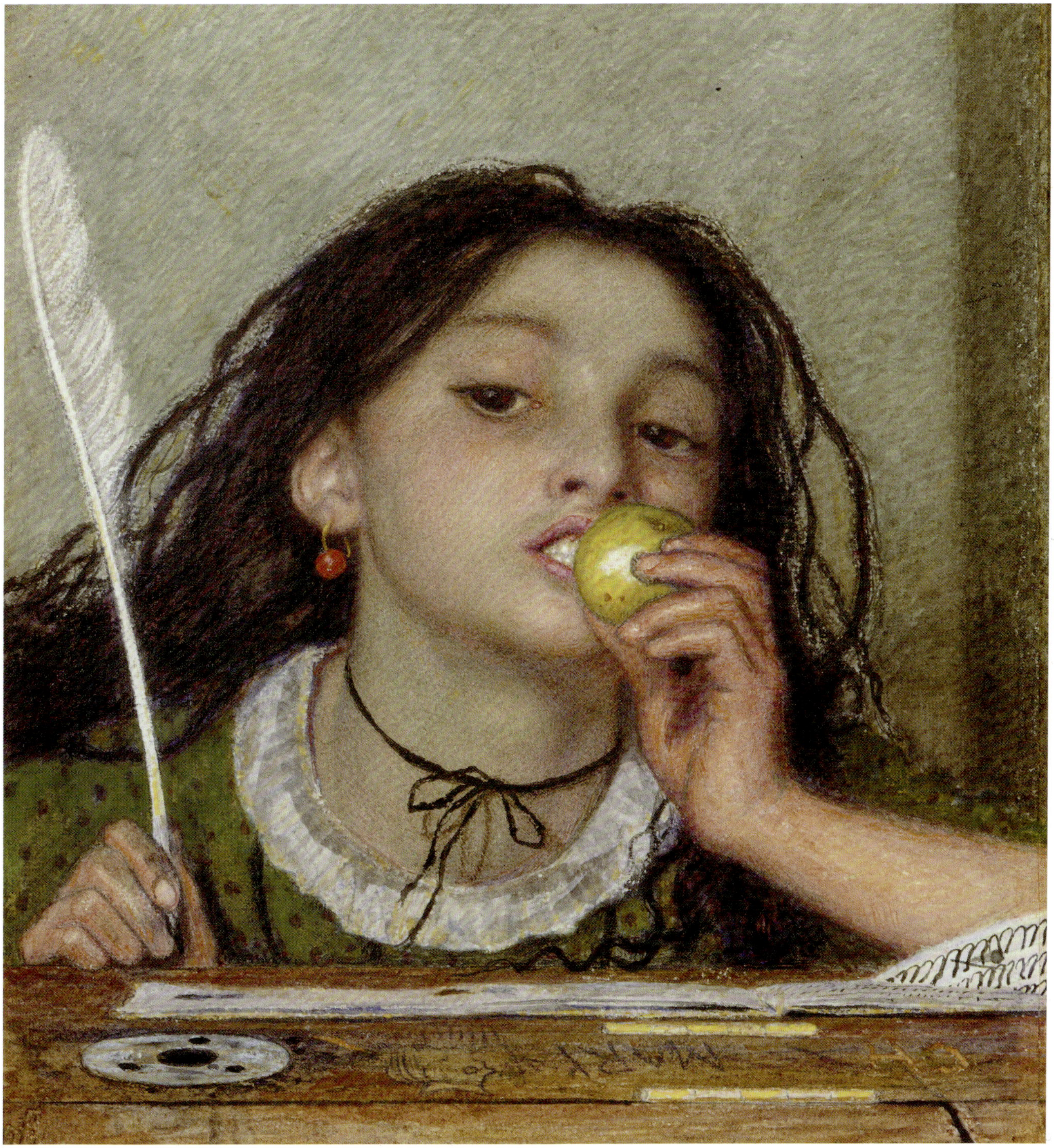

Controversy

You may think that art is harmless enough, but it can provoke intense feelings and reactions. A lot of people have strong opinions about what art should or shouldn't be and controversies surround countless works, over such things as interpretation, ownership, history or value. If the artist has not written down his or her intentions, disputes can continue for generations, while other conflicts or differences of opinion can be short-lived. Then again, what might have been shocking or challenging to some when a work was new, usually loses its initial impact within a relatively brief space of time.

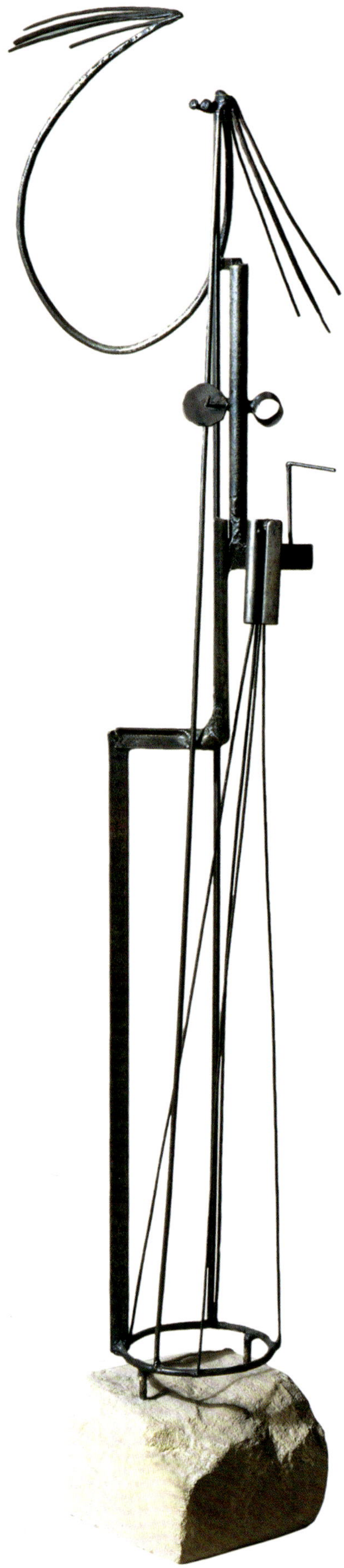

Two types of observation

A method preferred by many art historians is actually two loosely structured approaches used together. One approach is quite objective: you concentrate on a work's visual and physical aspects, pondering how it was made, its lines, shapes, colours, textures, composition and so on. This is called 'formalism', or formal analysis. The other approach is slightly more subjective. Known as 'contextualism', or contextual analysis, you judge and interpret works of art in terms of the times and places they were made, the experiences and ideas of the artists, and the works' purposes and meanings. There is no strict or exact formula for these two approaches, but the following lines of questioning will help you to get started.

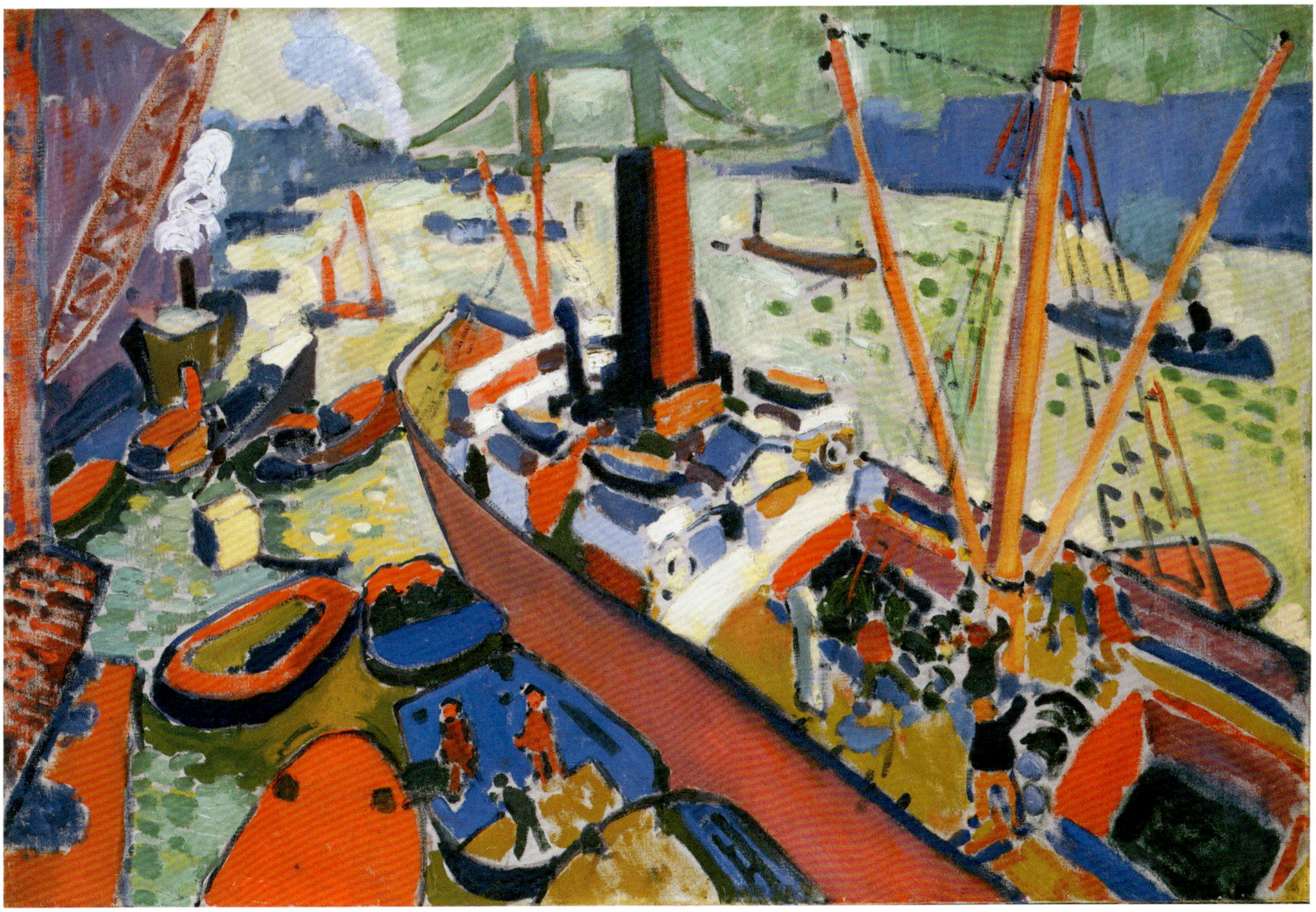

Julio Gonzalez, *Maternity* 1934, steel and stone, 130.5 x 40.6 x 23.5, Tate

Sculpture is traditionally made by three main processes: assembling, carving or modelling. This work has been assembled. Gonzalez (1876–1942) originally trained as an ironworker and welder, and his sculpture has been welded together out of steel rods, tubes, rings and discs. In how much detail do you think Gonzalez planned the work? It looks almost like a three-dimensional outline drawing. At first glance, it appears to be abstract, but figurative references can be detected, especially when related to the title. Compare this mother figure with the work by Henry Moore on page 9. Words like thin, curved, angled, spike and tension could describe some of its formal qualities.

André Derain, *The Pool of London* 1906, oil on canvas, 65.7 x 99, Tate

What is your first impression of this work? What do you think of the colours? The composition? The artist's viewpoint and paint application? Consider descriptions such as 'long and short brushstrokes', 'bold contrasts', 'vivid', 'patchy', 'direct' and 'freely handled'. Note down your first thoughts. Does the painting remind you of anything that you have seen or experienced before? Derain (1880–1954) painted four versions of this view, the River Thames from London Bridge. At the time, he was an important member of the Fauves, a group of painters in Paris who had been given the nickname meaning 'wild beasts' because their work was so bright and seemingly unrestrained. He had been sent to London by his dealer, Ambroise Vollard (1866–1939), specifically to create a Fauvist image of the popular Thames views that had been painted by Claude Monet (1840–1926) a few years earlier.

Formal questions

As you are aiming to be objective, avoid using emotive, judgemental words like strange or beautiful. What is the work – a painting, sculpture, building or something else? Does it represent the real world or is it abstract? What is being portrayed? Describe the composition or structure. Use words like line, curve, shape, rhythm or scale. Does it seem planned? What materials and tools have been used? Are they traditional or 'found' materials? Try to understand some of the artist's techniques or processes. How big is the work? Describe any lines, using adjectives such as soft, firm, broken, heavy, thin, indistinct or irregular, and shapes, using words such as small, large, overlapping, triangular or adjacent. Is the work bright and colourful, or subdued and dull, for instance? Identify colours or pigments if you can. Are these warm or cool – or a mixture? Are there strong tonal contrasts? Has light been shown, either natural or artificial, and where is it coming from? What about the surface of the work? Are different textures actually present, or are they illusions?

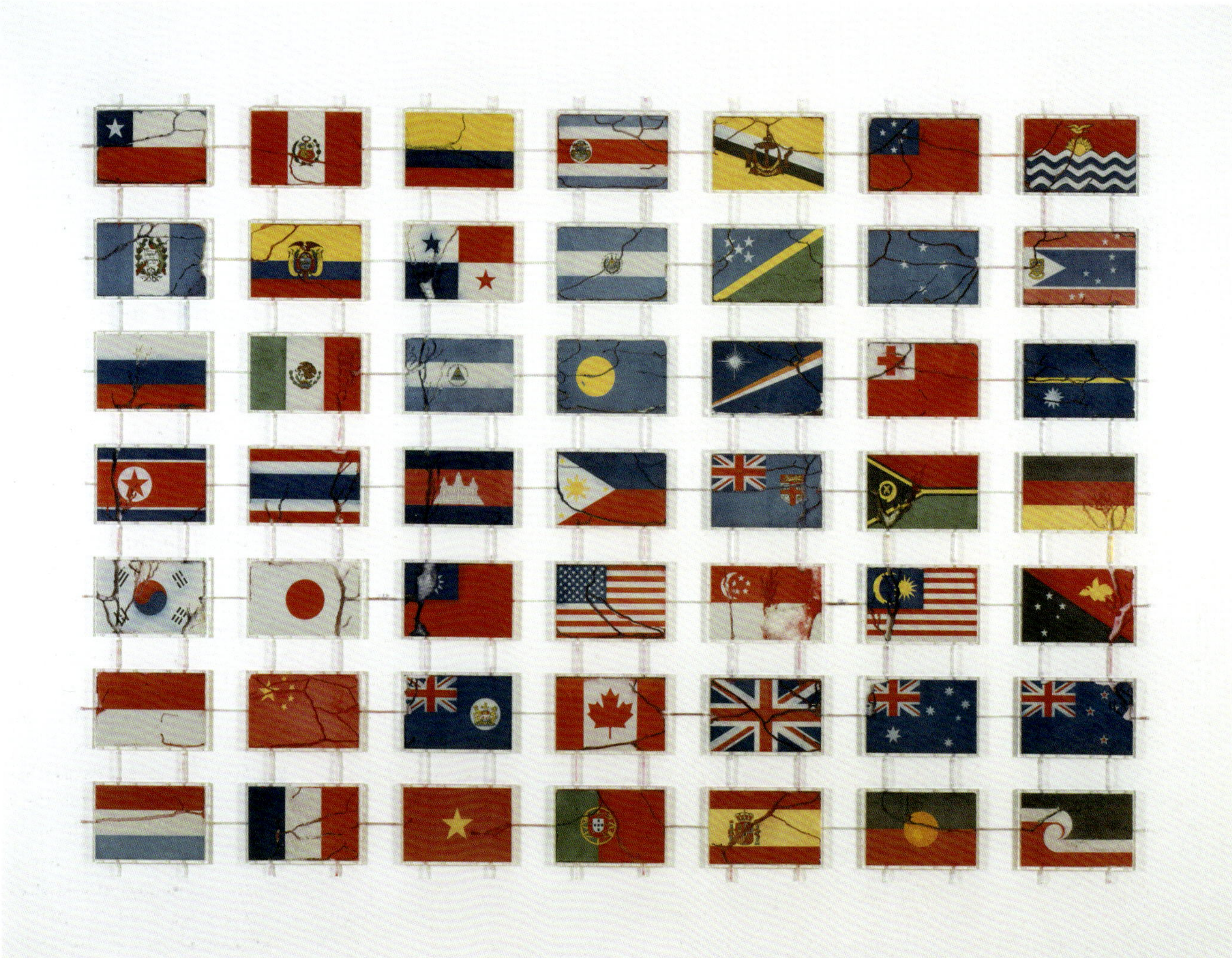

Yukinori Yanagi, *Pacific* 1996, forty-nine Perspex boxes, plastic tubes and artificial sand, 282 x 405 x 1.8, Tate
Yanagi (born 1959) filled several interlinked Perspex boxes with coloured sand to represent the flags of forty-nine different nations. He then released thousands of ants into the boxes. Their busy movements moved the sand around and gradually changed and dismantled the borders between different nations, creating new designs. Yanagi said: 'I question the concept of a nation. A nation, its border and national flag, has become an imaginary fiction.' What do you think about the concept behind this work? Do you think it's clever? Do you think it's not art? Is there anything you feel strongly about that you could make a symbolic statement about through your own art? (No ants were harmed in the making of this work!)

Karel Appel, *Questioning Children* 1949, gouache on wood, 87.3 x 59.8 x 15.8, Tate
Appel (1921–2006) made this work by nailing discarded pieces of wood to an old window shutter. The simplicity of the 'figures', the bold colours and rough painting style are intended to resemble children's art. Appel belonged to a movement called CoBrA, whose artists believed that by using unwanted objects and trying to return to a more spontaneous approach to art, they would arouse awareness of the futility of the Second World War, both literally in the bombed landscapes and spiritually in the social deprivation and shortages. The Dutch title for this work also means 'begging children' and intentionally reminds viewers of the poverty Appel had seen in postwar Germany. Does this background information make you reconsider the work? Does it change your opinion of the artist?

How has the artist used space and are there open and closed-off areas? Has space been distorted or is perspective used accurately? What effect does this have? Look for negative and positive use of space: positive space appears as objects; negative space fills the areas in between. Is the amount of negative and positive space balanced, or not? Is there a strong foreground or background? What other elements can you see in the composition? What about movement? Has this been portrayed, or does the work actually move? How have these effects been achieved?

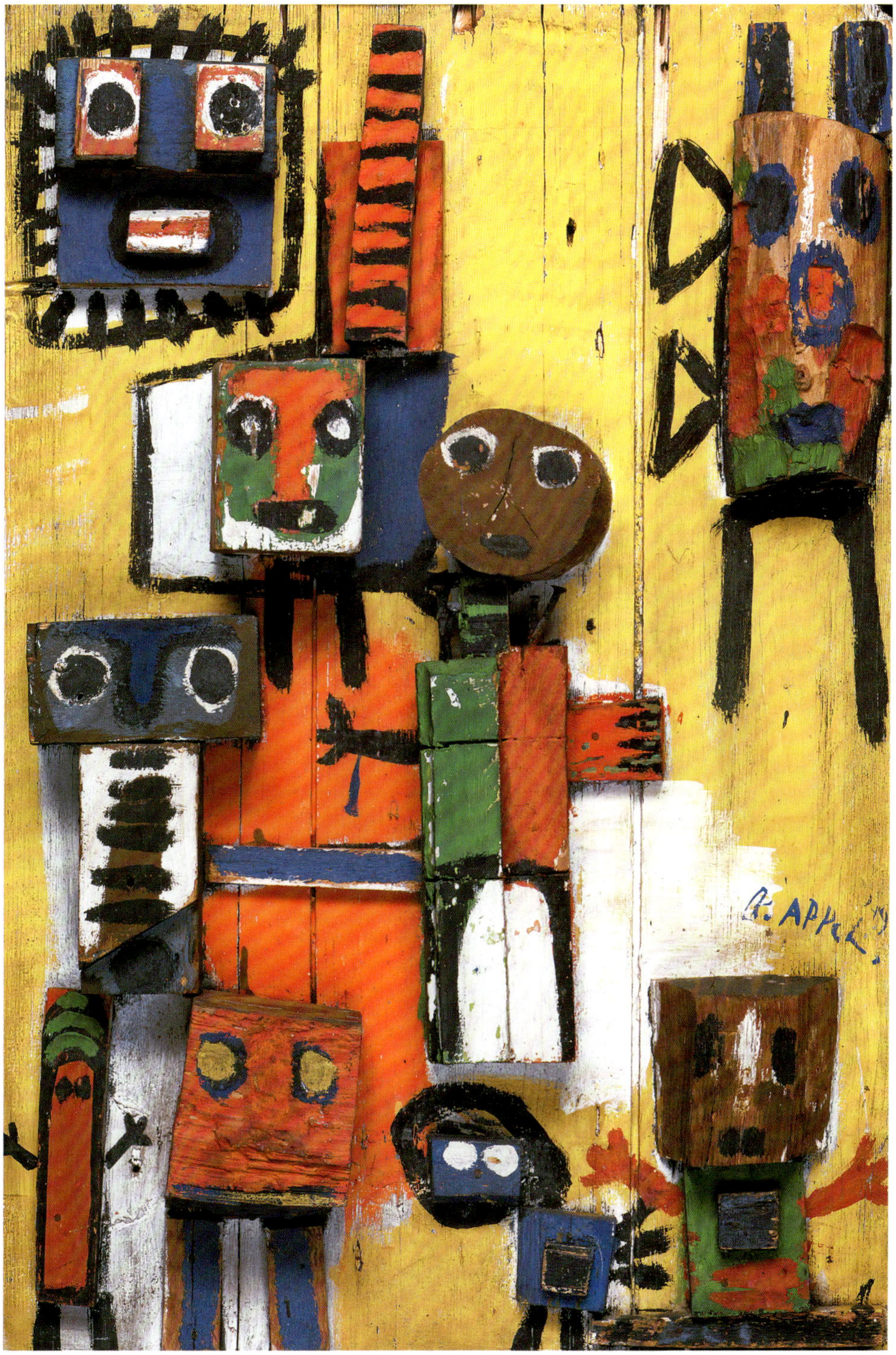

Learning from labels

Galleries and museums usually place labels near works of art to give more information about them. Sometimes the label simply gives an artist's name, the title of the work and its date. Sometimes it includes the artist's dates and nationality, materials used, the work's dimensions, the period, culture or movement, where the work is usually housed, such as 'private collection' or 'on loan from'. If the artist's name is not known, it may say something like 'artist unknown', 'attributed to', 'after', 'follower of' or 'workshop of' (followed by an artist's name). Some galleries and museums also give a short piece of information about the work. The date of execution may be precise or approximate. If approximate, the label will probably say 'c.' followed by a date or dates. The 'c' stands for the Latin word *circa* meaning 'around'. 'Exhibited' or 'exh.' is also sometimes used. This is the date the work was first exhibited and usually means that the date it was made is not known. BC after a date means 'before Christ', or any date before the year zero (now often referred to as BCE, 'before the common era'). AD after a date stands for *Anno Domini*, which is Latin for 'in the year of Our Lord', and means after the year zero (now often referred to as CE, 'the common era').

Contextual questions

Look at the artwork's label. Note the title and dates, and the artist's name and dates. When was the work made and where? Who was it made for? What can you find out about the artist? When and where was he or she born? Is the work part of an art movement? If so, which one and does it correspond with that movement's ideals? What do you think the artist was trying to say? What's the work about? Does it convey a story or a message? Are there symbolic or other underlying meanings? How has the artist portrayed this? How does this work relate to traditional art themes, such as religion, history, portraiture or landscape? Can you make any connections between the work and the place and period in which it was made? Does it reflect the social or political history of the time? Can you link the work to other arts of the period, such as film, fashion, music or literature, for example? What about contemporary developments in science, philosophy, geography or ecology? How do people view the work today – is this different from the opinion people had of it when it was made? If you lived at that time

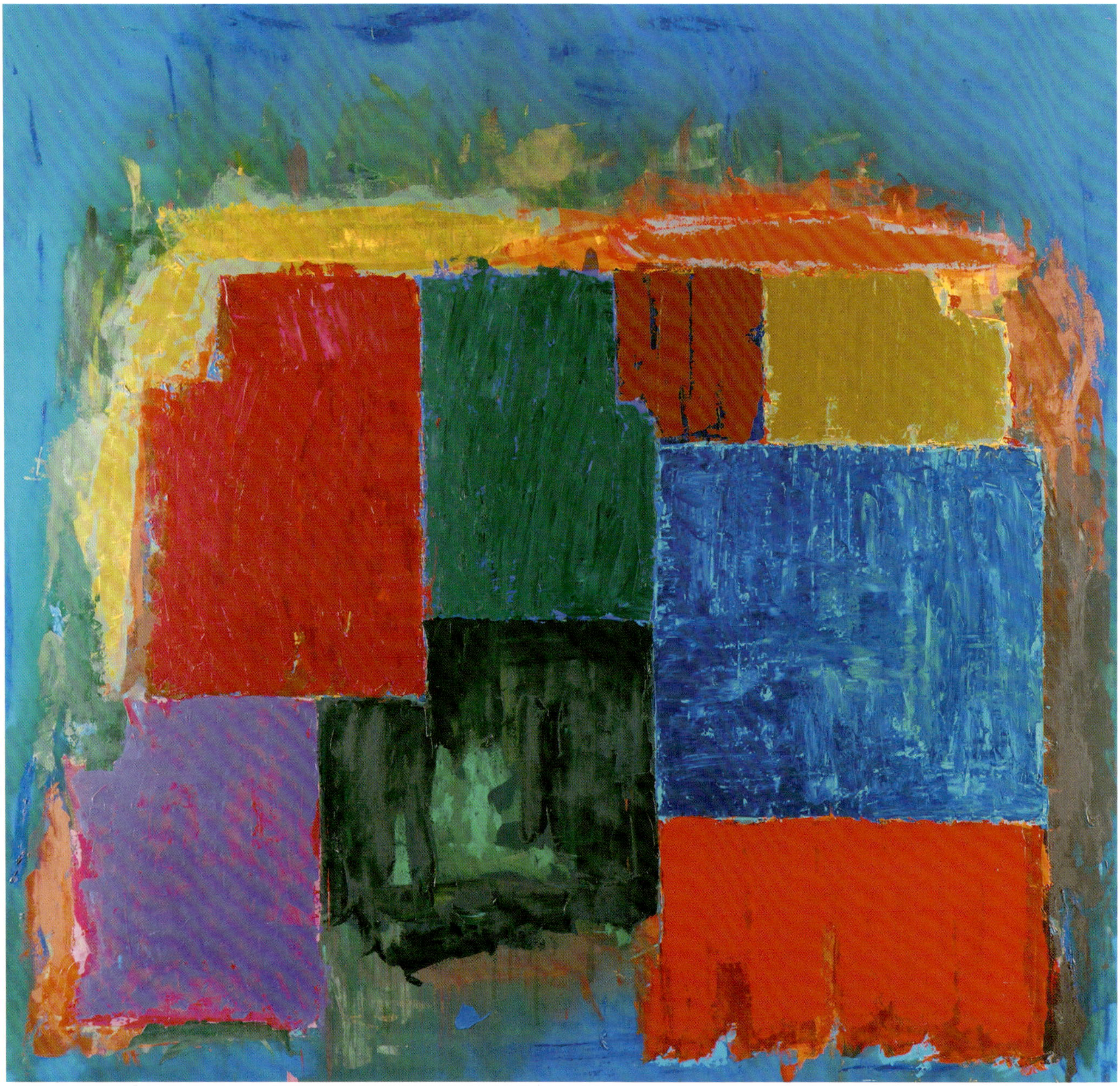

in that place, why might you have made this work? What might you have done differently? Does the work evoke a mood or atmosphere? What is this and why has this been portrayed? What evidence supports your interpretation? How original or innovative is the work (for the time it was made)? Why do you feel this? How does the work make you feel? Uncomfortable? Uplifted? Happy? Reflective? Do you think the artist was deliberately trying to provoke viewers' responses and, if so, why and how?

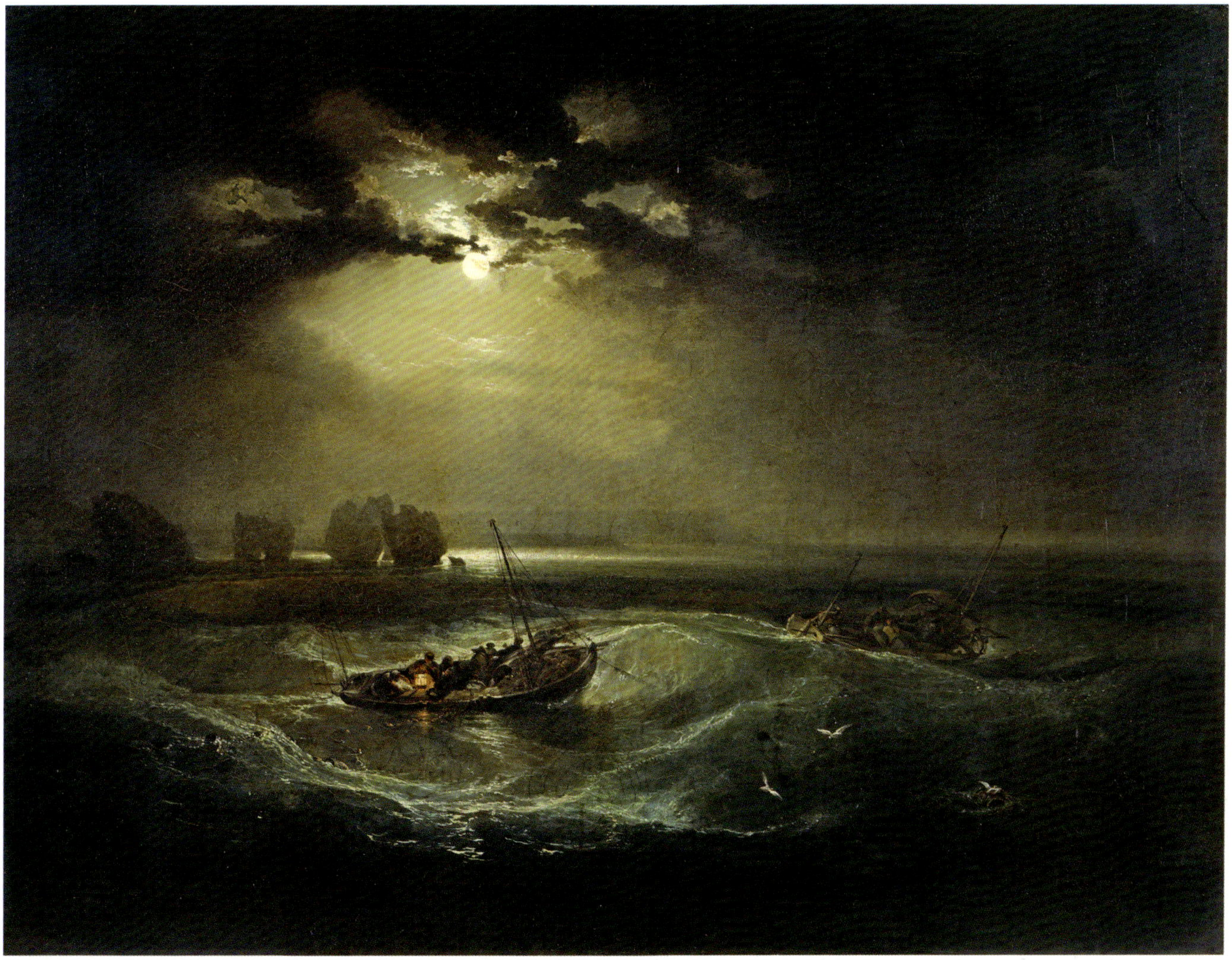

John Hoyland, *North Sound* 1979, acrylic on canvas, 228.6 x 243.8, Tate
The display caption of this work reads: 'Shortly before painting *North Sound* Hoyland stated: 'Paintings are not to be understood, they are to be recognised. They are an equivalent to nature, not an illustration of it'. Hoyland (1934–2011) produced his first abstract works in 1958 and they have always been independent from the world around us. In the 1960s he was mainly involved with issues of scale, colour and shape. In the 1970s he began to present these elements with greater expression, and consequently, as this painting demonstrates, his style became looser. He explained: 'The structure of form is meant to be a container for colour, a container of feeling.' Focus on what you can learn from this gallery label, including Hoyland's opinion and his methods. It's useful to research and compare other art of the time as well.

J.M.W. Turner, *Fishermen at Sea* exhibited 1796, oil on canvas, 91.4 x 122.2, Tate
The caption next to this painting in the Turner wing at Tate Britain reads: 'This was the first oil painting Turner exhibited at the Royal Academy, just after turning twenty-one. It was conceived to position him as an artist worth watching. In differentiating between the types of light passing over the water, Turner (1775–1851) displayed his technical proficiency. Connoisseurs would have recognised borrowings from an earlier fashion for nocturnal subjects. A more contemporary source was Philip de Loutherbourg who had some influence on this stage in Turner's career. The setting has always been linked with the Isle of Wight. But rather than the Needles, at the western tip of the island, this seems to depict Freshwater Bay.' From this label, you can work out when, where and even why Turner painted this when he did.

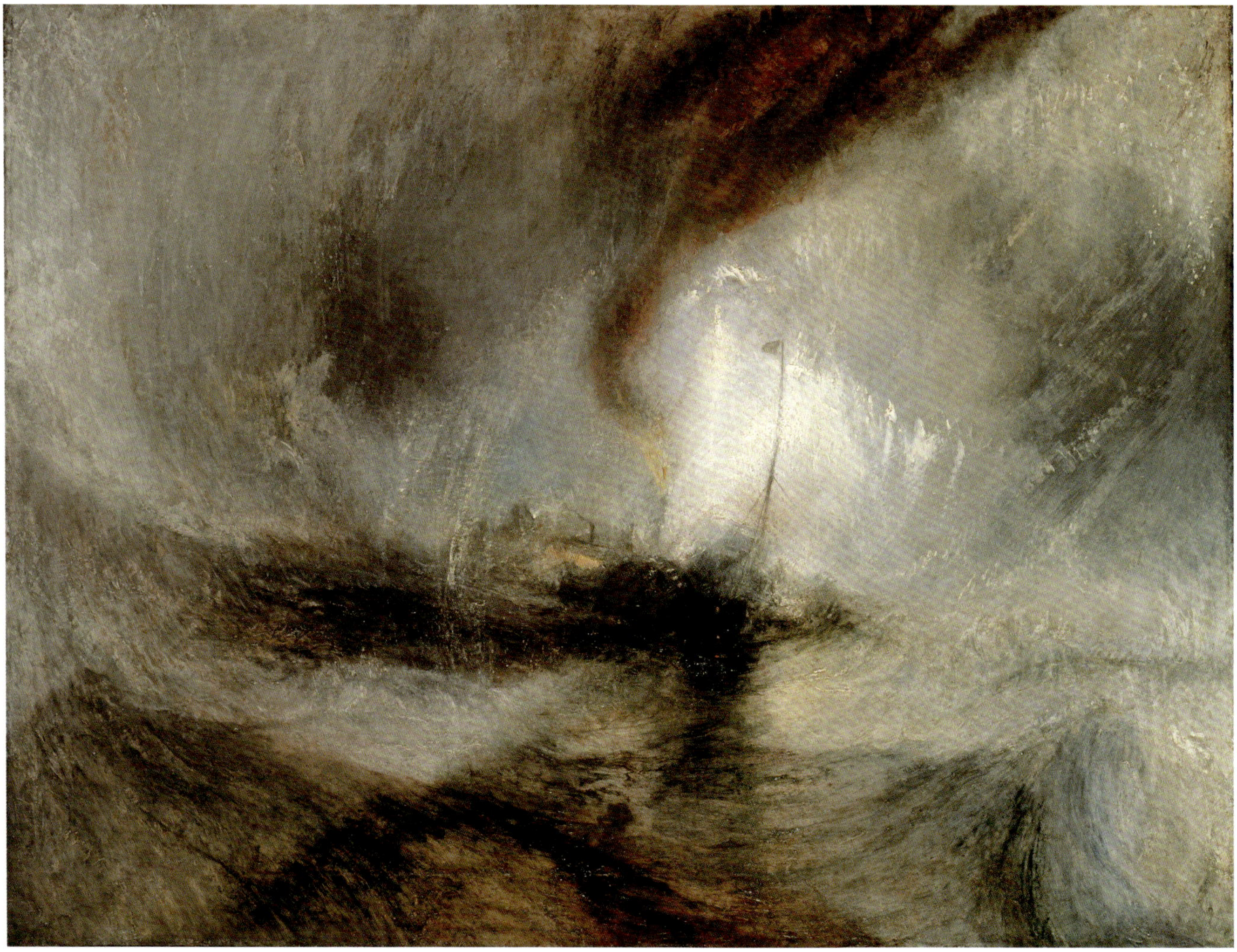

J.M.W. Turner, *Snow Storm – Steam-Boat off a Harbour's Mouth making Signals in Shallow Water and going by the Lead. The Author was in this Storm on the Night the Ariel left Harwich* exhibited 1842, oil on canvas, 91.4 x 121.9, Tate

Unlike typical paintings of the time, there are no details here, as Turner painted a general effect. The dark central shape is a paddle steamer in the vortex of a storm surrounded by the steamer's smoke, waves and snow. A white flare can be seen, one of the 'signals' in the title. Although steamboats were sturdier than sailing boats, they were still defenceless against nature's forces. Turner said he had witnessed this while lashed to the mast of the ship *Ariel* for four hours, but the story seems unlikely. Disliking the lack of detail, critics described the painting as 'soapsuds and whitewash'. Turner grumbled: 'Soapsuds and whitewash! What would they have? I wonder what they think the sea's like?'

A response to Turner's *Snow Storm – Steam-Boat off a Harbour's Mouth*, chalk pastel and pencil on paper

Key points to note:

- Directional brushwork gives the impression of an agitated wild mood, action, dynamism
- Marks changing from long and angled to short, to softly rendered
- A 3B pencil was used to make quick marks, while looking mainly at the painting
- Strong tonal contrasts
- The focal point is the boat, but this is undefined
- Difficult perspective – the horizon is not clear because of strong curving waves
- A spiral builds up the composition and gives a sense of perspective – the middle point in this painting is far away, almost seen through a telescope
- Blurred, hazy effects evoke a sense of texture and confusion

VISUAL THINKING

'Art has increasingly become the concern of the artist and the bafflement of the public.'
Paul Gauguin

Although you don't have to follow all the suggestions in this book, any combination of them will help you to understand art better and to think in a more visual way, which will help you to appreciate a wider variety of art in more depth, and you'll be able to develop your own creative ideas from them. You can train yourself to become a visual thinker by pondering art from different angles that will help you to make links between your own art and the work of others.

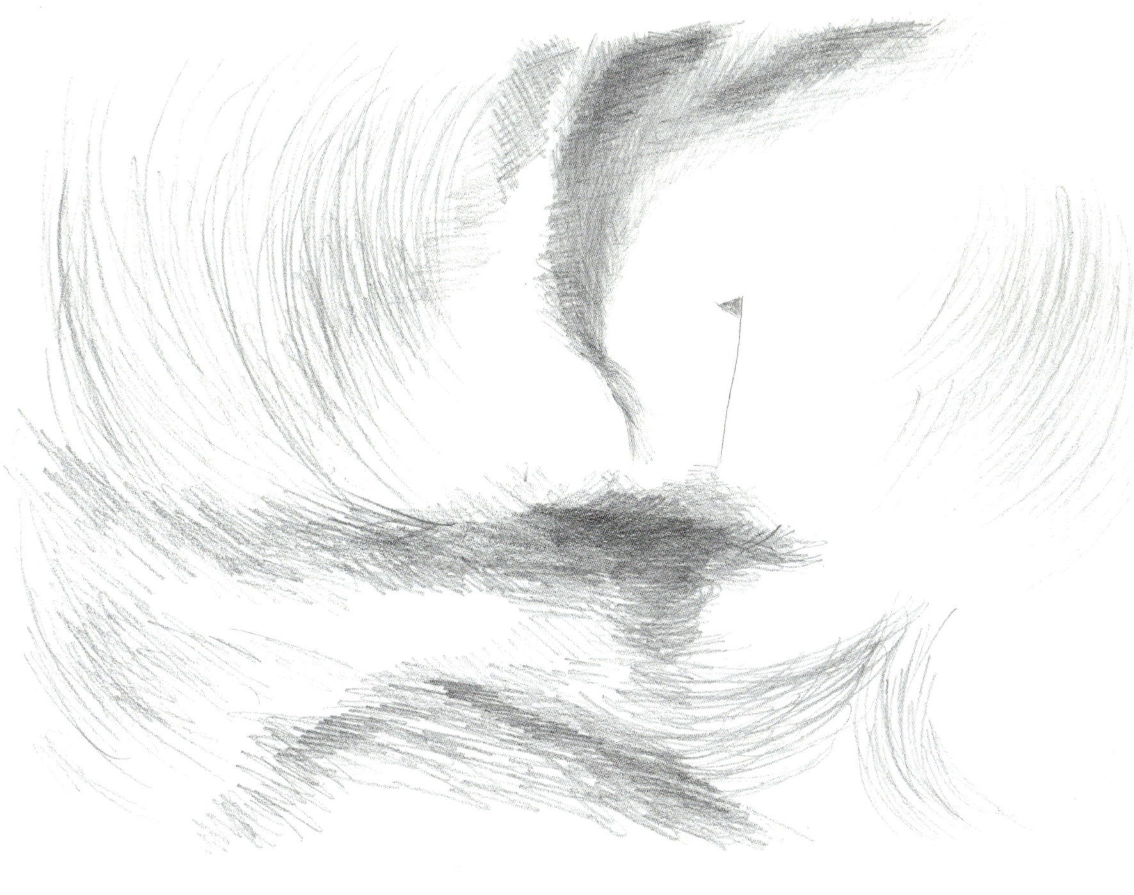

The language of art

There is no one style or form of art, and there is no one, fixed formula for interpreting it, but there are certain approaches that will help you to work out many of the themes, theories and ideas. Having considered an artwork from your personal viewpoint, you need to develop greater critical thinking skills and to be able to match words to images. There is a 'language of art', a vocabulary of words that can be used to describe it and help you to explain what you are seeing. These words appear throughout this book and are also in the vocabulary section at the back.

People make art for many reasons, ranging from personal adornment to illustrating historical or political narratives, to projecting power or evoking emotions. A lot of artwork has more than one interpretation or meaning. If you are in a gallery, there will be some information given about the work, such as its title, date of creation and the dates and nationality of the artist. This might give you some indication about where and why it was produced and you might either know, or be able to research, whether something significant was happening in that part of the world at that time. At the time the work was made, perhaps religious views were particularly potent, there might have been unrest in the build-up to a war or revolution, or there could have been economic or social problems. On a personal level, the artist may have endured a tragedy or be celebrating something. Artists always use influences from their own experiences and reflect their societies and cultures, so a little background information can help you gain a fuller picture. The title might help you too, but be aware that sometimes an artist names his or her work, sometimes a contemporary art dealer or gallery owner might label it, and sometimes a title is given to the work after the artist has died, so it might not always signify the original meaning. For instance, a c.1647–51 painting by Diego Velázquez (1599–1660) in the National Gallery in London is known as *The Rokeby Venus*. It is of Venus and Cupid, but acquired its name after its location in the 19th century at Rokeby Hall in County Durham in the north of England.

Frank Auerbach, *To the Studios* 1990–1, oil on canvas, 169.5 x 149.4, Tate
Auerbach was born in Berlin in 1931 to Jewish parents. His father was a lawyer, his mother a former art student. In 1939, when he was eight years old, Auerbach was sent to England to escape the Nazis, while his parents stayed in Germany and subsequently died in concentration camps. As a Jewish refugee in England during the Second World War, he went to boarding school in Kent and was then evacuated to Shropshire. From 1948 to 1955, he went to art school in London, and made friends with David Bomberg (1840–1957) and Leon Kossoff (born 1926). They became part of a group called the School of London painters. From 1954, Auerbach worked in his studio in Camden, north London. The entrance to it is represented here, and the steps up to the building. Circular elements suggest a bike leaning against the gate that leads to the alley and studio. A flash of red draws the eye to the entrance, while messy, hatched brushstrokes in yellow, green and red imply a block of flats nearby. At the centre is the sign at the entrance: 'To the Studios'. Thick, vigorously applied paint shows Auerbach's painting technique, of scraping away and then reapplying paint in strong colours of purple, ochre and sharp yellow. This is an *abstraction*, but it's not completely abstract; it suggests things from the real world to give an impression of the surroundings. Space and form are described with a dense lattice of lines, swirls, scribbles and patches of colour, and perspective is not used in a traditional way.

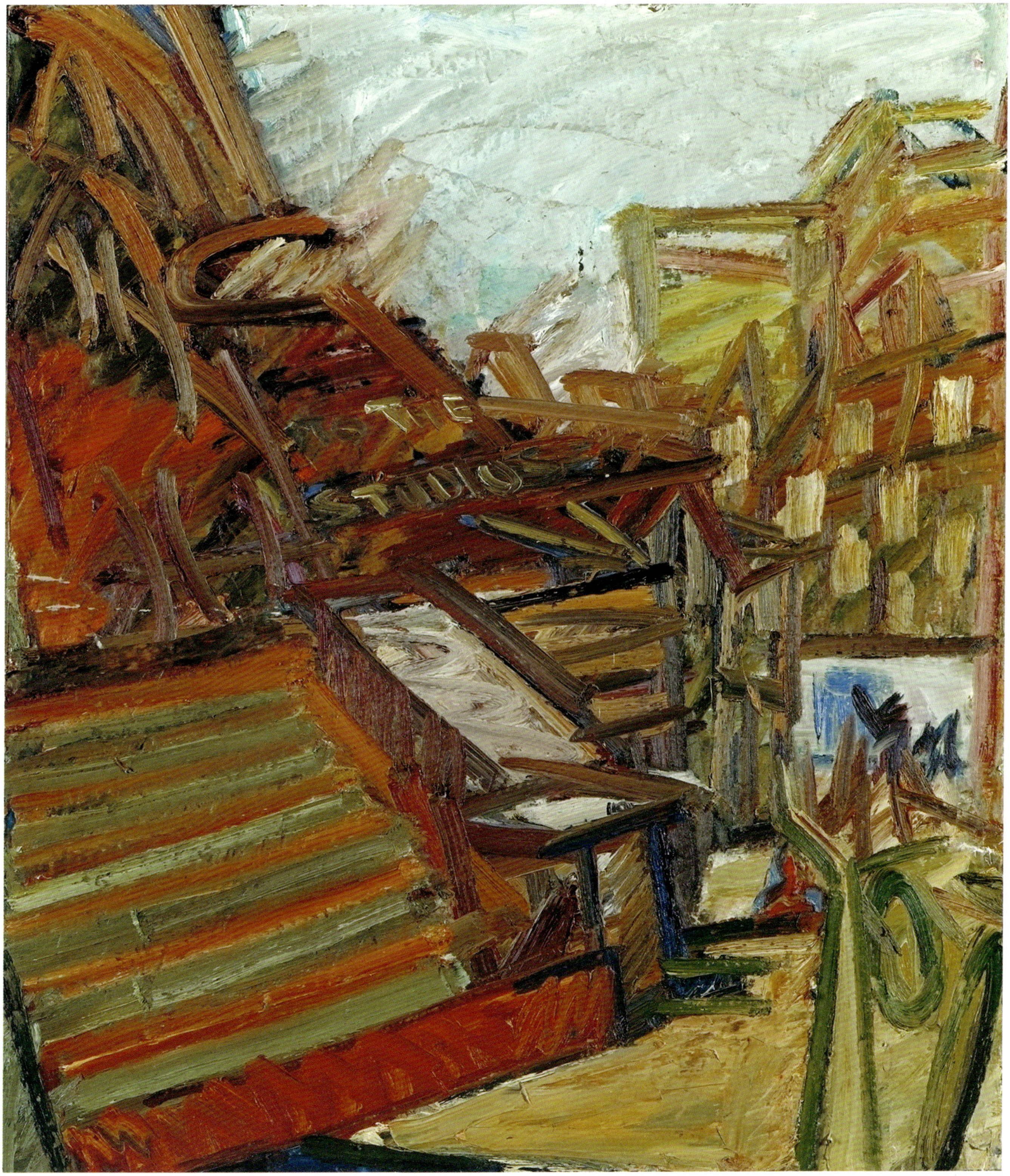
THE
STUDIO

Sketching to generate ideas

Making sketches or drawings from works of art is the traditional, centuries-old way that artists have learned from each other. In doing this, you will engage with a work and an artist's approach even if you previously knew nothing about it. If possible do this whenever you can, not from a postcard, the internet or a picture in a book, but from the actual work itself. This is useful because it forces you to look closely at the work and to consider elements you might not have noticed before.

While you can set up an easel in a gallery or museum only if you have applied for permission to do so before your visit, you can draw in a sketchbook whenever you like, as long as you adhere to a few rules. You can stand near a work of art, or sit on the floor, or a chair or stool if they are available. Make sure you don't block walkways or draw with anything messy – use materials such as pen or pencil. Don't touch any artwork or objects on display and don't rest your clipboard or sketchbook on display cases or plinths, for example. Before you begin drawing, think about how the art has been

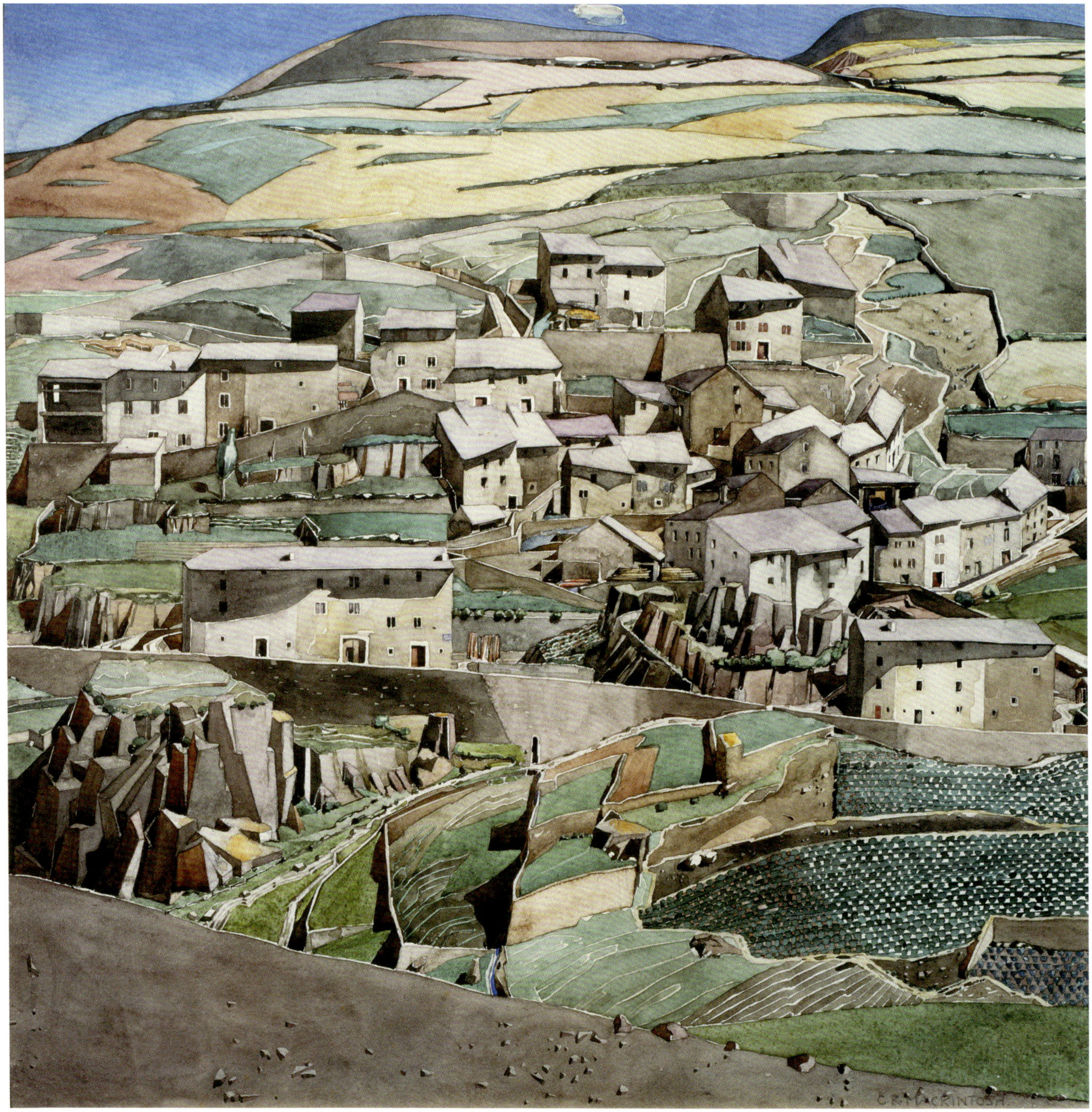

displayed and how it connects with other work in the room. You will probably have a theme, movement or an artist or style to focus on, so choose a work that fits your criteria. Find a comfortable place to stand or sit where you can see the work clearly. As before, note the name of the artist, the work's title and date, as well as the dimensions and materials used. If possible, find out the artist's nationality and where the work was made.

To begin, study the lines, shapes or tone of the work. You could make a sketch of the whole thing, plus a detailed drawing of a small section of it. You may want to concentrate on one aspect, such as features or patterns in the composition. You might make a sketch to use later as the basis for a painting or construction. Your drawings do not have to be perfect, they just have to be simple records of what you have seen, or aspects of the work that interest you. Your main aim is to engage with the work and to think about it in new ways. Consider some of the artist's ideas. Annotate your sketch, perhaps mentioning contrasts, materials or unfinished elements.

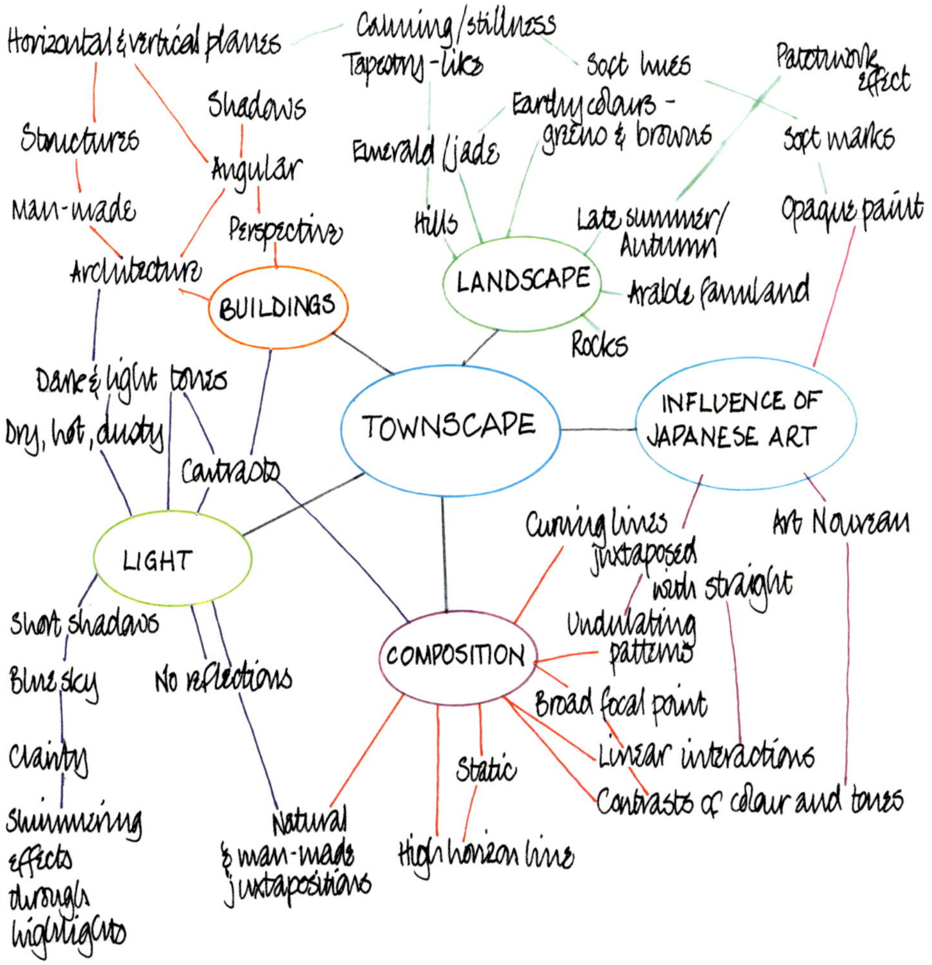

Annotations

Written notes – or annotations – made next to an image about it are extremely helpful when analysing art, as they enable you to process and clarify ideas and develop a personal response. Annotating your own sketches or reproductions of artworks will help you to foster new ideas, question what you are looking at and think objectively. Annotating postcards or printed images is also useful, as it makes you think more intensely and organise your thoughts. To do this, collect relevant images and stick them in your sketchbook. Leave space to add annotations that remind you of aspects of the art you noticed in the real thing, or highlight elements of the work that seem important. Annotations help to reveal your thought-processes to others and enable you to reach considered conclusions. Any answers you gave to questions in the previous chapter can form part of your annotations to generate new thoughts and ideas.

Charles Rennie Mackintosh, *Fetges* c.1927, watercolour on paper, 47.4 x 48, Tate
This is one of a group of watercolours painted by Mackintosh (1868–1928) in the south of France during the last few months of his life. He was an innovative architect and his watercolours contrast with his angular designs. Take a viewfinder or two L-shaped pieces of paper or card and focus on a section of this painting. Once you block out other elements and concentrate on one small area, your impressions of the work will change. What do you notice? Is the part of the work you are looking at surprising? How would you describe it? Perhaps angular, strong, subtle, natural, jagged or soft? Does your opinion of the work change knowing that the artist was also an architect? Looking again at the entire work, what can you say about the composition? Find out about Art Nouveau, Art Deco and Mackintosh's work, and see if your initial impression of the work alters.

A mind map exploring the theme of 'townscapes'.
This is an example of a mind map responding to Mackintosh's painting. Mind maps are explained in more detail on page 26. Use this one as a starting point for your own ideas and thought processes, and build on it.

Outside what box?

You might think that just by looking at a work of art, sketching some or all of it and annotating it, your opinion of it won't alter. But copying all or parts of an artwork that someone else has made will force you to look at it in greater depth and think about it differently. As you look and draw, ask yourself questions about the work, but rather than focusing on your first impressions as you did before, now consider it from a different angle or viewpoint. What would your opinion of it be if you were alive at the time it was made? How would you feel if you'd been caught up in a war or revolution? Try working from, literally, a different angle. Find an image of the work, take a print of it and turn it upside down. Or use a viewfinder to study a small section in close-up detail and copy it six or seven times the size. All these things will change your impressions and challenge your assumptions about any work. 'Thinking outside the box' is an expression that originated in the USA in the late 1960s. It has been used so often that it's become a bit of a joke now, but it implies the notion of thinking imaginatively and freely

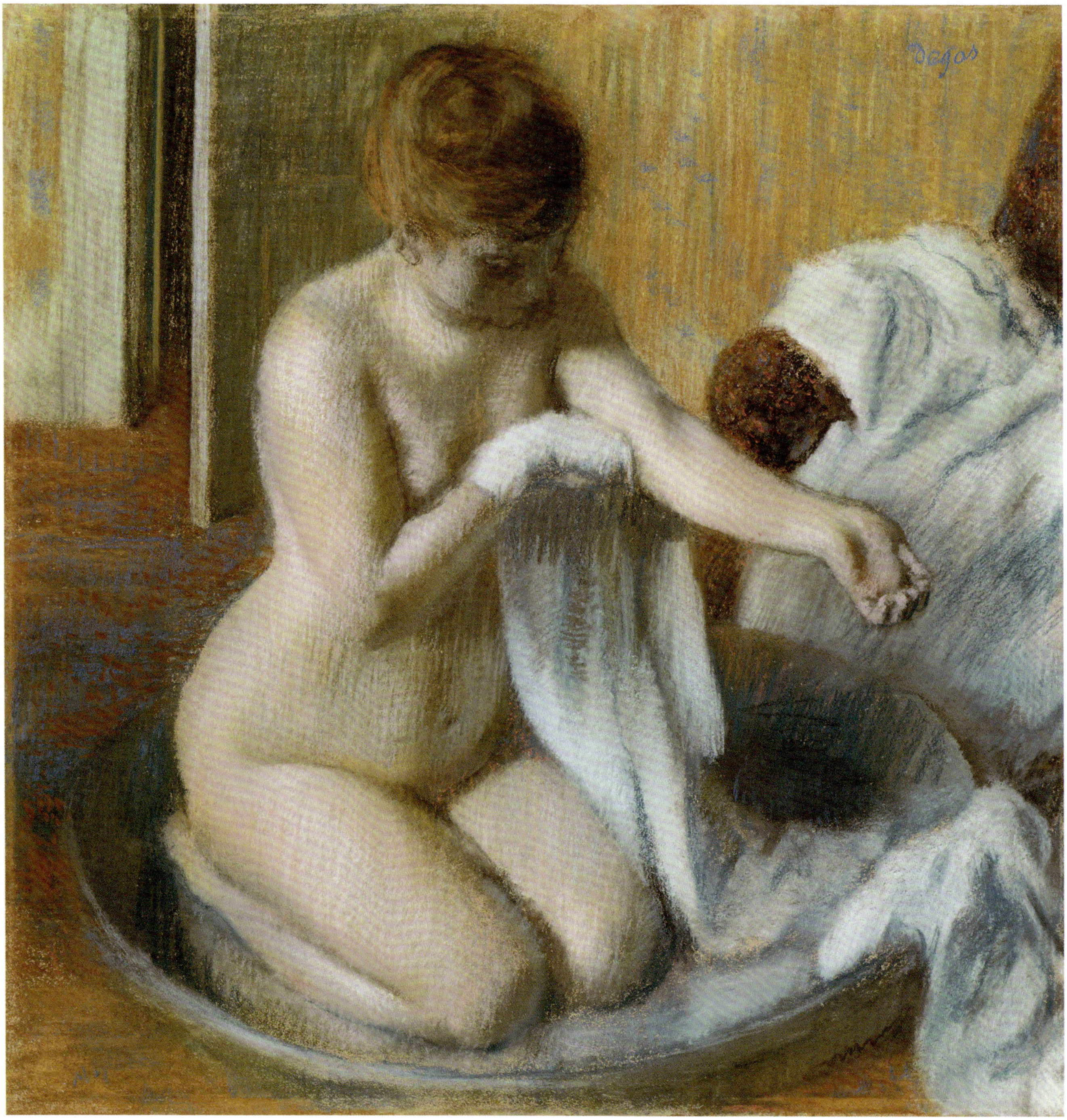

– similar to 'blue-sky thinking', which came from a comment in a newspaper in 1945. Both 'thinking outside the box' and 'blue-sky thinking' describe the idea of thinking beyond our usual thought patterns, which should result in unexpected and creative solutions to any problem. The ideas are also related to 'lateral thinking', which was first used in 1967 in the UK by the psychologist and inventor Edward de Bono (born 1933) to describe his method of building creativity. To develop your own lateral, blue-sky thinking, keep asking yourself questions. They can be general or specific, such as about the techniques used. Who commissioned it, or why was it made? Was it innovative when new? Was it shocking – and if so, why, who was shocked by it and when did it stop shocking them? Is it made with costly materials? Have materials been used conventionally or unusually? Can you see any tool marks or fingerprints? You might not be able to answer all these questions, but you can probably make some thoughtful guesses. Your ideas and opinions will generate new ideas to help you to think outside the box – or to throw away the box altogether.

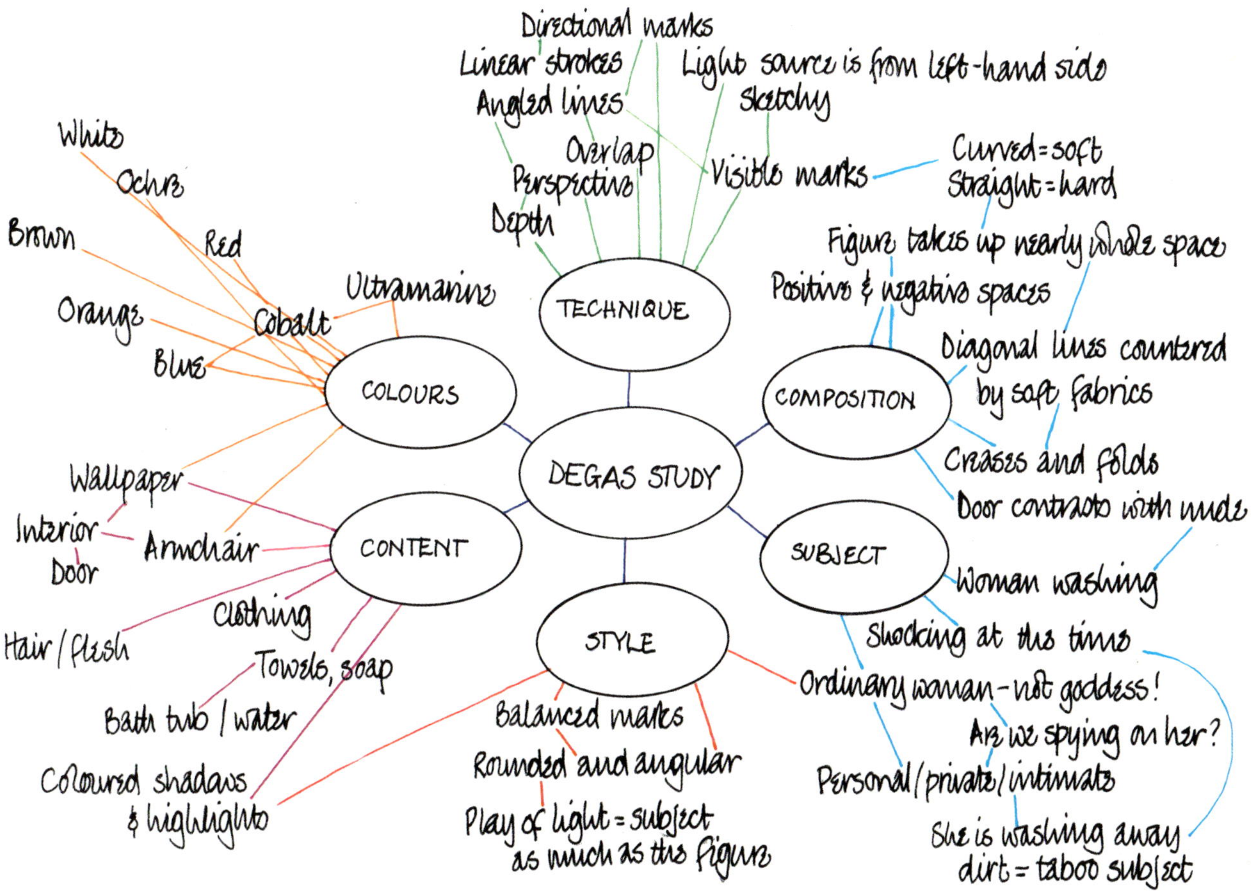

Edgar Degas, *Woman in a Tub* c.1883, pastel on paper, 70 x 70, Tate
A delicate pastel and one of a series of studies of women at their toilet by Degas (1834–1917). When Degas produced these works, critics varied in their reactions. Some praised the way he showed modern women rather than idealised goddesses, while others complained that the models were ugly, probably prostitutes, and that portraying anyone washing was too personal and vulgar for art.

This mind map is an exploration of the work by Degas opposite.
See how it can help you to think around a topic in a more creative way – and read on the next page how to make your own mind maps.

Making maps

There are lots of ways you can invigorate your thinking and stimulate your creativity. Mind mapping is a powerful method for exploring a theme and helping you to direct and expand your ideas. Mind maps are a form of visual planning using a combination of words and images. They are visual diagrams, usually developed around a word or phrase, with ideas and words radiating out, creating a kind of spider's web design (which is why they're also sometimes called spider diagrams, or brainstorms). Although the term 'mind map' was first used on a UK television programme in the 1970s by an educational consultant, Tony Buzan (born 1942), one of the earliest examples of mind mapping is thought to have been developed by an ancient Greek philosopher known as Porphyry of Tyros in the third century, only he didn't call it a mind map. Before you start, look at the mind maps on pages 23 and 25 for ideas. To make yours, write a word or phrase or draw an image related to your topic in the centre of a page and circle it. Draw lines radiating away from it

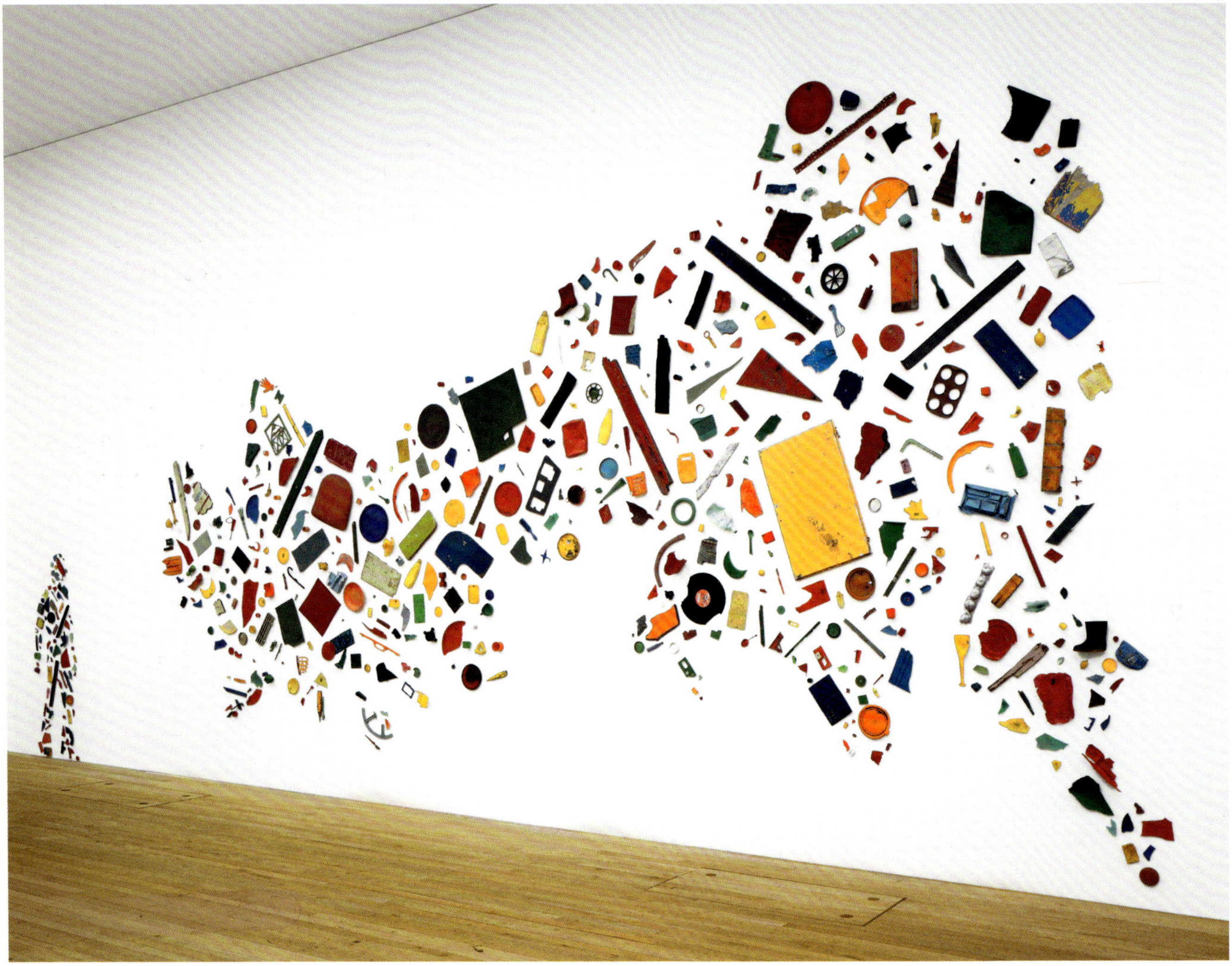

Tony Cragg, *Britain Seen from the North* 1981, plastic, wood, rubber, paper and other materials, 440 x 800 x 10, Tate
British-born Tony Cragg (born 1949), who lives in Germany, made this during a visit to Britain in 1981 when he witnessed the country struggling with social and economic difficulties. The figure to the left is a self-portrait and implies that he was viewing Britain from the point of view of an outsider. The work is made up of many small objects found discarded on the streets and waste sites and arranged to form the large image. Cragg made it in London for an exhibition he was having at the Whitechapel Art Gallery in early 1981. By making a recognisable image of the British Isles and tilting it on its side, with him as a standing male figure looking at it, he was exploring a theme that included his vision of his native country viewed from his new, distant perspective. To understand the work further, it would be helpful to read about events in Britain and the world in 1981. You can also judge the work on its composition, colours and scale, for instance.

and on these, write words that link to your theme. Draw more lines radiating away from these words and add further words or ideas that connect to them. Keep adding more words as they occur to you. Use colours if it helps and be as imaginative as you can. Even if you don't think the final mind map has inspired you, keep it and add to it later. The process will have given you fresh thoughts and could help you later.

Opening your mind

There are so many ways you can become a visual thinker and so many ways of considering art. Leonardo da Vinci (1452–1519) was a great example of a visual thinker (he certainly had 'blue sky thinking'). Help yourself to be as visual a thinker as possible:

- When considering any artwork, theme or style, look for several reasons why the artist worked in that way, used those materials or represented that subject. There's rarely only one answer.
- Don't hold back! Consider crazy meanings and reasons behind artworks as well as sensible ones.
- Never judge a work of art simply because you don't like the look of it (or you do), because you've never liked that artist, or because the work isn't well known, for example.
- Make a mind map or list all your ideas about your topic Don't spend too much time on this and don't worry if they're right or wrong, just write them down. Look at this the next day or in a couple of days' time. New thoughts will nearly always present themselves to you.

Art games

There are lots of ways you can break out of your old patterns of thinking and use art to expand your creativity. Try some 'art games'. First, find a work of art that appeals to you or fits in with a theme you are exploring, then try any of the following:

- Write a detailed description of the artwork for someone who hasn't seen it (try imagining you're a radio presenter, telling listeners about it).
- Write another detailed description of the work for someone who is visually impaired.
- Write down just six words to sum up the entire work.
- Imagine the work has a mind of its own. Write its diary entry for today.
- Draw the work, but only the negative spaces around the main shapes.
- Imagine you are advertising the work of art and you want to attract as many people to see it as possible. What would your poster or press ad look like and say?
- Give the work a new title.

None of these activities should take much time. Spend just five to ten minutes on each and don't worry if they're not perfect. They're simply ways of opening up your mind to new perspectives and to make you consider subjects differently.

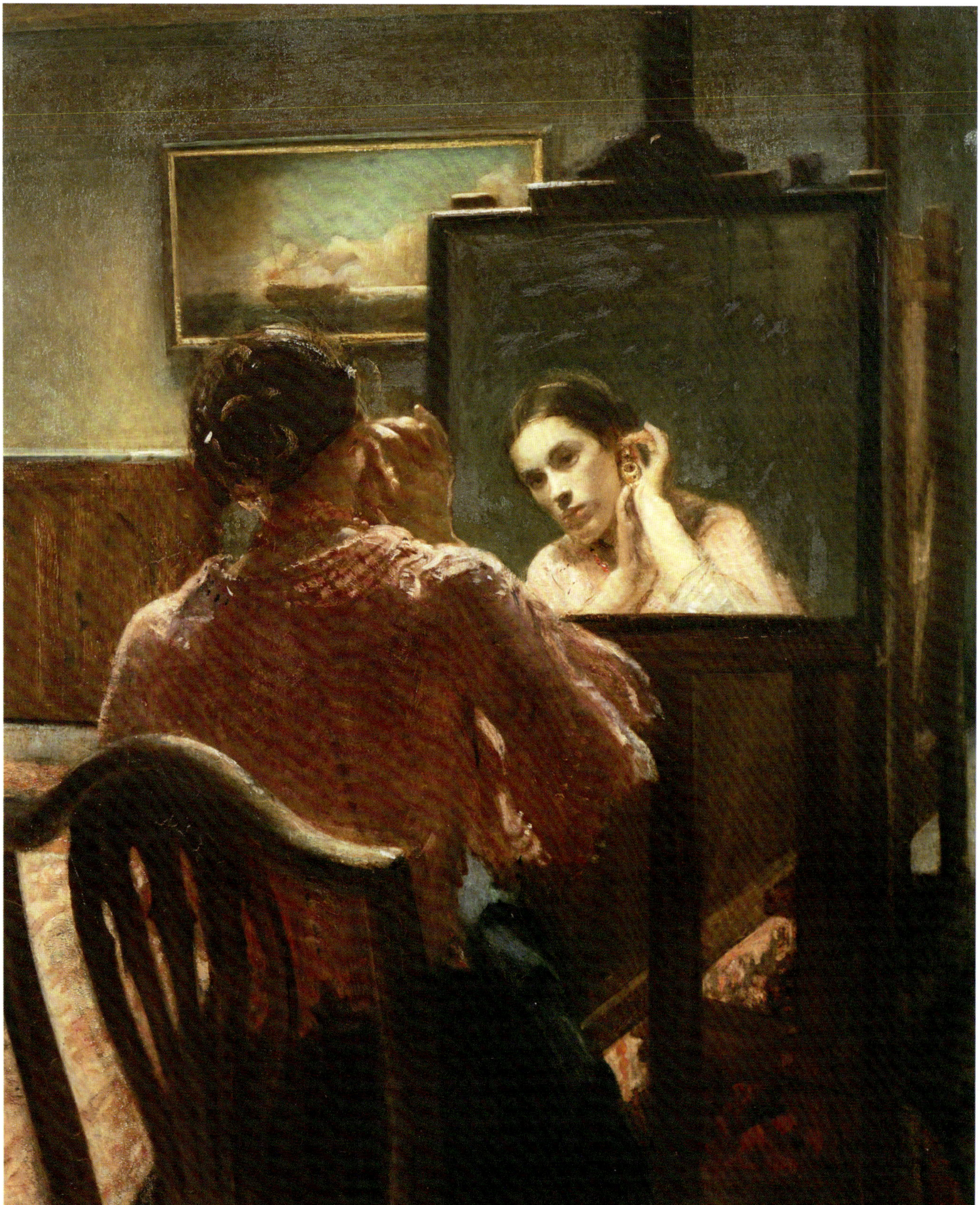

SUBJECTS

'Art is not what you see, but what you make others see.'
Edgar Degas

The next chapters include suggestions for exploring, interpreting and building ideas around different subjects or themes. Most of these ideas are universal and can be used for almost any topic. After brief backgrounds to each subject, suggestions for generating greater understanding and developing creativity are given. They will all help you to enjoy and appreciate art, but remember that, like art itself, there are no rules.

Ambrose McEvoy, *The Ear-Ring* exhibited 1911, oil on canvas, 76.2 x 63.5, Tate
Influenced by James McNeill Whistler (1834–1903), McEvoy (1878–1927) worked with well-known artists of his time, including Augustus John (1878–1961), William Orpen (1878–1931) and Walter Sickert (1860–1942).

He first exhibited landscapes and interiors, but later became known as a portrait painter of fashionable society ladies, usually in watercolour, in a loose, sketchy style. This painting could fit into several themes including: portraits, reflections, looking through, adornment, contemplation, interiors, angles, time, change, identity, gender, solitude, examination, scrutiny, preparation, shadows, appraisal, intimacy or many others. Simply ask questions that fit with your theme, such as, how has the artist created a mood of intimacy, or what effect does the reflection have on viewers?

Painting hierarchy

From the late 16th century onwards, when membership of one of the art academies across Europe increasingly became the only way an art student could progress to being a successful artist, a hierarchy or order of importance for painting themes was established. The first and most highly respected category was history painting, which has always encompassed story-telling works alongside descriptions of actual events. History paintings are often large and their subjects can be historical episodes, allegories or stories from the Bible, mythology or literature.

Next in the line of importance came portraiture. Portraits were often made to express power and authority, and before photography was invented, were the only way to extend the memory or record the likeness of a person. But art frequently means different things to different generations or cultures. The meaning of a single painting can change over time. For instance, the *Mona Lisa* (c.1503–6) by Leonardo da Vinci has perhaps become the most significant, enigmatic and revered portrait in the world. Yet it was probably originally commissioned by a man who simply wanted a portrait of his wife to hang in their new home and to celebrate the birth of their second son.

Landscapes and 'genre' paintings rank next in order of importance after history and portraiture. Some of the earliest landscape paintings were produced by ancient Greek and Roman fresco artists as well as Chinese painters. Both Roman and Chinese paintings were usually grand and imaginary panoramas, and in the East landscapes were considered the most prestigious form of art. But for centuries in the West landscape was seen only as a background to historical, religious or mythological works or portraits. By about the 17th century, however, landscapes in their own right began to be popular, particularly stimulated by the Dutch Golden Age, and later by Romanticism. Genre paintings are scenes of everyday life, featuring people at 'ordinary' tasks and activities, and contrast with history paintings and portraits, as the subject matter is not monumental and the people depicted have no individual identity.

The last theme in the hierarchy was still life, paintings of everyday inanimate objects.

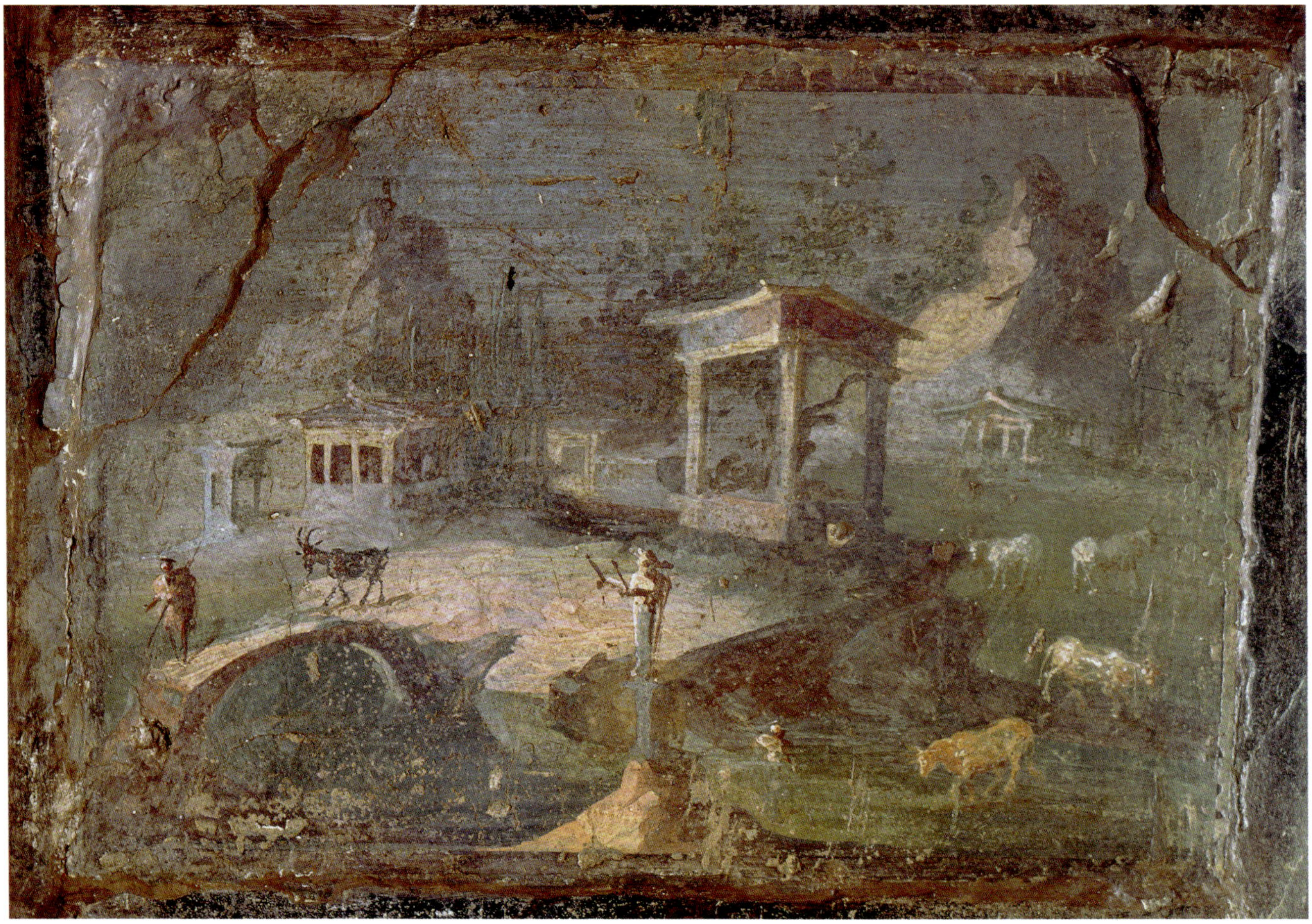

Inspiration and stimulation

This order of importance no longer matters to contemporary artists or viewers, but if you are looking at a work from any of these time periods, bear it in mind. Contemporary art, in contrast, is often made with non-traditional art materials, such as video, installation or discarded or recycled objects, and you can't measure subjects and themes in the same way as in the past. But whatever theme or subject you are looking at really depends on you and how you interpret and respond to it.

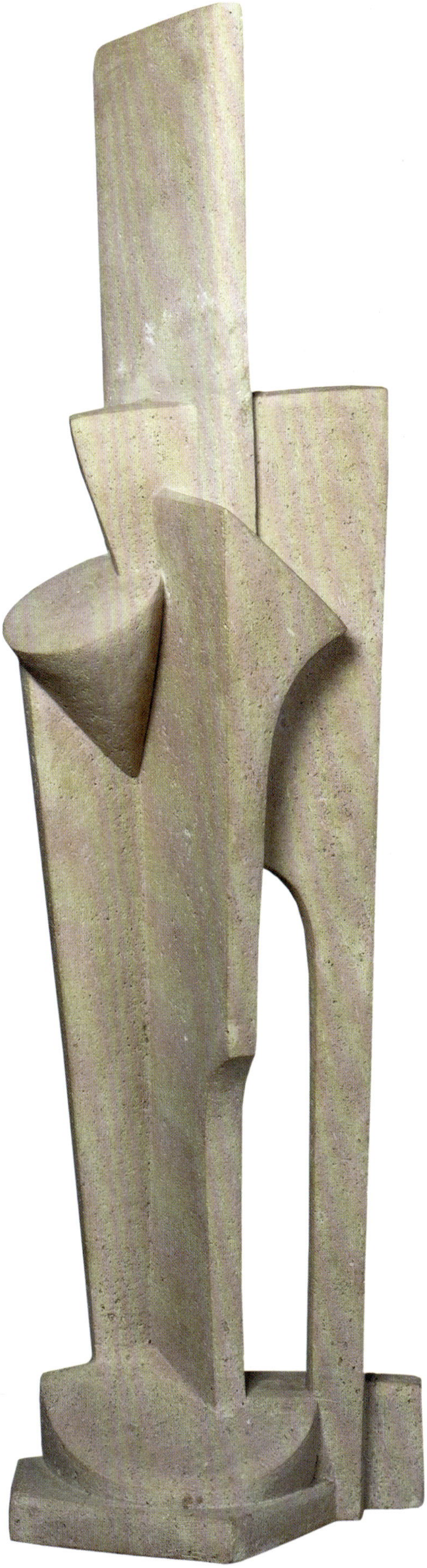

***Idyllic Landscape* 1st century BC–AD 79, fresco, Museo Archeologico Nazionale, Naples**
Landscape was an important genre in the ancient Roman period. Although not as accurate as it became after the 15th century, perspective – both linear and aerial – has been used here to create a believable imaginary world.

Jacques Lipchitz, *Sculpture* 1915–16, limestone, 98 x 28 x 18, Tate
Lipchitz (1891–1973) described this and other similar works as 'abstract architectural sculptures'. He wrote that he was 'building up and composing the idea of a human figure from abstract sculptural elements of line, plane and volume'. He's suggesting that this is based on a person sitting at a table. The work lends itself to many subjects, such as architecture, change, structures, tradition, discovery or Cubism.

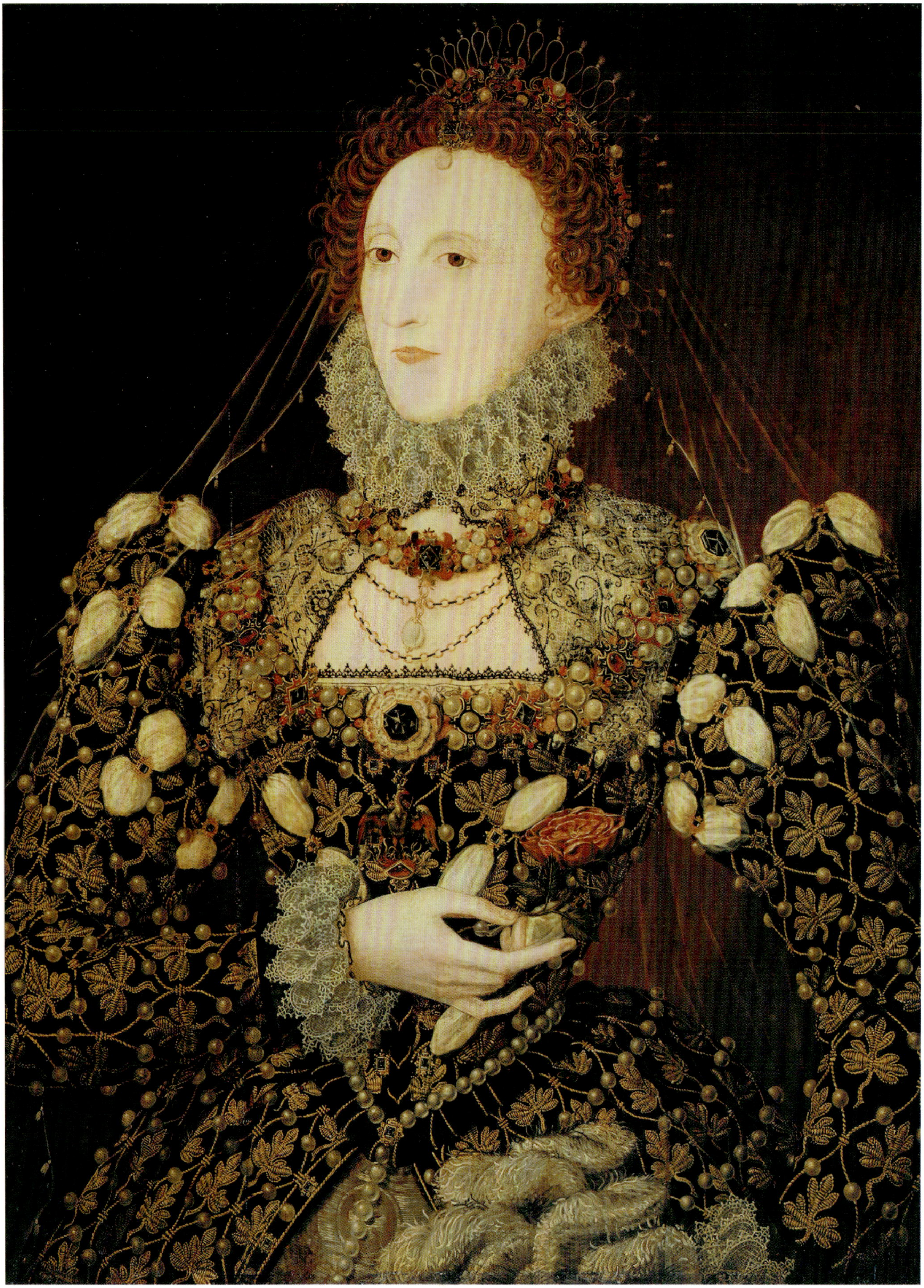

PORTRAITS

'Who sees the human face correctly: the photographer, the mirror, or the painter?'
Pablo Picasso

Portraits have been created for centuries for numerous reasons, including exploring changes in age, fashion, identity or mood, or asserting power, wealth and social standing. As with all artistic themes, however, styles, methods and functions of portraits have changed over time and across nations. Many portrait artists have confronted social and moral issues, while others have conveyed feelings, or used portraits to explore new art styles and techniques. The face fascinates and many portraits have been commissioned by rich patrons to indicate the importance of the sitter or to commemorate someone worthy. The works also proclaim the success of the artist, as only the most skilled are likely to be commissioned by powerful people. Conversely, many self-portraits are created by artists who can't afford to pay models (but this isn't the only reason self-portraits are made).

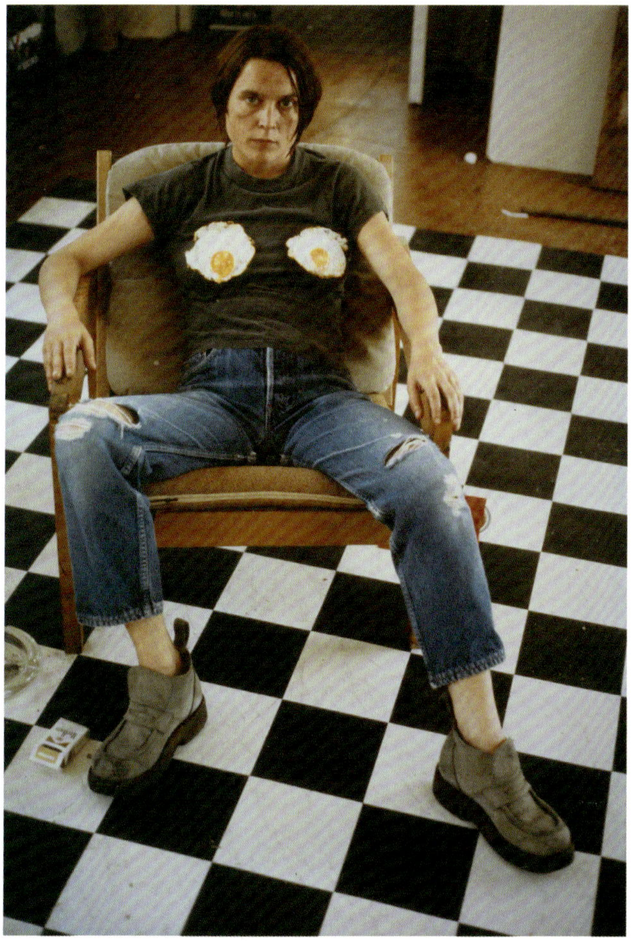

Attributed to Nicholas Hilliard, *Queen Elizabeth I* c.1575, oil on wood, 78.7 x 61, Tate
This is thought to be one of only two 'normal'-sized portraits that the miniaturist Nicholas Hilliard (c.1547–1619) painted. From 1572, Queen Elizabeth I preferred him to paint her portrait in his flat, shadowless style that resembled religious icons. Her face is white and her dress is heavily embellished with embroidery, pearls and other gems. She holds a rose, which symbolised virginity as well as being an emblem of the Tudor dynasty. Above her hand is a jewelled pendant of a phoenix, a mythical bird that represented immortality, power, virginity and chastity. Portraits like this were made to impress, so it emphasises the Queen's wealth, purity and power.

Sarah Lucas, *Self-portrait with Fried Eggs* 1996, digital print on paper, 74.5 x 51.4, Tate
This is one of twelve photographic self-portraits created by Lucas (born 1962). In the works, she exploits what she perceives as her 'masculine' appearance, posing in deliberately confrontational ways, challenging stereotypical representations of the female and exploring her own identity, gender and sexuality. Her clothes, pose and facial expression are all deliberately defiant. Food as symbols for sexual body parts is a common theme in her work, used mainly to rebel against traditional attitudes about the female nude and imagery that turns ordinary women into goddesses.

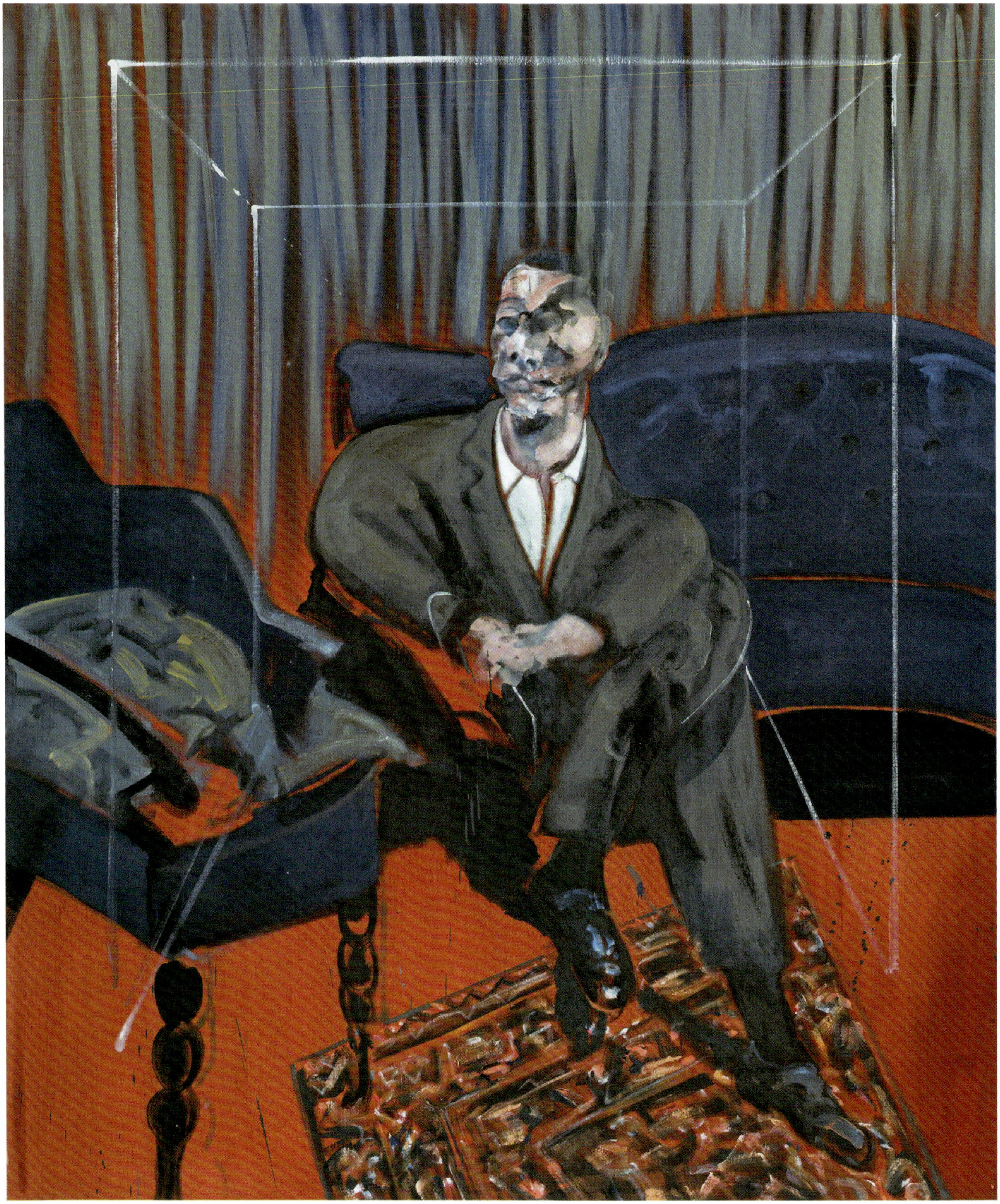

Artist, patron and sitter

A portrait is the result of an arrangement between sitter, patron and artist (who can sometimes be the same person!). Before photography was invented, a painted or sculpted portrait was the only way to record a person's likeness. Portraits were often commissioned to celebrate important events, such as births or marriages. They may have been commissioned to project a public persona, to declare beliefs and allegiances, or simply to be kept as a private image of a loved one.

Knowing a bit about the artist and patron can help you to understand a portrait, but there are other ways of investigating it too. Because portraits represent people and we all, whether consciously or unconsciously, 'read' our fellow humans, analysing portraits is something many of us can do instinctively. When you have chosen a portrait, view it from a distance and then step closer to examine details, such as structure or expression. If you don't understand or relate to it, don't disregard it, but try to find something that tells you why it looks as it does.

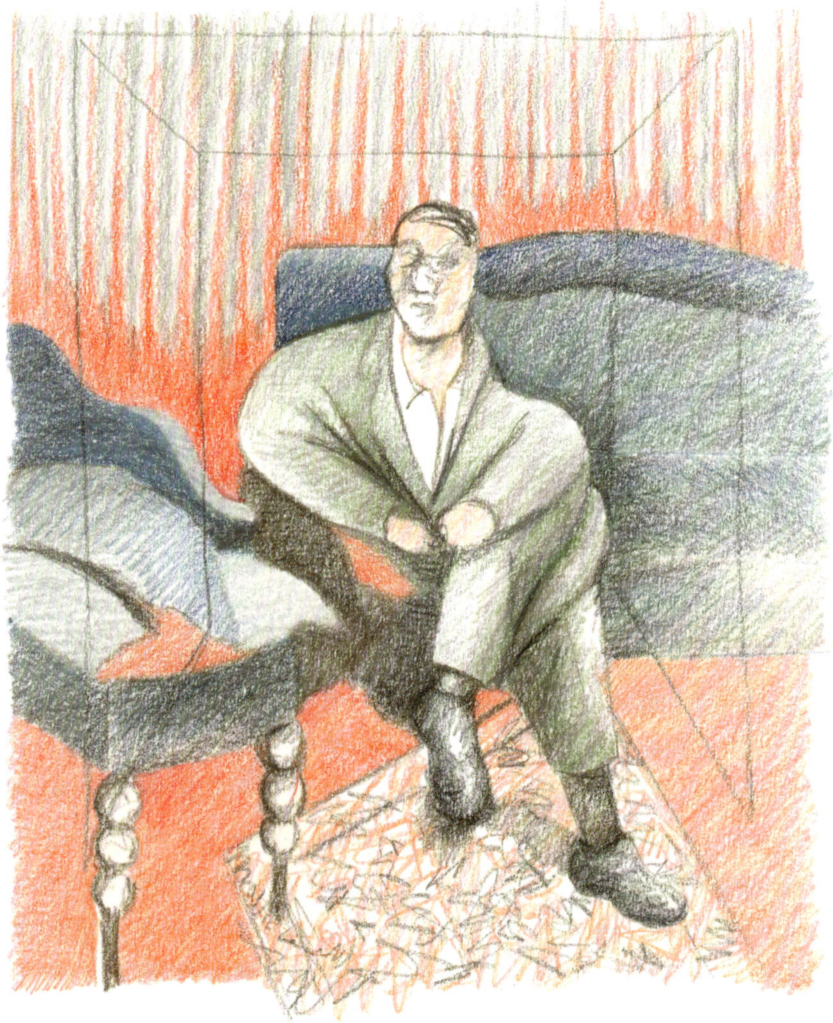

Francis Bacon, *Seated Figure* 1961, oil on canvas, 165 x 142, Tate
Many of Bacon's sitters are anonymous. Rather than portraying an individual, Bacon (1909–92) focuses on the 'human condition' here, with his model sitting in what appears to be a glass box, one of Bacon's favourite methods of creating a sense of isolation and claustrophobia. Few colours are used and paint has been smeared on in places, while other areas are heavily scumbled.

A response to Bacon's *Seated Figure* 1961 – coloured pencil sketch to understand colours, composition and methods
Key points to note:

- Saturated red paint on unprimed canvas
- Paint applied quickly, dripped in places
- Combination of real and distorted
- Long grey brushstrokes
- Lines suggesting a glass box
- Limited palette
- Colour links and holds the composition together – mainly reds and greys
- Tasteful furniture, disturbing, sinister image

Identity

Having your portrait made is a way of being seen and immortalised. Portraits can show the world who you are, or would like to be. But more than simply a superficial physical depiction, a portrait also aims to convey something about the individual, about his or her interests and social status. By interpreting such things as facial expressions, gestures, clothing, stance and symbols, we can learn something about the person beneath the surface.

Artists capture many intangible or intrinsic things about their sitters, such as social roles, status and self-perception. The image of ourselves we choose to present to the world is only the way we perceive ourselves, not necessarily how we appear to others. Many artists expose a person's opinion of themselves in contrast to what the rest of the world really sees. Symbols are often featured to reinforce some of these ideas. We usually recognise symbols that belong to our own times and cultures, but symbols from the distant past or from different cultures may be obscure and need to be researched to uncover their meanings and significance.

In the past, symbols were often important elements of portraits, while some more modern portraits also contain symbols that the artist has unintentionally included, and which can also be 'read'.

A helpful way to investigate any portrait is to choose one, and then make a note of the artist, the title of the work and the date it was made. Make a simple outline sketch of it. As you draw, think about the importance of each area of the image. If it's a sculpture, draw it from several different angles. Mark your drawing with arrows or lines to indicate areas that caught your attention and write, briefly, your reasons.

Write down adjectives that describe your impression of the work, such as brooding, proud, attractive or wistful. If the caption or label to the work gives you more information, add some of this to your notes and then study the work again. Knowing an artist's dates and nationality can help you to understand what was important to him or her, as well as what was fashionable at the time the artwork was created. Examine fine details. Ask yourself these questions:

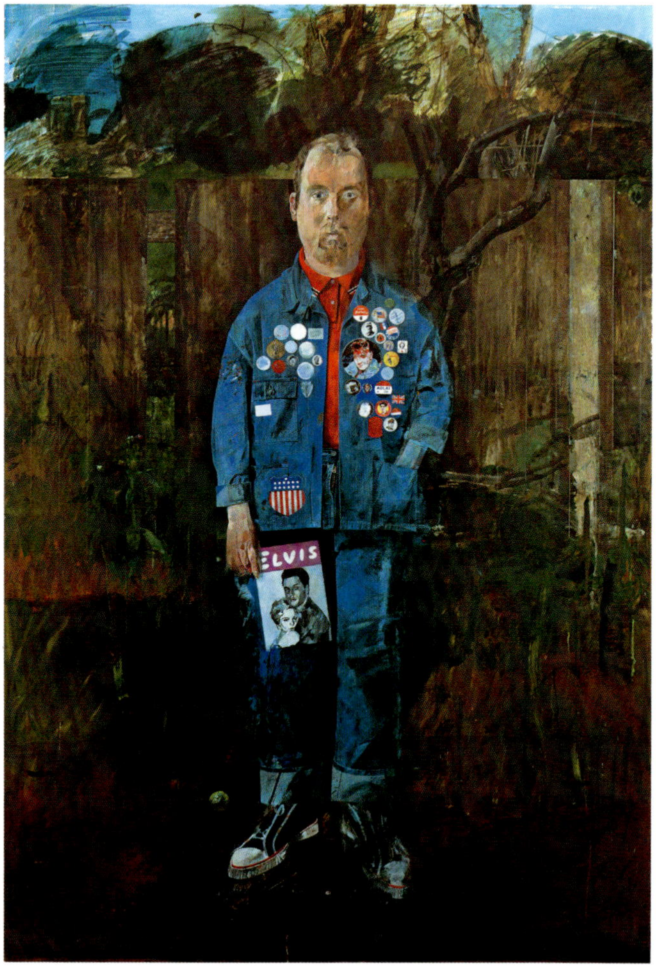

Peter Blake, *Self-portrait with Badges* 1961, oil on board, 174.3 x 121.9, Tate
One of the British Pop artists, Blake (born 1932) began making paintings of recognisable popular subjects while he was an art student in the 1950s. Painted the same year as Bacon's *Seated Figure*, this is a self-portrait, showing off the artist's collection of American badges and his all-American attire. (Baseball boots, jeans and denim jackets were at that time only really worn in the US.) The flatness of the commercial objects in the picture, that is, the badges, sewn-on patches and magazine, emphasises the actual painting surface. They are all bold, bright and new, while behind him the garden appears indistinct and drab. His own appearance is shapeless and distorted. To better understand this painting, you need to research the 1960s in Britain and America: the explosion of consumerism in the US and of fashion and music in the UK – and of youth culture in both countries.

- What is your first opinion of the portrait? Would you like to meet this person? Why or why not?
- What does this work say about the person depicted? What does the facial expression tell us? What about the posture or gestures of the sitter?
- Who is the subject? Why has this person been depicted? Does he or she have any particular significance in history?
- Do the clothes or appearance of the sitter say or reveal anything about the person's occupation or status? Can you work out from the way he or she is dressed when the work was made?
- What do you know about the artist? How does this compare to his or her other work?
- Who asked for this portrait to be made and why?
- Describe the setting. Is it real or imagined? What about other features or objects? Is there any symbolism in the work and, if so, what does it mean?
- Is the work realistic or distorted? In what ways does this make the work stronger or weaker?
- How would you describe the mood of the work? Calm, dramatic, cold, warm, eerie, or happy perhaps? If it is a painting, where is the light source? Is it natural light or artificial?
- Can you see how the work has been produced? What are the materials, techniques and processes?
- What do you think the artist was saying about the subject? What do you think the sitter wanted this portrait to communicate? What do you see that makes you say that?

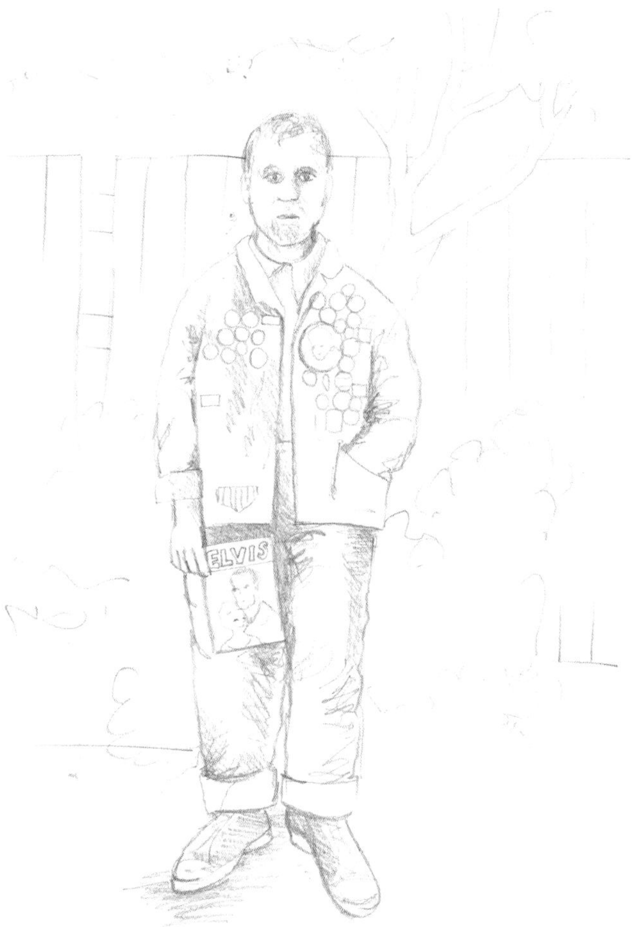

A response to Blake's *Self-portrait with Badges* 1961, pencil on paper
Key points to note:

- Many different sized badges all over jacket
- Sewn-on patch
- Denim, head to toe
- Elvis, the US singer featured on his magazine, helped popularise this style of dressing
- Scruffy, nonchalant
- Blake seems older than twenty-nine
- Staring eyes, no personality – objective portrait, difficult when it's the self
- Grass is green over brown – earthy colours in the background contrast with the blue and red of the figure
- Background is rough and sketchy, figure is in focus, more detailed, prominent
- Traditional full-length portrait pose, but executed in a modern way

Stanley Spencer

Stanley Spencer (1891–1959) painted his first self-portrait in oils over three months during 1914. (He had painted four self-portraits using other materials in 1913.) Although Spencer aimed to copy the style of Old Master paintings, and the colours and tones are reminiscent of Caravaggio (1571–1610) and Rembrandt van Rijn (1606–69), the vulnerability of his personality emerges unconsciously in the picture, as his expression seems filled with anxiety. His dark eyes and curved eyebrows convey slight astonishment. At the time of this painting, Cubism was influencing artists and Spencer's work was viewed by many as old-fashioned. He built up the face with broad brushstrokes, creating a fairly thick impasto surface, while scumbled marks define soft contours, and some areas have been stippled. He studied at London's Slade School of Art, where the training was traditional, concentrating on drawing rather than painting. But by the end of his life he had radically changed his approach, as can be seen in the second self-portrait, in which he seems to have discarded all superficial pretence, exposing his inner thoughts and an awareness of the person he had become.

Ideas for comparing portraits

- Find two portraits that are either completely different or have something in common. In your sketchbook, sketch the two images on facing pages.
- Note any differences in expression; what makes the sitter's emotion obvious or obscure? What mood has been created in each work?
- Note any differences in colour, tone or paint application – can you see the brushmarks? What materials and techniques has the artist used? What colours?
- Words you might use: realism, distortion, care, smeared, curved, texture, scale, close-up, line, intensity, detail, soaked, isolation.
- What do you like about each work? What do you dislike, and why?
- How do you think this work might influence you?

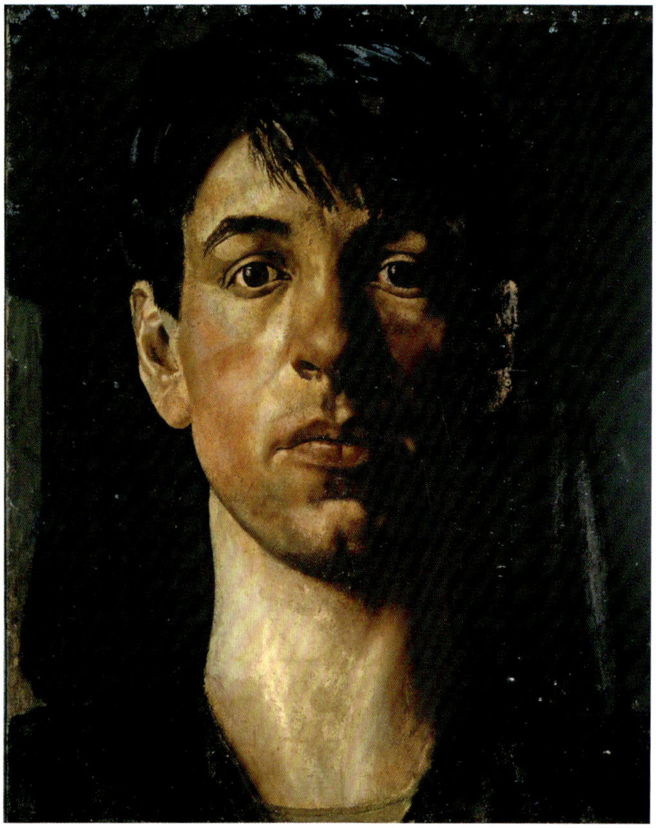

Stanley Spencer, *Self-Portrait* 1914, oil on canvas, 63 x 51, Tate
His first self-portrait in oils, this was painted by Spencer in his bedroom in Berkshire when he was twenty-three, just weeks before the outbreak of the First World War. He was attempting to emulate the style of an Old Master painting, supposedly after seeing a reproduction of a head of Christ by the artist Bernadino Luini (c.1480–1532) and paintings by Botticelli (1445–1510) in the National Gallery in London.

Stanley Spencer, *Self-Portrait* 1959, oil on canvas, 50.8 x 40.6, Tate
This is Spencer's final self-portrait, produced forty-five years after his first. He painted it while staying with friends in Yorkshire, five months before he died from cancer. Although ill, he painted it in just five days, as before, working in a bedroom and using his – by then – characteristic method of quick paint application and candid style that conveys a raw sense of physical and emotional intensity.

Comparing portraits

How do Spencer's two self-portraits compare? What was he most concerned with in the first painting? Had that changed in the second? Why do you think this? From his young self to his older self, how did his approach change? Contrasting two works is a good way of discovering what is distinctive about each. Comparing two works by the same artist is also useful for understanding artists' creative developments and for working out what may have changed in their lives.

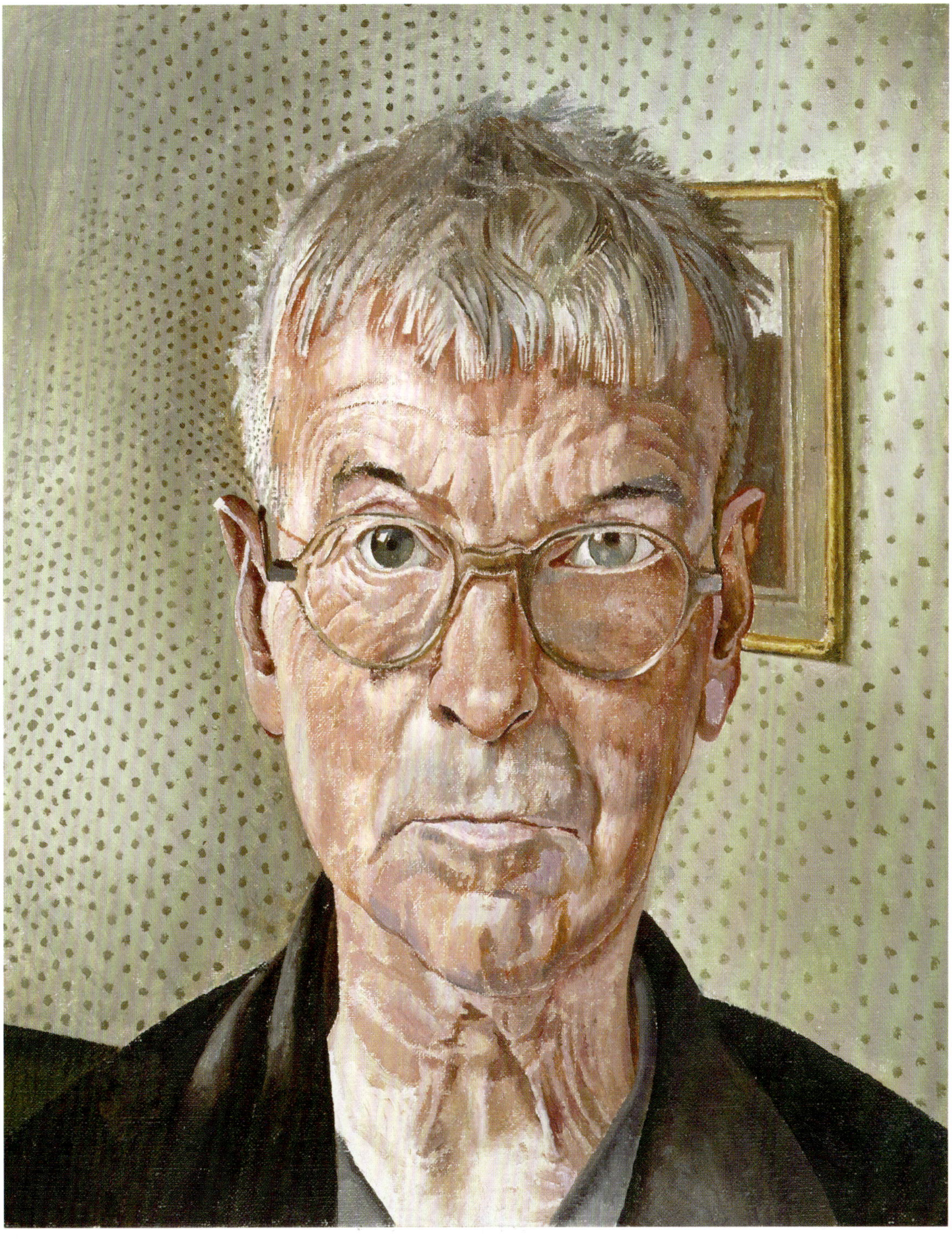

Self-portraits

Artists have commonly used self-portraits for self-expression. Many have explored their own genders, cultures and sexual orientations, and others have used them as marketing tools for self-promotion.

By the 15th century, once mirrors had progressed from the earlier disks of polished bronze, tin or silver, more artists began creating images of themselves. Self-portraits were cheap and the models were readily available! Sometimes artists created self-portraits simply to practise their skills. Artists such as Albrecht Dürer (1471–1528) produced self-portraits that reflected their physical appearances, while others such as Rembrandt and Vincent van Gogh (1853–90), created intense self-studies, revealing complex personalities. Making up approximately one-third of all her work, the self-portraits of Frida Kahlo (1907–54) functioned as a kind of therapy. After a traffic accident in 1925, she was in pain and unable to walk properly for the rest of her life. Influenced by this, her self-portraits explore her emotions, her heritage and her gender.

Learning more about any self-portrait

- What is the sitter's expression?
- How is the sitter dressed? What is happening in the background? Are these features relevant?
- When was the portrait painted? Does the date have any relevance? (The country in which it was painted may also be significant.)
- How do you think the sitter was feeling – can you tell? What can you learn about the artist's personality from this work?
- Is the work distorted or realistic? How does this affect your opinion of the work? What do you think the artist was trying to say?
- What time in history was the painting produced – does this have any implications for what he or she was trying to show?
- How have the materials been used? Is this significant?
- In what ways is this a) similar and b) different from a self-portrait you have produced?
- Make several observational studies of yourself using different materials. Note how your face changes depending on your expression or feelings.

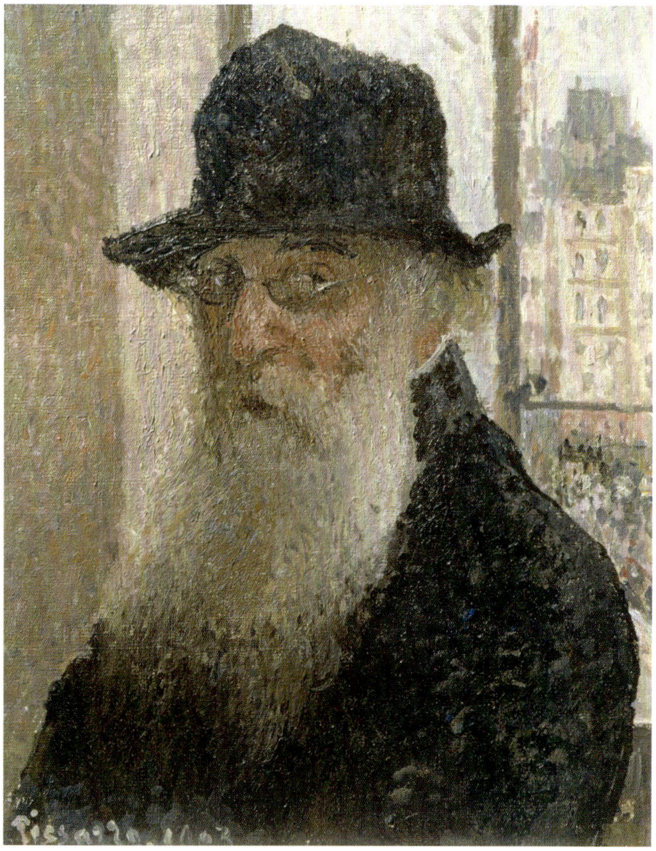

Camille Pissarro, *Self-portrait* 1903, oil on canvas, 41 x 33.3, Tate
This is the last self-portrait painted by Impressionist artist Camille Pissarro (1830–1903), made in the year of his death – the same year he received official recognition from the art authorities in Paris. It is painted with the small patches of paint that he applied in many of his works, in a style that was no longer original and shocking, but that had become popular across Europe.

George Frederic Watts, *Self-portrait* 1864, oil on canvas, 64.8 x 52, Tate
Watts (1817–1904) was one of the busiest and most successful portrait painters in Britain during the Victorian era. Although this self-portrait was painted forty years before Pissarro's, the styles of the men's fashions are similar. Both have beards, both are in dark clothes, both wear hats. Compare the two portraits using the questions in this chapter, or the 'content, form, process, mood' method (see page 42).

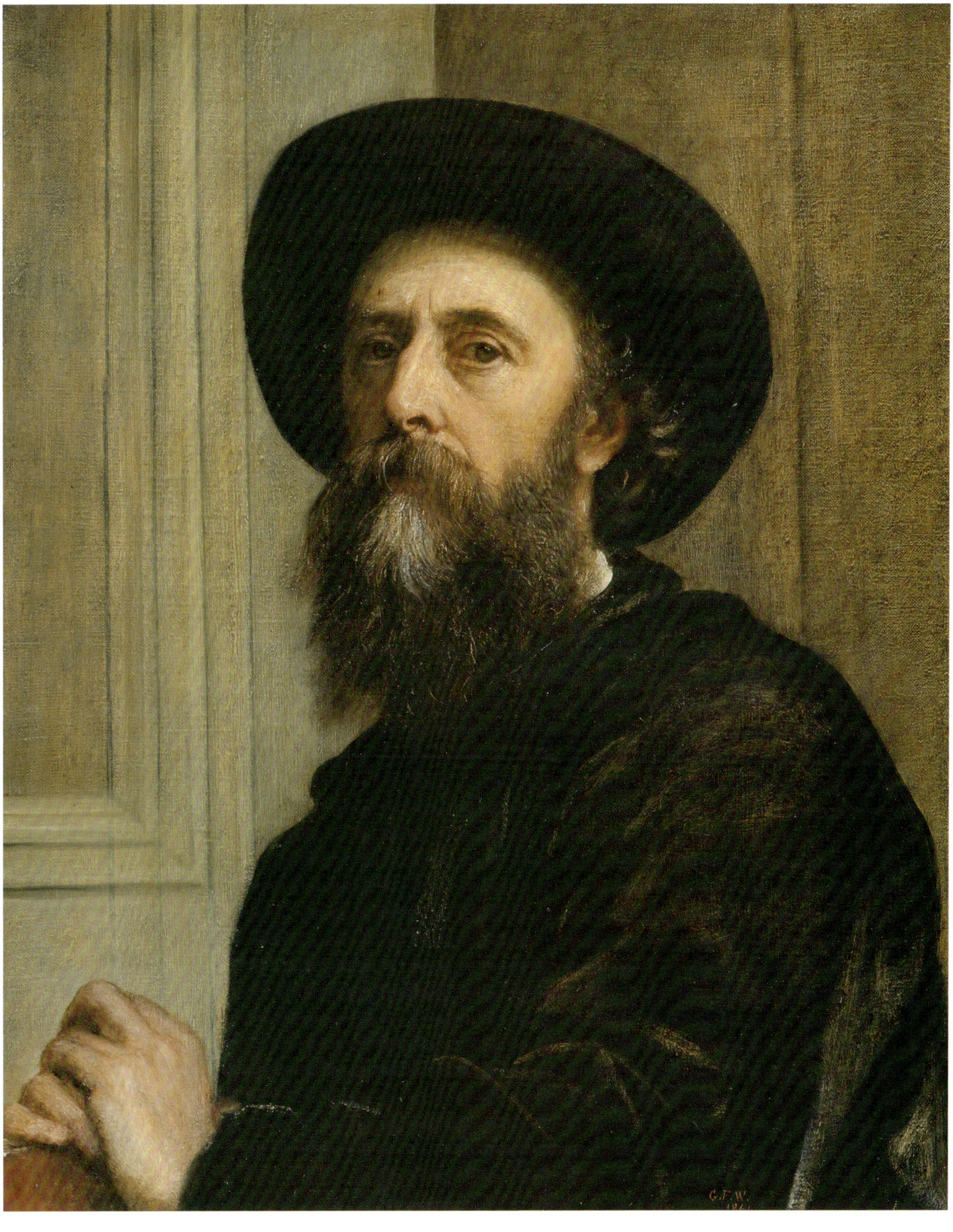

Picasso's *Weeping Woman*

A woman is in her best hat, on her way to market. But what she sees overhead is reflected in her eyes – German bomber planes. All around her is death and destruction; innocent people like her, mainly mothers, babies and children, killed and maimed. As the woman weeps at the horror of it all, her face distorts, changing shape and colour.

Picasso was painting a portrait of emotion rather than trying to capture a physical likeness. It was a protest against the horrors of the Civil War in his native Spain. The jagged shapes around the woman's mouth as she bites on her handkerchief resemble ice or broken glass, and the jarring colours and thick black outlines add to the discomforting feeling the image evokes. Picasso has created his own symbolism to comment on the event. Is he telling the truth? Do you think he was a supporter or opponent of General Franco? How has he expressed emotion? Is the work relevant today? What makes you think this?

Picasso could draw realistically as a young child. By the time he was thirteen, he painted pictures that were as

Content, form, process, mood

These headings represent a common and effective method for gathering information about a work of art. They can be used alongside the personal, formal and contextual approach already discussed, or on their own as the initial steps in understanding a work of art. Apply your own questions under the four headings:

Content

What is the work of art about? Did the artist observe the subject matter directly or is it imagined or remembered? Is the subject realistic, or is there exaggeration or distortion? If so, what effect does this create? Can you see any symbols or hidden meanings in the work? Is it a common theme – have other artists produced work with similar content? If so, how does this differ?

Form

How has the artwork been arranged? Are there combinations of shapes or patterns – and, if so, what? Are there repeated shapes? Have colours or tones been used deliberately to create a sense of solidity? What textures are in the work? Does it seem balanced? How does negative space balance with positive shapes? Is negative space an important part of the work? How has it been used?

Process

What materials and techniques has the artist used? Did he or she work in a studio or elsewhere? In front of a subject or somewhere because the materials dictated where it was best to work? Did the artist use sketchbooks, photographs or other preparatory methods in planning the work? Was it made quickly or over some time?

Mood

How does the work of art affect you? Does it arouse your emotions? Can you imagine what the artist might have felt while producing it? What is your impression of the work's 'mood'?

Pablo Picasso, *Weeping Woman* 1937, oil on canvas, 60.8 x 50, Tate

One of the worst atrocities during the Spanish Civil War of 1936 to 1939 was the bombing of the Basque town of Guernica by the German air force, which lent its support to General Franco. Hundreds of civilians were killed and the town was devastated. Picasso responded to the massacre by painting the vast mural *Guernica*, and for months afterwards he made supplementary paintings based on one of the figures in the mural: a weeping woman holding her dead child. This is the last and most elaborate of these. For Picasso, the vision of the woman crying epitomised the distress, destruction and desolation of the war. The woman's features are based on Picasso's lover Dora Maar, who had encouraged Picasso's political awareness.

Key points to note:

- A woman crying is a universal image of suffering. The woman's Sunday-best hat seems almost ludicrous in the circumstances
- German bomber planes are reflected in her eyes
- Paint is applied in flat, smooth and fairly thick marks
- As the woman weeps at the horror of it all, her face distorts, changing shape and colour
- The harsh palette and angular brushstrokes emphasise her pain
- Picasso has mixed viewpoints and angles on the flat surface, to show the subject from different directions at once
- The face fills the composition, creating a strong impact
- Emotion is shown in the eyebrows, teeth and fingers, which have been painted as sharp, angular and jarring
- Even though the event happened in the last century, the work will always be relevant

skilful as many in art galleries made by extremely experienced artists. So he invented new ways of drawing, painting and making things. He was outstandingly productive and his ideas were subsequently followed by other artists. This portrait was painted after he had pioneered Cubism with Georges Braque (1882–1963) and he was comfortable with portraying objects from various angles on one flat surface. So the woman's mouth, for example, is shown from a different viewpoint from that of the nose and eyes.

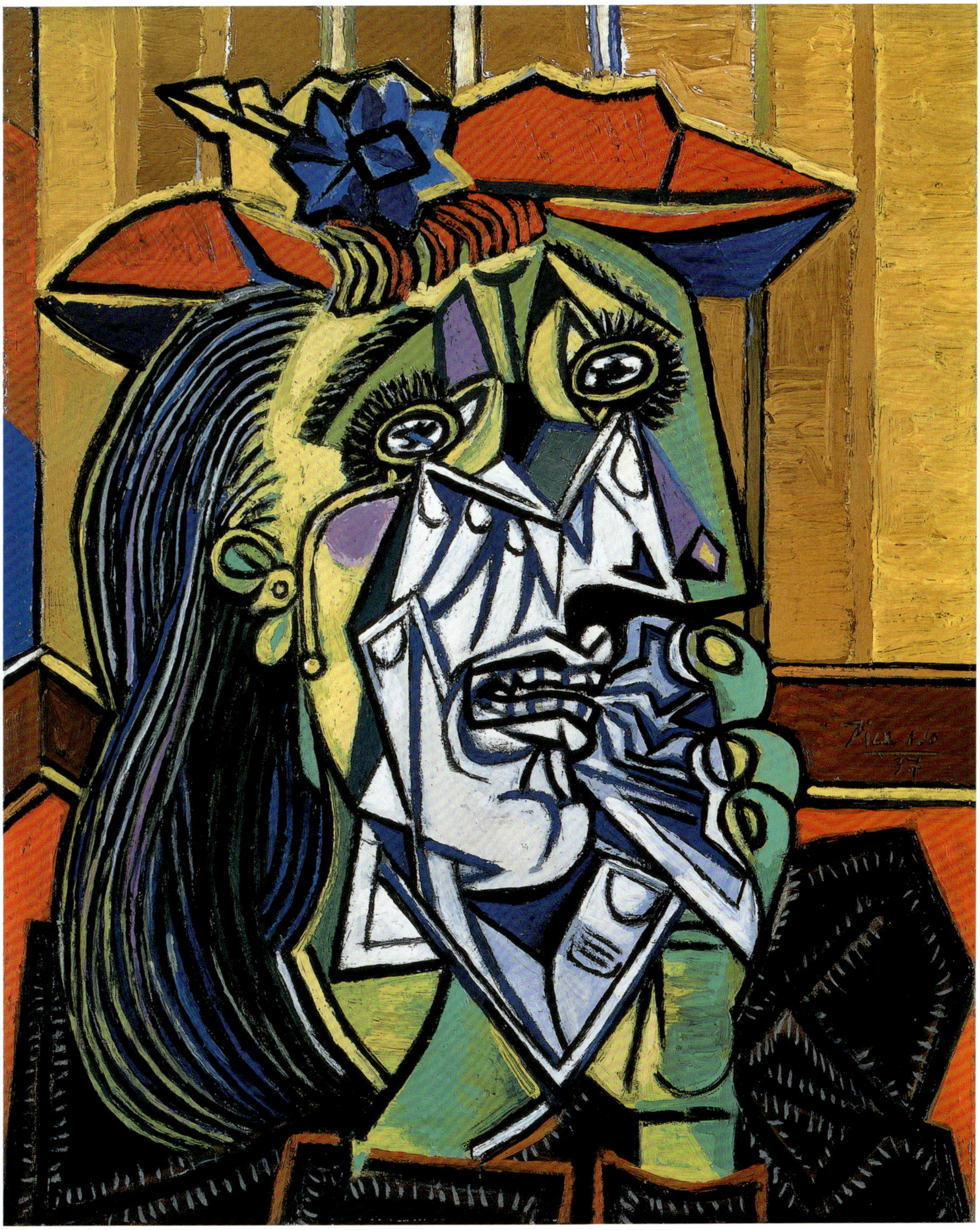

Expanding on your creativity through portraiture

- Draw a 'normal' portrait of someone you know. Make another drawing of the same person, expressing an emotion through colour and shape as Francis Bacon did in *Seated Figure* (see page 34).
- Ask your subject to think of an event that he or she has experienced that was dramatic and emotional.
- Now plan a third work to express the emotion your sitter felt during that event. Look at other artists' portraits to get some ideas on how you might do this. Consider scale: will this make a difference to the impact of your work? What about materials, texture or colour? Will you include symbols for viewers to work out? Will there be any elements in your work to express the drama and emotion of the event? Will you convey movement too? How?
- Finally, produce the portrait, showing your sitter surrounded by or expressing that dramatic, emotional event. After you have completed the work, make notes about whether or not your work was successful and why.

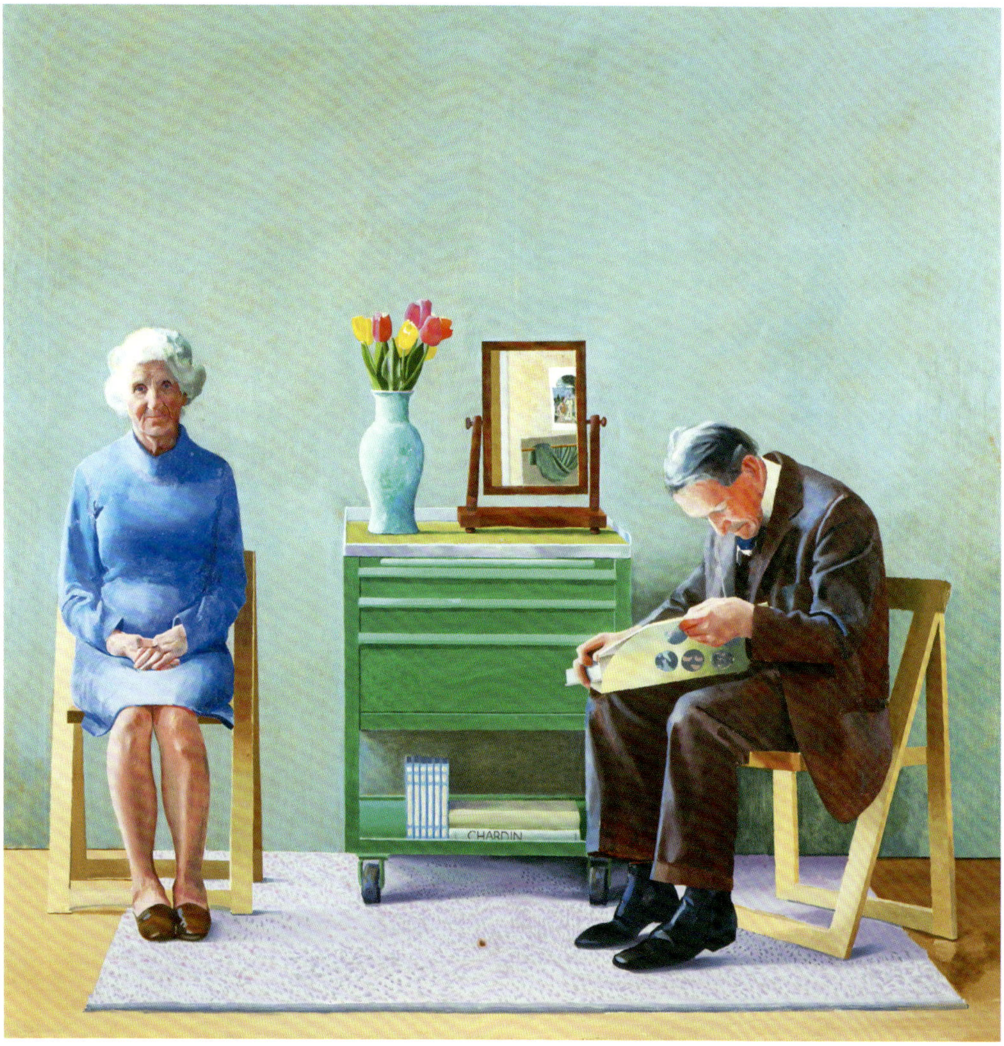

David Hockney, *My Parents* 1977, oil on canvas, 182.9 x 182.9, Tate
Painted a year before his father's death, in this work Hockney (born 1937) explored his parents' individual personalities. His mother sits attentively, posing patiently for her son, while his father has lost interest and is reading a book. Other (relevant) books can be seen on the shelf. A well-known Renaissance painting and another of Hockney's own works are reflected in the mirror. To produce this painting, Hockney made sketches from life and also worked from photographs. His parents were strong-minded individuals; his mother was religious and a vegetarian – unusual at the time. His father was an anti-war campaigner and a fierce opponent of smoking. Like an Old Master painting, the image is filled with symbolic objects and clues about the sitters.

Family portraits

As well as single portraits, family portraits have been a common subject for artists for centuries. From formal portraiture to candid, relaxed images of family life, artists have found great scope in exploring relationships and the impact of influences, juxtapositions and situations. As commissioned and formal portraits became less popular, artists extended their scope and individuality, creating works that expose more of the underlying issues between groups of relatives and also indicate the social concerns of the time in which the work was made.

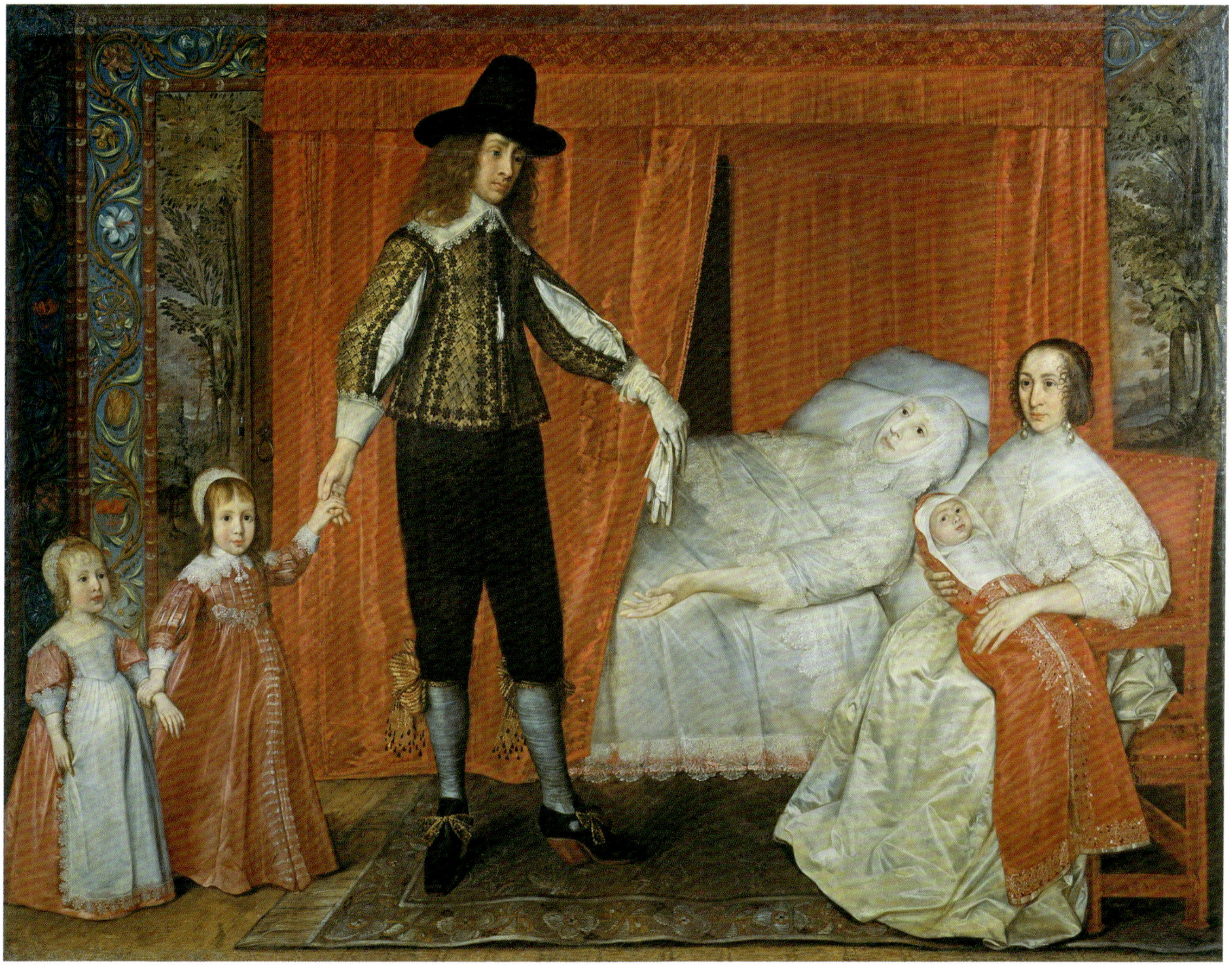

David des Granges, *The Saltonstall Family* c.1636–7, oil on canvas, 214 x 276.2, Tate
Employed as a miniaturist by King Charles I of England (1600–49), des Granges (1611/13–75) supported the Royalists during the English Civil War and painted many miniatures of the future Charles II (1630–85). This painting is of Sir Richard Saltonstall (1595–1650) of Oxfordshire, with his family. The figure in the bed is a posthumous image of Sir Richard's first wife, Elizabeth Basse, pointing towards their two surviving children, Richard and Ann. The smaller child is Richard; boys and girls were dressed the same until they were about nine, when boys were 'breeched', or put into male clothing and had their hair cut. Three years after Elizabeth's death, Sir Richard took a second wife: Mary Parker, the richly dressed woman sitting by the bed. The baby in her arms is the couple's son Philip, born in 1636. The red bed hangings and the rich tapestry are signs of wealth and high status. The inclusion of Sir Richard's first wife in the picture was quite normal at the time, to show the family line.

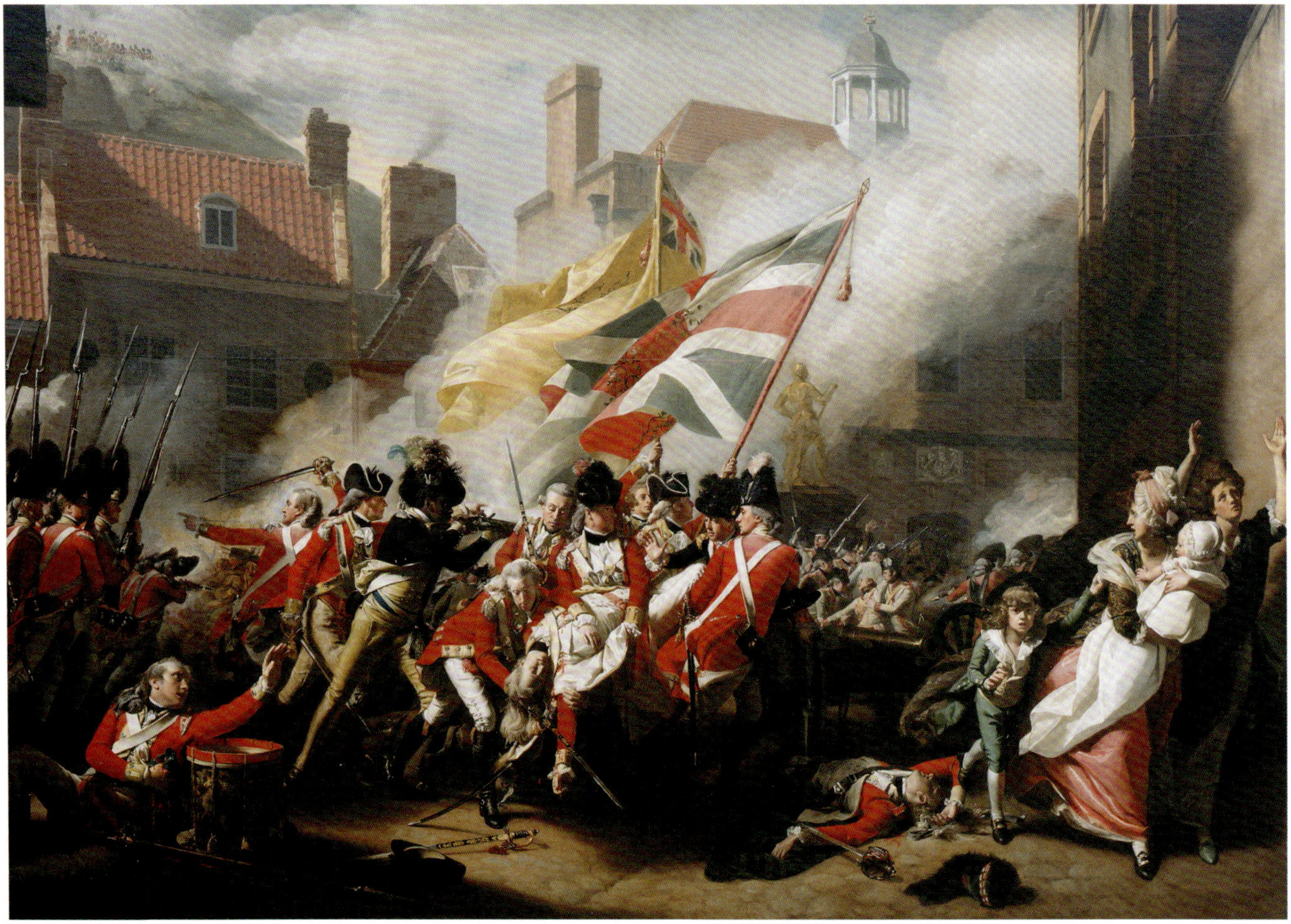

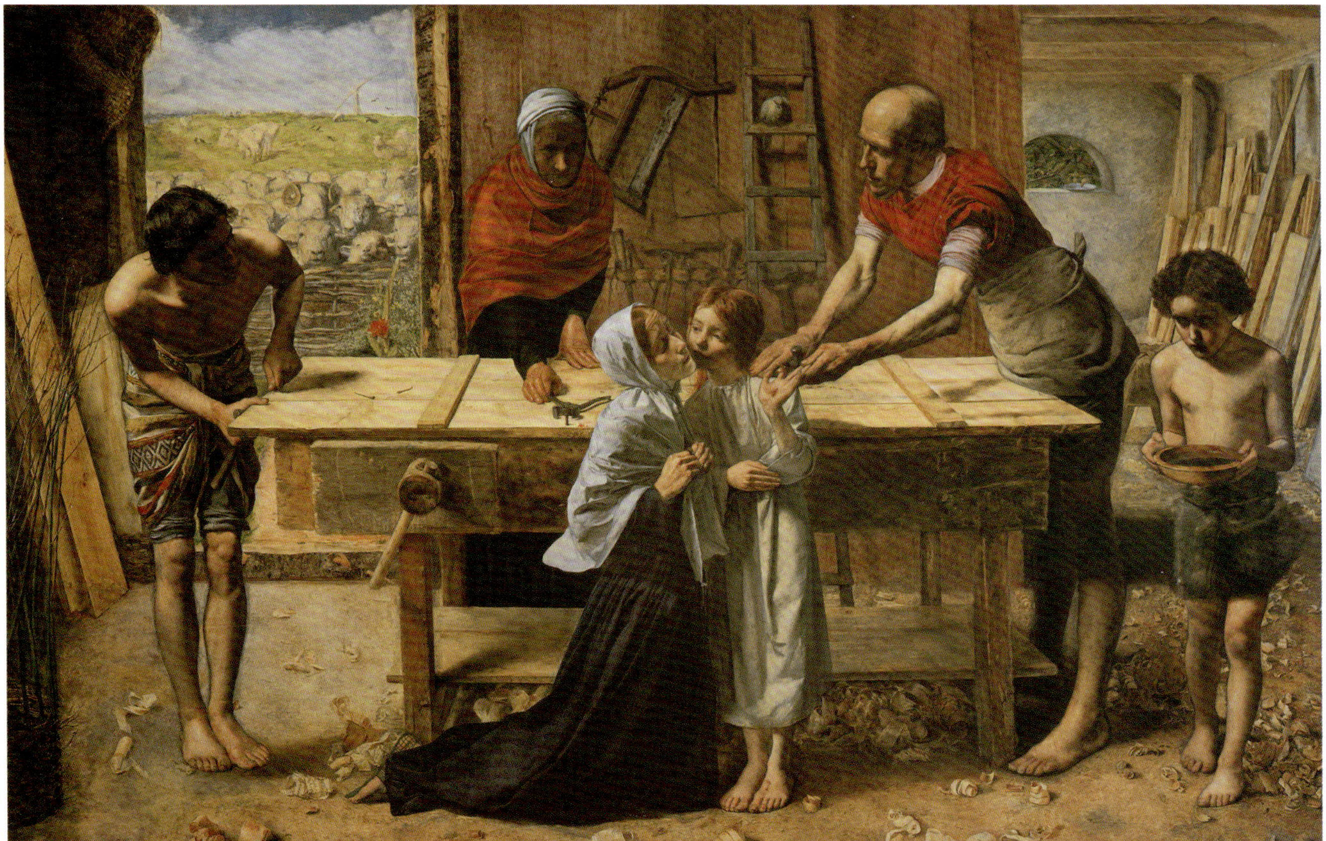

FIGURES

'It is through the human figure that I best succeed in expressing the nearly religious feeling that I have towards life.'
Henri Matisse

Since the earliest times, artists have drawn, painted and carved images of the human figure, and for centuries, depictions of the human form were prized more highly than those of still life, animals or landscape. In early societies, the significance of the figure in artefacts was often supernatural, to evoke or embody gods or spirits. Later, the reasons for depicting humans expanded, and from the 13th century in the West, anatomy became an essential part of an artist's training.

John Singleton Copley, *The Death of Major Peirson, 6 January 1781* 1783, oil on canvas, 251.5 x 365.8, Tate
In 1781, French soldiers attacked the Channel Island of Jersey. The British Governor was taken prisoner and ordered his troops to surrender, but a young officer, Major Peirson, ignored the order, took command and counter-attacked, defeating the French. Peirson, however, was killed by a French sniper and, in retaliation, his servant Pompey killed the sniper. This history painting by Copley (1738–1815) illustrates all these events as if they were happening at once. Major Peirson is dying, Pompey shoots the French sniper, and the moment coincides with the British victory, even though Peirson was actually killed earlier. When first exhibited in 1784, crowds thronged to admire the picture. What is your opinion of it? Even if the subject is no longer as relevant as it was, what about the dynamism of the figures and the composition?

John Everett Millais, *Christ in the House of His Parents* 1849–50, oil on canvas, 86.4 x 139.7, Tate
This scene from Christ's childhood is unlike any other religious art of the time. It horrified many. The *Times* described it as 'revolting'. Charles Dickens described it as 'mean, odious, repulsive and revolting', and Christ as 'a hideous, wry-necked, blubbering, red-headed boy in a bed gown.' The shock was that Millais portrayed the holy figures as grubby and poor, rather than immaculate and beautiful. Christian symbols appear throughout the picture. The sheep represent the faithful, the dove the presence of the Holy Spirit. The carpenter's triangle on the wall symbolises the Holy Trinity, while the wood and nails, and the blood on the boy's hand and foot indicate the Crucifixion. Young St John carries a bowl of water to bathe Christ's wounds, drawing attention to his role as Baptist. What do you think of this work?

Changing purposes

From ancient Greek wall paintings to Renaissance frescoes, and from commemorative statues to 19th- and 20th-century explorations of the human condition, story-telling has been an important aspect of art for centuries. Representation of the figure changed as human needs and artistic expression evolved, from the 'Venus' figures of Ice Age Europe and rock paintings of southern Africa, to the ornate, often frivolous figures of 18th-century Rococo styles, or the deliberately exaggerated and distorted works of the early 20th century. Early figure imagery seems to have been mainly created to explore religious beliefs. In ancient Egyptian art, figures were stylised and followed a formula for thousands of years while, later, ancient Greek and Roman figures became more natural-looking and descriptive. By the Middle Ages, figures appeared in religious and medieval scenes and, by the Renaissance period, artists strove to make them as lifelike as possible. After the invention of photography in 1839, artists became even more experimental.

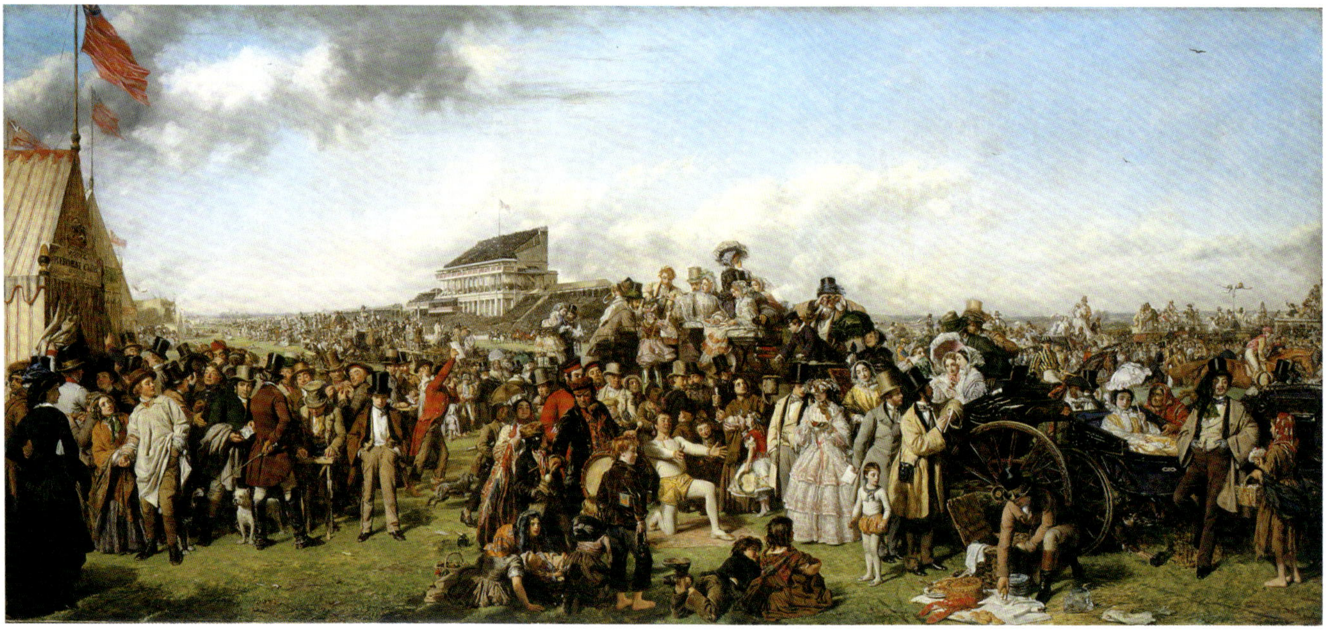

William Powell Frith, *The Derby Day* 1856–8, oil on canvas, 101.6 x 223.5, Tate
Frith's paintings were exceptionally admired at a time when there was no television or cinema. This is one of his narrative scenes of modern life which, when it was first exhibited at the Royal Academy, was so popular that a rail had to be put up to protect it from the crowds. It presents a scene of Victorian life featuring various characters conforming to their social stereotypes, such as young men flirting with young women in a carriage, minstrels, gypsies, touts, beggars, policemen and a fortune teller. Frith worked on this painting for fifteen months, producing two large sketches in addition to the finished work. Viewers enjoyed picking out different groups of people in various activities, such as conmen, courtesans, acrobats, swaggering young gents and servants.

Joseph Wright of Derby, *An Iron Forge* 1772, oil on canvas, 121.3 x 132, Tate
From the mid-1760s, Wright began painting scenes of contemporary scientific and industrial life, often with strong chiaroscuro effects. In this scene of a small iron forge, an iron-founder and his family are bathed in warm light cast by a white-hot iron bar that has just been taken from the furnace. Wright compressed the scene for dramatic effect to accommodate the machinery and figures. In the centre is the iron-founder, glancing proudly at his wife and children. Most forges were run by families at the time and, by including the elderly man too, Wright introduced the theme of the 'Ages of Man', showing three generations together and a link to the past. While the painting hints at the massive changes occurring through the Industrial Revolution, it also suggests that to many happy families the changes will not necessarily be positive.

History painting

History paintings usually depict a moment in a story and feature several figures rather than a single subject like a portrait. The term essentially means 'story painting', rather than painting exclusively historical scenes. History paintings can depict religious and mythological stories, commemorations or allegorical scenes. In 1435, the Italian polymath Leon Battista Alberti (1404–72) wrote a treatise, *Della Pittura* (*On Painting*), and declared history painting (*istoria*) to be the highest form of art. He outlined 'rules' that all history painters should adhere to, including featuring several figures in different poses and the need to show variety and originality. He emphasised the importance of depicting interactions between figures through poses and gestures, and he said that history painting was the most difficult type of painting, but it had the greatest potential to affect viewers. Largely through the influence of Alberti's ideas, history continued to be considered the most prestigious genre – or type – of Western painting until the 19th century.

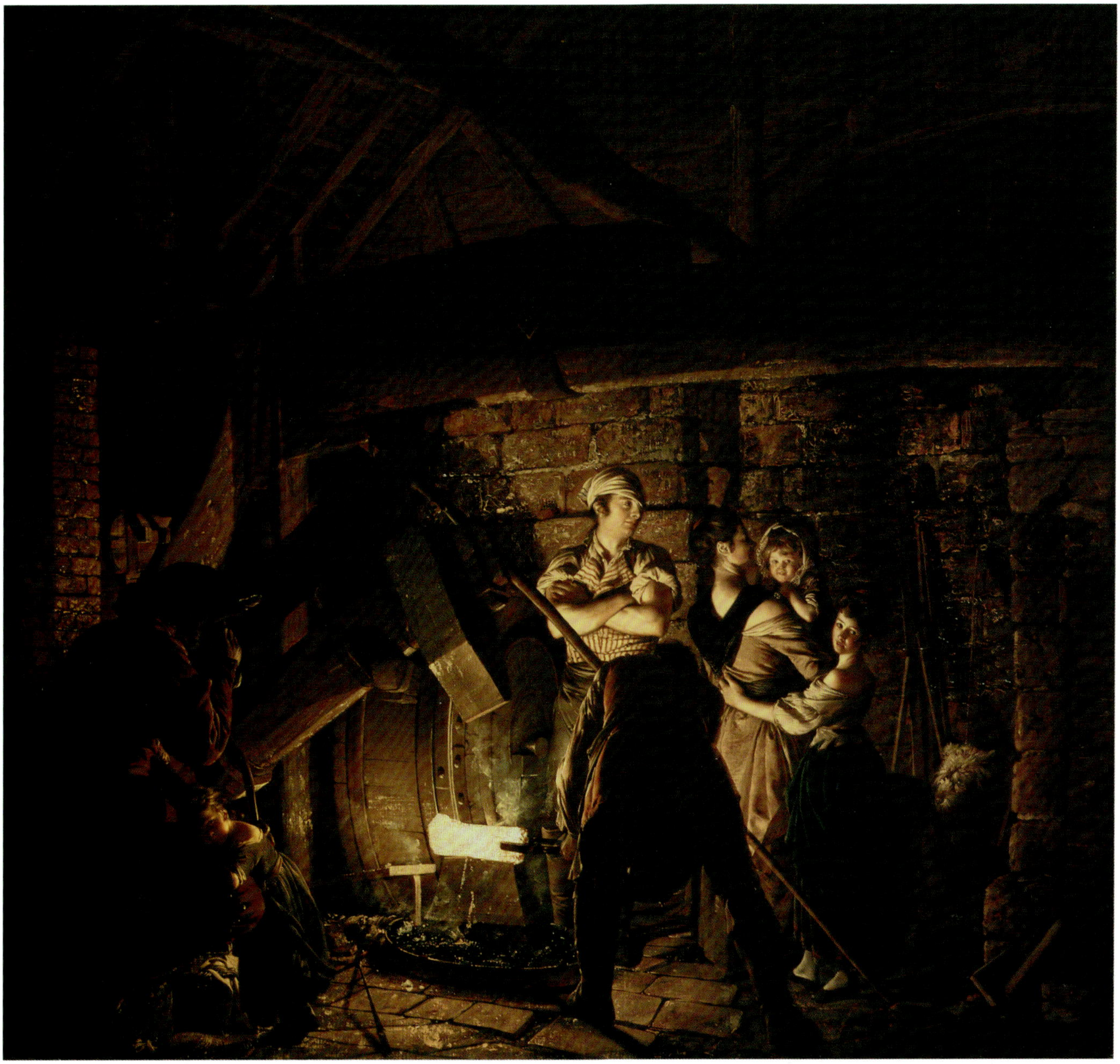

Narrative

All history painting is narrative, but not all narrative art is history painting. Narrative or story-telling in art is a universal method for communicating messages and imparting cultural values. Some of the earliest evidence of human art features stories told through pictures, and artists have developed many ways to do this. Although there are some features common to all narrative art, different cultures have developed distinctive ways to narrate stories through images. Once these messages become unfamiliar to viewers over time and place, however, they can lose their power to communicate or acquire different meanings. To read a work of narrative art from any time or culture, here are some questions to ask yourself:

- What is happening?
- How does the artist help us to understand this?
- What clues reveal the work's meaning?
- Imagine that you are describing the work to someone on the phone. List everything you see.
- What can you find out about the artist and the work?
- What moods or feelings can you detect?
- What techniques and materials have been used?

To respond to the work on a practical level, study the composition. As many narrative paintings include numerous figures, it is probably impractical to try to replicate the entire work, so focus on smaller areas:

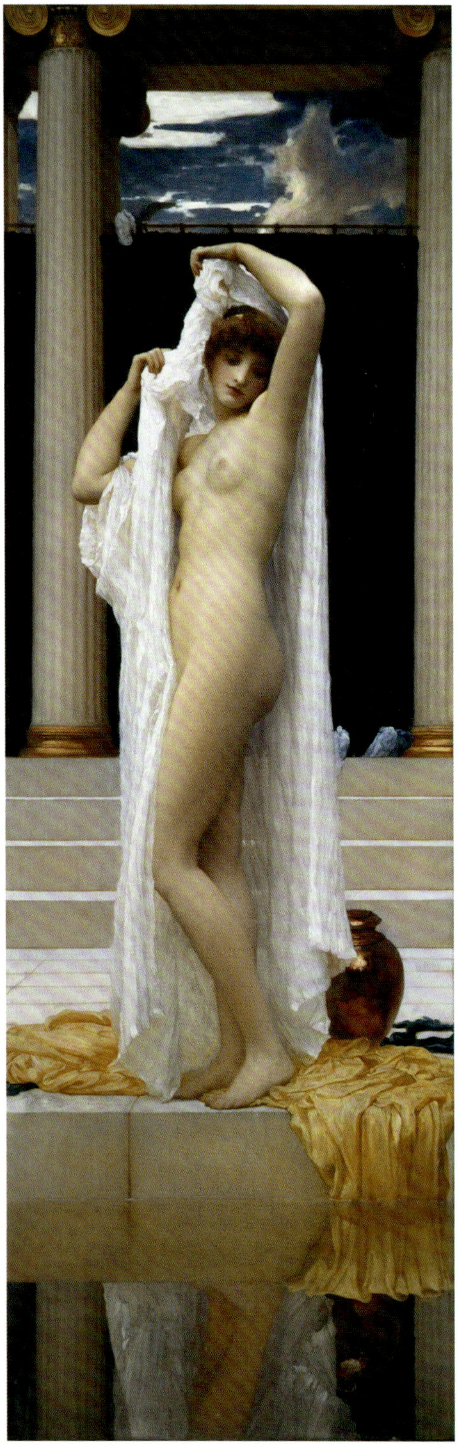

Frederic, Lord Leighton, *The Bath of Psyche* exhibited 1890, oil on canvas, 189.2 x 62.2, Tate

In Roman mythology, Psyche, the beautiful daughter of a king, attracted the love of Cupid, the god of love. However, she angered him so he left her. She roamed the Earth looking for him. Eventually Jupiter took pity on her, made her immortal and re-united the lovers. This myth became extremely popular during the second half of the 19th century. Leighton (1830–96) based Psyche's pose on an ancient statue of Venus he had seen in Naples in 1859, making the beautiful nude an acceptable work of art at the time, simply because he called her a goddess. A naked mortal woman would have shocked Victorian viewers.

1. Find a history or narrative painting, such as *The Derby Day* 1856–8 by William Powell Frith (1819–1909), *An Iron Forge* 1772 by Joseph Wright of Derby (1734–97) or *Christ in the House of His Parents* 1849–50 by John Everett Millais (1829–96).
2. Make an outline sketch of the work, summarising the main masses of the composition.
3. Isolate a detail within the work – to do this, hold a viewfinder over an image of the work until you find an area that interests you.
4. Draw your chosen detail of the work.
5. Find and draw another detail.
6. Continue in this way several more times and then copy your details on to a larger space, arranging them in a different composition.
7. Alternatively, select certain figures from the work and put them in your own narrative composition; same pose, different purpose. Translating other artists' figures was a common way for many artists to work in the past.
8. Be creative with the scale, composition and materials.

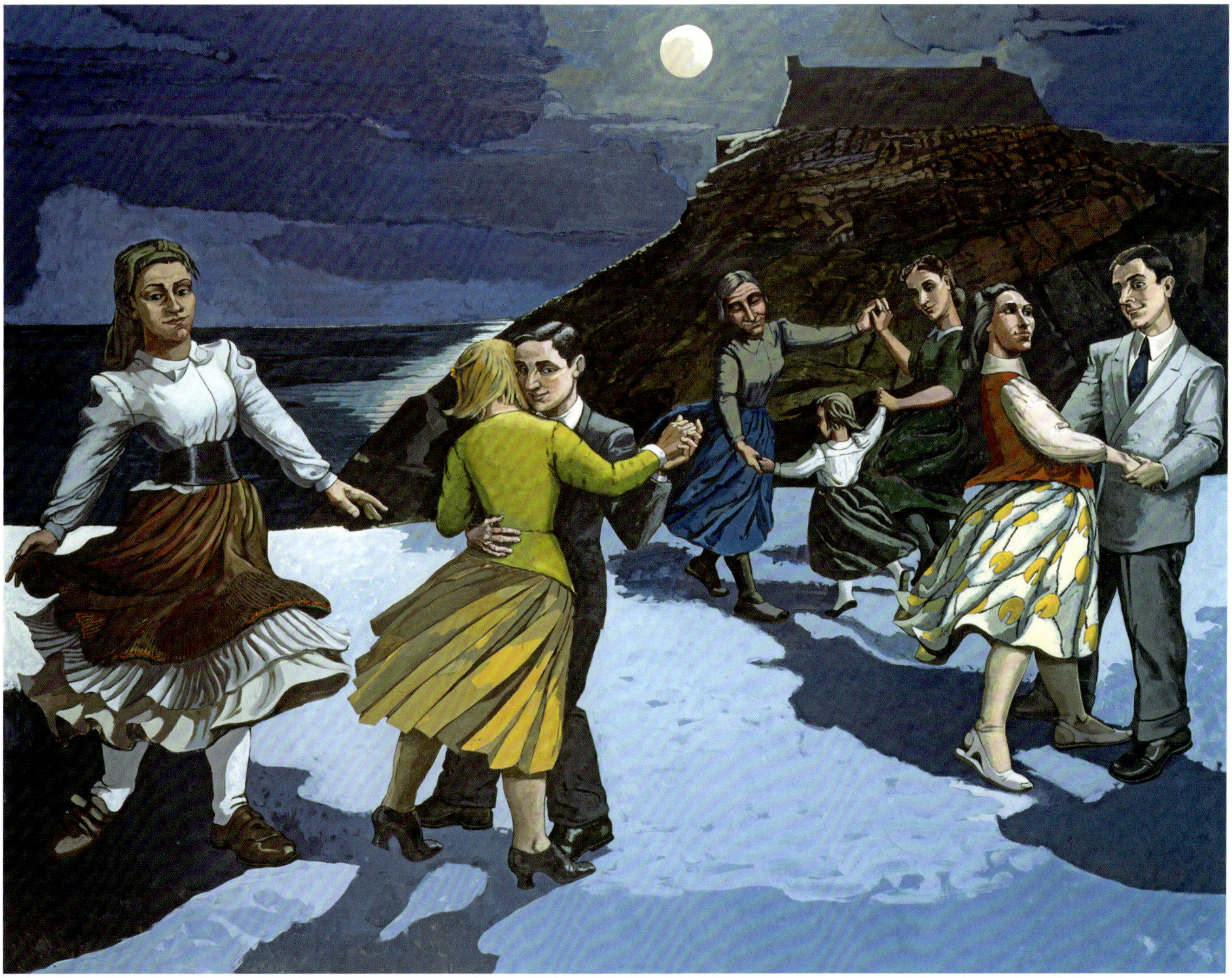

Paula Rego, *The Dance* 1988, acrylic on paper on canvas, 212.6 x 274, Tate
Inspired by her early life, Rego (born 1935) captured an image of a folk festival, or *festa*, in her native Portugal. Highly symbolic, the dance represents a dance of life, featuring the stages of a woman's life from childhood to old age. The dynamic and rhythmic composition has been created through the figures, which contrast with the motionlessness of the background, suggesting constant changes in human life set against the stability and continuity of nature. The colours and distorted figures create a strange, almost dream-like quality. The work was also a memorial to Rego's husband, who suggested the theme but died before the painting was finished.
Key points to note:

- The three ages of woman: innocence, courtship, marriage and pregnancy – child, young woman, old woman
- Diluted washes of colours including dull pink and brown
- Fluid outlines in black paint
- Thicker paint over thinner, leaving visible the black brushed outlines
- As in Millais's work on page 46, the white of the support makes some of the paint appear brighter, especially where the paint is thin
- The man resembles Rego's late husband
- Awkward, self-conscious, clumsy looking and unattractive, the adolescent girl feels she doesn't fit in
- The glowing light of Portugal suggests Rego's memories
- Limited palette, few colours, the only brightness is coming from the light of the moon

The nude

For as long as art has been produced, the nude has been an enduring subject for artists. Across time, nudes have been voluptuous or slender, usually expressing the fashionable proportions of the day or the personal preference of the artist. From ancient female fertility symbols to the male athlete (*kouros*) statues of ancient Greek art, and from the fleshy goddesses of Peter Paul Rubens (1577–1640) and Titian (c.1488/90–1576) to the slim figures depicted by Egon Schiele (1890–1918) and Frederic, Lord Leighton, nudes have nearly always conveyed a sense of the earth mother as well as exemplifying immortal beings.

Nudes in art have appeared at various times in different societies across the world. In Europe, as Christianity became the dominant religion, the depiction of nudes decreased drastically. Representations of Adam and Eve were almost the only instances where nudity was acceptable in medieval Western art, but from the 13th century, with the rediscovery of classical antiquity, nudity began to appear more often. By the 15th century, drawing from life became part of

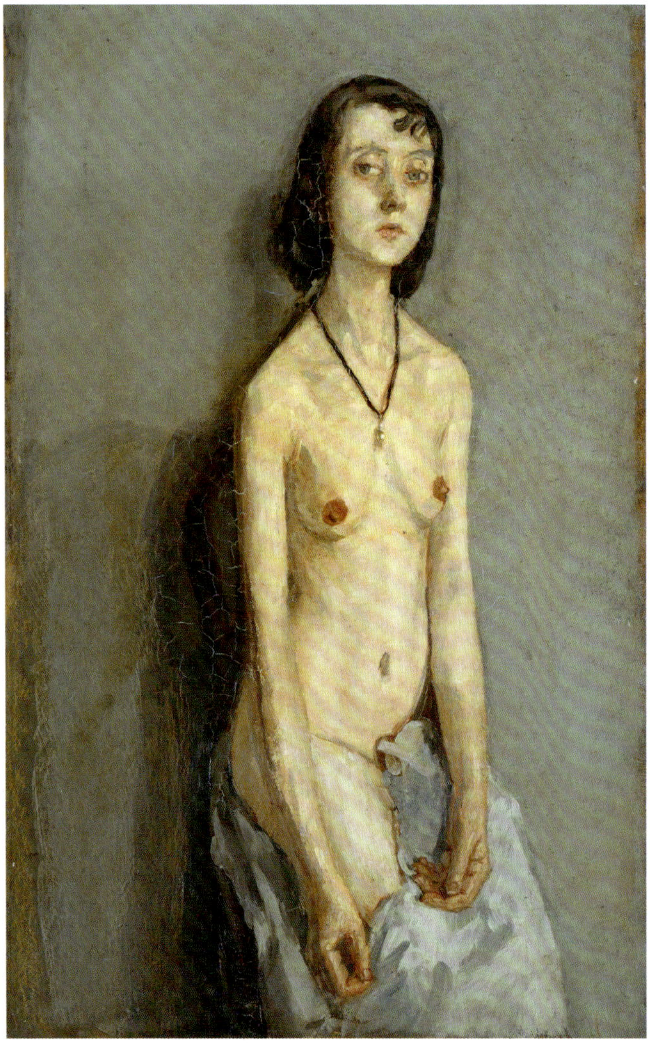

Gwen John, *Nude Girl* 1909–10, oil on canvas, 44.5 x 27.9, Tate

Although a traditional subject for male artists, the nude was considered an unsuitable subject for female artists. Even as late as the turn of the 20th century, it was perceived as questionable for women artists to depict nudes. Gwen John (1876–1939), however, went against convention, boldly painting this model and flaunting her nakedness. As a female, John's perception of the subject was completely different from a man's and the model appears as a contemporary woman, standing self-consciously with no clothes on. This was no goddess, beauty, or object of admiration or fantasy. John was far more realistic.

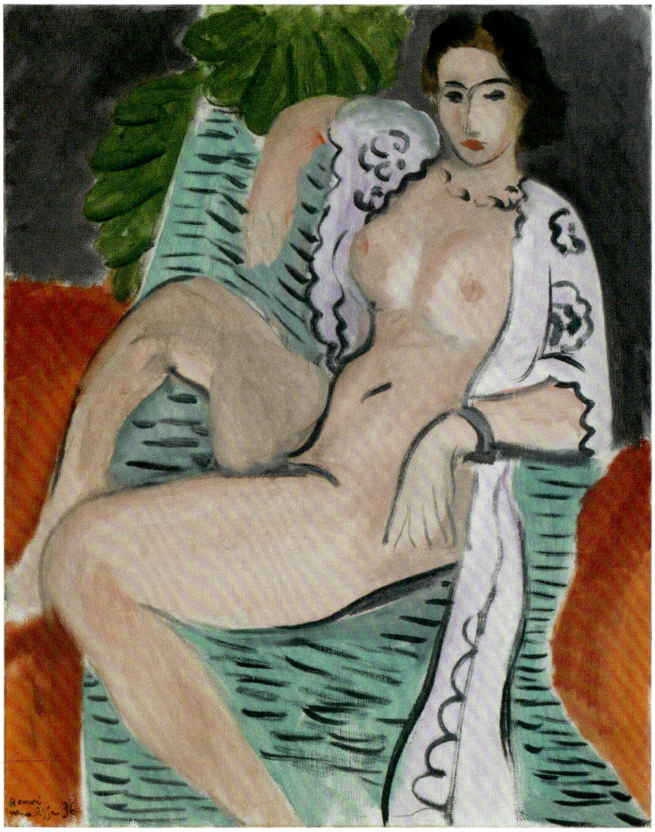

Henri Matisse, *Draped Nude* 1936, oil on canvas, 45.7 x 37.5, Tate

This is one of a series of four paintings, all the same size, produced by Matisse (1869–1954) in the spring of 1936. In this, the second of his series, Matisse filled the canvas with a voluptuous figure, creating a powerful, bold statement. The floral pattern of the woman's robe, her confident, relaxed pose and the exotic plant behind her suggest one of Matisse's favourite themes: the odalisque, or a woman in a harem. Had Matisse been working a century earlier, he would probably have pretended that she was a goddess, but by this time in the 20th century, the nude was accepted as a theme in its own right.

all artists' training, although only men, and not women, were used as models. The idea became established that drawing the naked body accurately was an indispensable test of an artist's skill. By the 16th century, artists such as Botticelli, Leonardo and Michelangelo (1475–1564) were portraying idealised figures. Gradually, naked figures in art became more sensual, but they continued to be described as depictions of goddesses rather than mortal women, which made it acceptable within Christian society for observers to gaze at the naked form without censure. In 1863, Edouard Manet (1832–83) was the first artist to deliberately use nudity to shock rather than to idealise in his paintings *Le Déjeuner sur l'Herbe* (1862–3) and *Olympia* 1863, and as the 19th and 20th centuries progressed, the nude appeared more in 'ordinary' settings of modern life, no longer necessarily projecting a divine status.

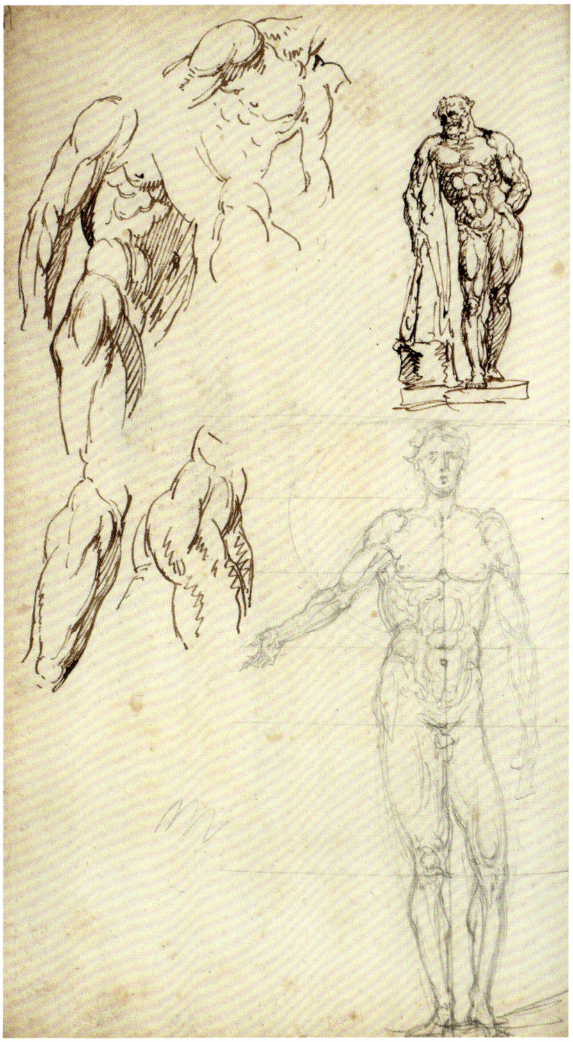

Joseph Highmore, *Study of the Farnese Hercules (Reversed), a Standing Male Nude, and other Anatomical Studies* date unknown, graphite and ink on paper, 35.4 x 23, Tate
This is a page from the 'sketchbook of figure studies after classical statues' made by Highmore (1692–1780). It's a collection of sketches, drawings, watercolours and engravings produced when he was twenty-one and training to be a lawyer by day. During the 18th century, it was still imperative (continuing from the Renaissance period) for any art student to study geometry, perspective, architecture, anatomy and drawing, before painting or sculpture.

Figurative art

Figurative art does not necessarily mean figures in art. While some figurative art includes the human body, it actually describes any form of art that features elements derived from objects we recognise from the world around us. Figurative art is therefore always representational and so is often considered to be the opposite of abstract art.

Some things to consider when looking at figures in art:

- What's happening? Is there a story?
- Are the figures in action? Are their poses convincing?
- Are the figures realistic or idealised, or has the artist distorted them?
- Can you detect any signs or symbols in the work? If so, what are they and what do you think they mean?
- Does the title describe the work well? If not, what title would you give it?
- Is a mood conveyed, such as mystery, happiness, calm or fear?
- How have materials been used? How have these materials affected the style of the work?
- How have the figures been defined? If it's a painting, for instance, are the limbs and contours darkened with strong tones? If it's a sculpture, are the forms rounded, smooth, rough or angular?
- Does the work seem timeless or does it represent a particular time? What makes you think this?
- Can you detect any relationships between the figures in the work? This could be emotional or compositional. Look at the placement, poses and spaces around and between the figures, as well as gesture, body language and eye direction.
- If it's a painting, are some figures cut off at the edges? What effect does this create?
- Are there any vigorous, twisted or contorted poses? Exaggerated gestures? What effect do these elements have on your impression of the work?
- Can you detect ambiguity (double meanings) within the work?
- What clothes, if any, are the figures wearing? What effect does this create?
- Is the purpose of the work religious or secular? Does this make a difference to the way you feel about it?
- Did this artist challenge convention? If so, how? Try to explain this in your own words.
- Who asked for this work to be made? Does this make a difference to the way it has been made, or its content?

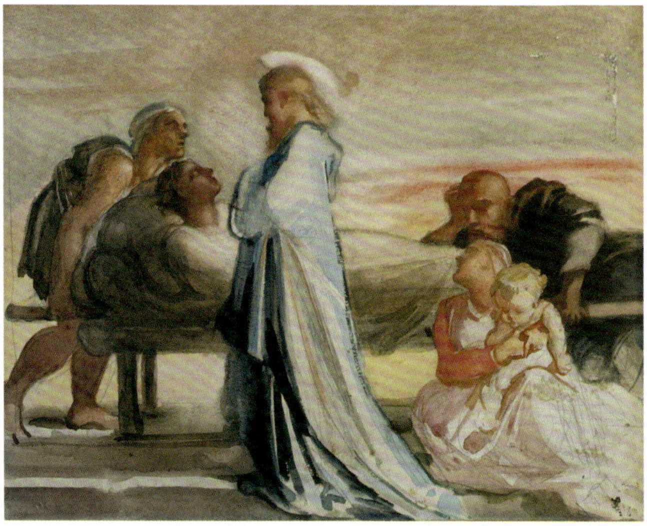

Louisa Anne, Marchioness of Waterford, *Christ Raising the Dead* date unknown, watercolour on paper, 28.6 x 36.8, Tate
Louisa Anne Beresford, Marchioness of Waterford (1818–91) was a Pre-Raphaelite watercolourist who spent her childhood in Paris where she received tuition in the arts. As a woman and member of the British aristocracy, she could never be more than an amateur artist, so her paintings did not appear in galleries until the 1870s, even though her tutors included Dante Gabriel Rossetti (1828–82) and John Ruskin (1819–1900). One of her particular skills was to create sensitive watercolours, using appealing colour combinations and stirring compositions.

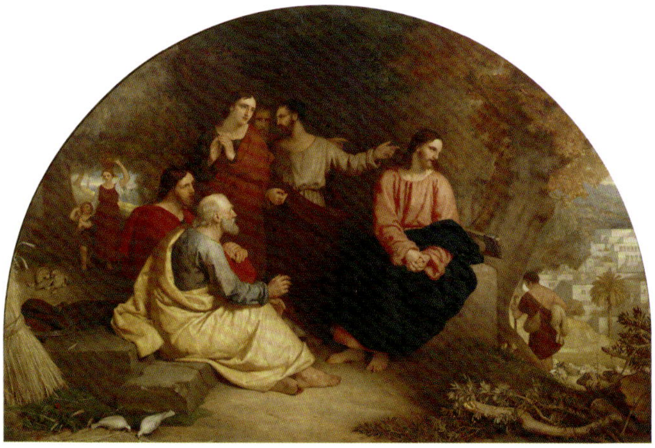

Charles Locke Eastlake, *Christ Lamenting over Jerusalem* 1846, oil on canvas, 104.8 x 156.2, Tate
This painting by Eastlake (1793–1865) was inspired by lines from the New Testament where Jesus predicts the destruction of Jerusalem. Within the painting are several symbols representing Christ's prophecy. For example, the axe in the tree suggests Jerusalem's fall, while the shepherd carrying a sheep implies Christ as the good shepherd.

Religious imagery

Religions across the world have sought different ways to define or explore the human relationship with a higher power. Each religion has its own beliefs, rituals and 'rules', and almost every set of beliefs has developed its own imagery. Christian imagery, for instance, grew out of pagan depictions and has been a huge influence on the representation of the figure. Before the advent of literacy, mosaics, frescoes, carvings, stained glass and illuminated manuscripts all featured figures to help worshippers understand and contemplate stories that explain the Christian message.

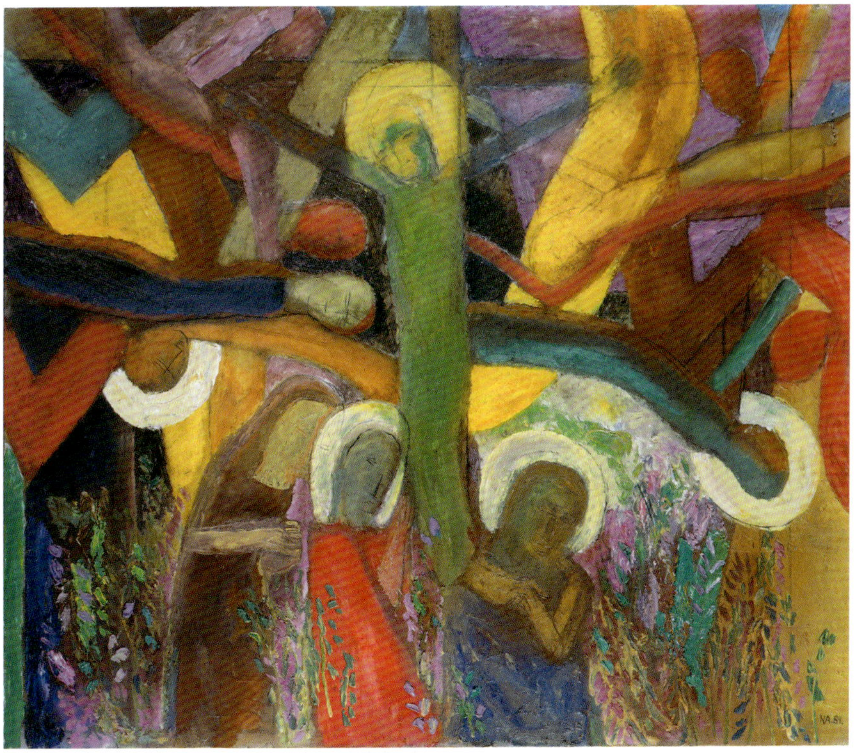

Norman Adams, *Christ's Cross and Adam's Tree* 1989, oil on canvas, 127 x 152.6, Tate
Adams (1927–2005) worked as a set designer, painted murals and designed ceramics. From the late 1980s, he was Professor of Painting and Keeper at the Royal Academy in London. This painting derives from a poem by John Donne (1572–1631). The Virgin Mary, St John and Mary Magdalene are at the cross. Adam's tree, from which the cross was made, is also there.

Compare the three Christian works here. Which appeals to you and why? Apart from relating to Christianity, how are they similar? How are they different? Are the figures' poses lifelike or not? Why is this? What about colours and tones? How do these enhance or detract from the compositions? Do the works seem dated, or fixed, to their own era? Why do you think this?

Making it real

From the early 13th century, European painters began to consider how to depict skin realistically and how to make figures appear solid. They began with an application of a green undercoat, known as *verdaccio*, covered with a second layer of paint, a blend of yellow, pink and white, to represent flesh. Highlights were picked out with white, and crimson was applied to lips and cheeks. This method of applying a contrasting, underlying colour was also used for clothes, and where the undercoat showed through in places, the vibrancy of the garment was enhanced. Dark and light tones were also added to give an impression of light falling on the skin and drapery.

Anatomy

The idea of creating figures of ideal proportions arose from a belief that the human body adhered to a set of precise, mathematical ratios. In approximately 1490, Leonardo drew his Vitruvian Man, a pen-and-ink image of a male figure in two positions within a circle and a square, accompanied by notes explaining the ideal proportions of the human figure. Leonardo's idea was based on the work of Vitruvius (c.80/70–c.15 BC), a Roman writer, architect and engineer. In his work, *De Architectura (On Architecture)*, Vitruvius described the proportions and ratios of the human figure, and he specified that the ideal body is eight heads high.

Most of these notions are still adhered to by artists. In *On Painting*, Alberti explained that the ultimate aim of an artist is to imitate nature, and he also wrote about how important it was for artists to be familiar with the structure of the body: 'When painting a clothed person, it is first of all necessary to draw a nude and then to drape it in garments. Similarly, when painting a nude, we must first position the bones and muscles and lightly cover them with flesh and skin, so that one can tell without difficulty where the muscles are.' It was from commentators like Alberti that ideas developed about studying the human body exceptionally closely, to attain even greater realism. In around 1447, the sculptor Lorenzo Ghiberti (1378–1455) began writing *I Commentarii (The Commentaries)*, three treatises on art history and theory from antiquity to his time. Although he never completed the work, several of his comments were to influence the practice of his contemporaries. For example, he wrote: 'It is necessary for sculptors wishing to sculpt a *statua virile* [male statue] to have observed dissections so that they know how many bones there are in the body and are also familiar with the muscles and all the sinews and their connections.' Published in 1550, *Lives of the Most Eminent Painters, Sculptors, and Architects* is a series of artists' biographies written by the Italian painter, architect and historian, Giorgio Vasari (1511–74). Vasari wrote that the Florentine sculptor, painter and printmaker Antonio Pollaiuolo (1431/2–98) was the 'first master to skin many human bodies in order

Stereotypes

Several artists have used the figure either to consciously challenge or unconsciously confirm stereotyping within their societies. For example, Sarah Lucas's self-portrait photographs challenge the misogynist culture and sexual stereotyping prevalent in British tabloid newspapers. She confronts viewers with androgynous, masculine portrayals of herself, contradicting typical images of females traditionally featured in the press. The works of Chris Ofili (born 1968) are vibrant and technically complex, often consisting of layers of paint, resin, glitter, collage and elephant dung. Concerned with issues of black identity, he explores and challenges racial stereotypes, drawing on a range of references, from the Bible to music, and from William Blake and Auguste Rodin (1840–1917) to pornographic magazines. The American photographer Cindy Sherman (born 1954) often photographs herself in costumes and poses parodying female stereotypes in scenes based on old films, TV soaps and magazines.

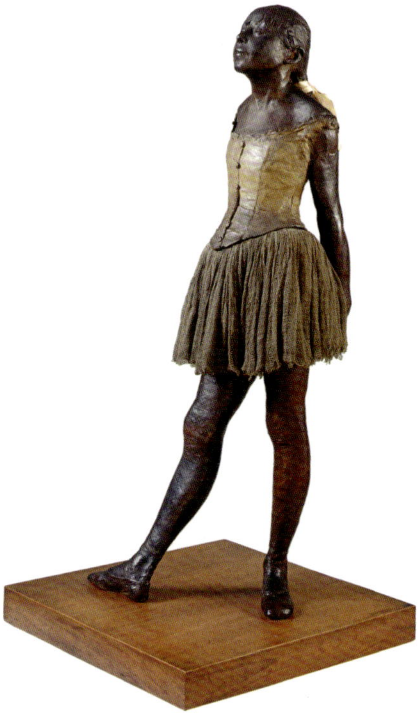

Edgar Degas, *Little Dancer Aged Fourteen* 1880–1, cast c.1922, painted bronze with muslin and silk, 98.4 x 41.9 x 36.5, Tate
Although he exhibited with the Impressionists, Degas studied the Old Masters. He said, 'No art was ever less spontaneous than mine.' The model for this work was Marie Van Goethen, a young ballet student at the Paris Opéra, where Degas often drew and painted. He first made a wax sculpture of her in the nude, then a three-quarter life-size wax sculpture of her and dressed it in real fabrics: silk for the bodice, tulle and gauze for the tutu, fabric shoes and a horsehair wig with a ribbon. Contemporaries were shocked by the realism of the work. It wasn't pretending to be beautiful, but was a depiction of a hard-working adolescent girl training to be a dancer. After Degas's death, a number of bronze casts, including this one, were made from his wax original.

to investigate the muscles and understand the nude in a more modern way', and that he 'dissected many bodies in order to study their anatomy'. The practice of dissecting bodies (cadavers) was illegal, so artists such as Leonardo risked life imprisonment or even death in their efforts to understand the structure of the human body. Soon, artists' anatomical investigations began to exceed much that was being taught to medical students at universities, and through their anatomical findings these artists set new standards in their portrayals of the human figure.

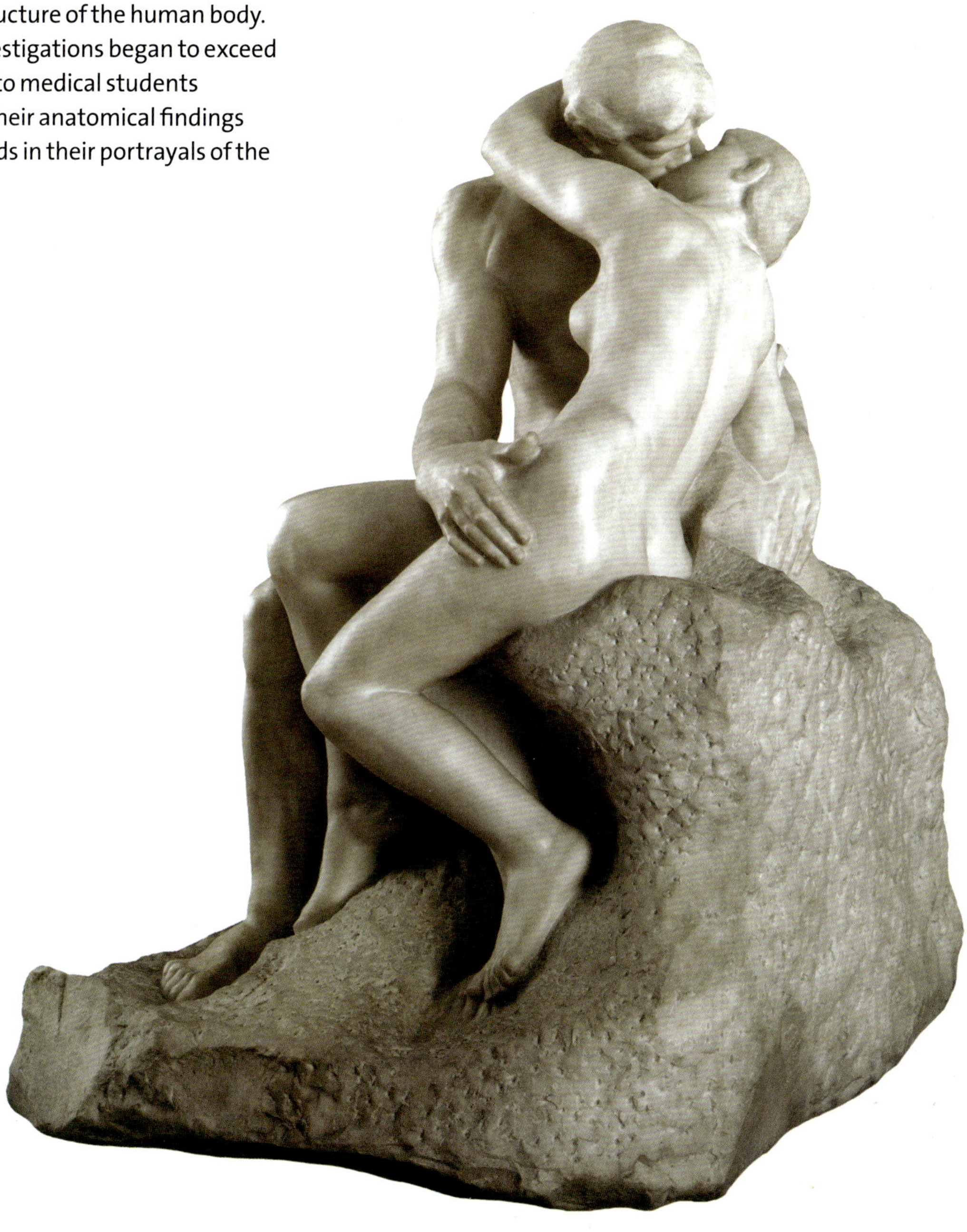

Auguste Rodin, *The Kiss*
1901–4, Pentelican marble,
182.2 x 121.9 x 153, Tate
Because we identify with them, figures are particularly effective in the projection and arousal of emotions. Which emotions are evident in this work? It illustrates a moment from *Inferno*, part of the 14th-century epic poem *The Divine Comedy* written by Dante Alighieri (c.1265–1321). The couple are Francesca da Rimini and Paolo Malatesta. Francesca was married to Paolo's brother, but she fell in love with Paolo, who was also married to someone else. In the story, Francesca and Paolo read the Arthurian legend of Lancelot and Guinevere together, and suddenly discover that they love each other. The statue encapsulates that moment, as the book can be seen in Paolo's left hand. After this, Francesca's husband discovers that his wife and brother are having an affair, and he kills them both.

Experiments and developments

While notions of depicting the figure in more lifelike ways developed during the Renaissance, the rules they set for artists were adhered to for centuries. For creating realism, they have yet to be surpassed. There are many ways you can build your own ideas and skills through these discoveries. Here are some suggestions:

- Look for ways that artists have applied knowledge of anatomy, or used tone and texture, to create illusions of reality. Make notes on how this enhances or reduces your enjoyment of the work.
- Research relevant aspects of anatomy – the bones, sinews and muscles – and how they all connect and enable movement. What ratios surprise you? (Consider: arm lengths, neck widths, size of ears!)
- Become familiar with the ways that bodies are formed and move, and practise drawing bones, muscles, sinews – and the clothed figure – in different poses. These could be quick sketches or more detailed studies.
- In your sketchbook, draw figures you see around you, wherever you are, whenever you can. Look at sketchbook figures by artists such as Raphael, Michelangelo, Annibale Carracci (1560–1609), Degas, Alberto Giacometti (1901–66) and others. Notice how they make marks and create tones.
- Practice making your figures appear to move by showing distortions that occur during the locomotion of limbs. Ask friends to let you draw them. Alternate the materials you use.
- If you're near a statue of a figure, draw it. View it from different angles and distances and draw parts of it overlapping on your page. Draw only the negative space around it, or just the dark tones, with no lines or other details. Or try drawing what you see with just one continuous line.
- Create a three-dimensional figure – following the styles of artists such as Giacometti or Rodin.
- Draw limbs over and again: arms, hands, feet, legs, from different angles and in various activities.

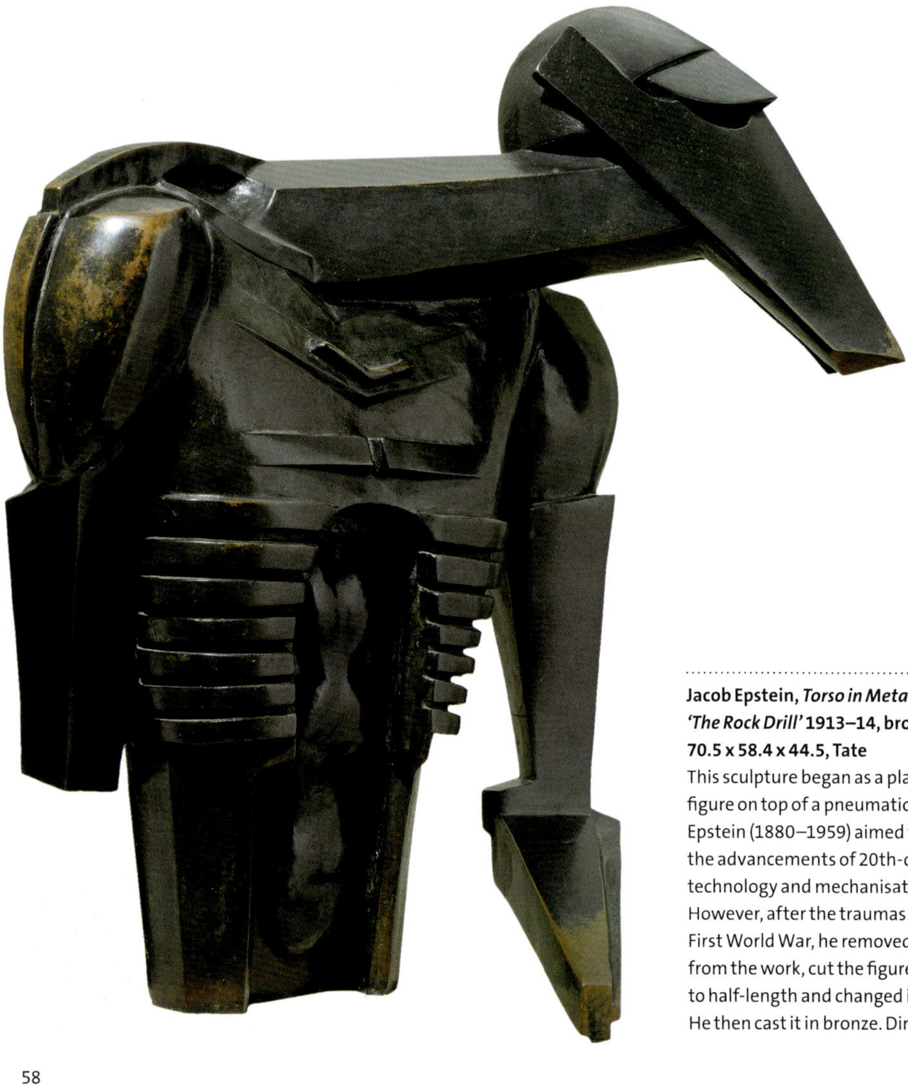

Jacob Epstein, *Torso in Metal from 'The Rock Drill'* 1913–14, bronze, 70.5 x 58.4 x 44.5, Tate
This sculpture began as a plaster figure on top of a pneumatic rock drill. Epstein (1880–1959) aimed to embody the advancements of 20th-century technology and mechanisation. However, after the traumas of the First World War, he removed the drill from the work, cut the figure down to half-length and changed its arms. He then cast it in bronze. Diminished in this way, the originally menacing work appears defenceless, perhaps another victim of the war. What do you think of it? What is that round shape beneath the ribcage? Does the work seem threatening or vulnerable? Why do you think Epstein remade it in this way? What would you say is the most important thing about this work?

Emotion

Since the end of the 19th century, many artists have expressed their inner feelings through their art, or have created art to stimulate emotional responses in viewers. The Expressionists of the early 20th century aimed to do both. They distorted their images to evoke moods or ideas and to express underlying meanings or emotional experiences rather than physical reality. Paul Gauguin (1848–1903), van Gogh and Edvard Munch (1863–1944) were earlier artists who expressed emotions through their art. William Blake also often distorted figures to depict and evoke emotion, as he believed that the source of thought and imagination is within us and not from the world around us. Following on, the Expressionists explored feelings of anguish, suffering and disillusionment brought about, for example, by their experiences of war and its effects. Since then, many other artists have conveyed emotive ideas in their art. Examples include Picasso's *Weeping Woman* 1937 (see pages 42–3), *The Broken Column* 1944 by Frida Kahlo or *Torso in Metal from 'The Rock Drill'* 1913–14 by Epstein. Each of these works was created in different eras, expressing a variety of emotions against a range of personal, political and cultural backgrounds.

How and why do works of art have the power to affect our feelings? Think about formalism and contextualism (see page 13). What about marks, lines, facial expressions or gestures? Are hands or faces obscured or exaggerated; are figures solitary or contorted? How do artists portray certain feelings, such as grief, solitude, anguish, happiness or anger?

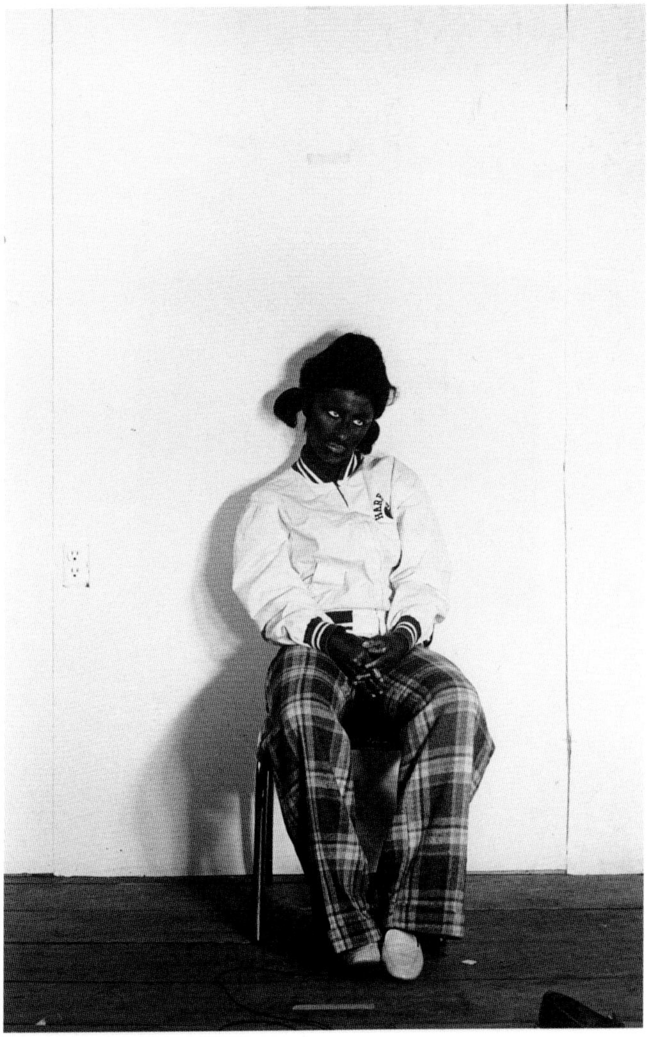

Cindy Sherman, *Untitled, Bus Riders* 1976, printed 2000, photograph, gelatin silver print on paper, 189 x 127, Tate
Bus Riders is a series of fifteen black-and-white photographs produced by Sherman shortly after she graduated from the State University College at Buffalo, New York, in 1976. She did not publicly exhibit them, however, until late in the year 2000. Like many of her works, the photographs are an exploration of staging and stereotypes. She based the characters she enacted on people she had observed on the bus. In each photo she appears in a different outfit, wearing wigs, glasses and make-up according to the character being staged. Against the wall behind her, a shadow of her character accentuates the contrivance of each image.

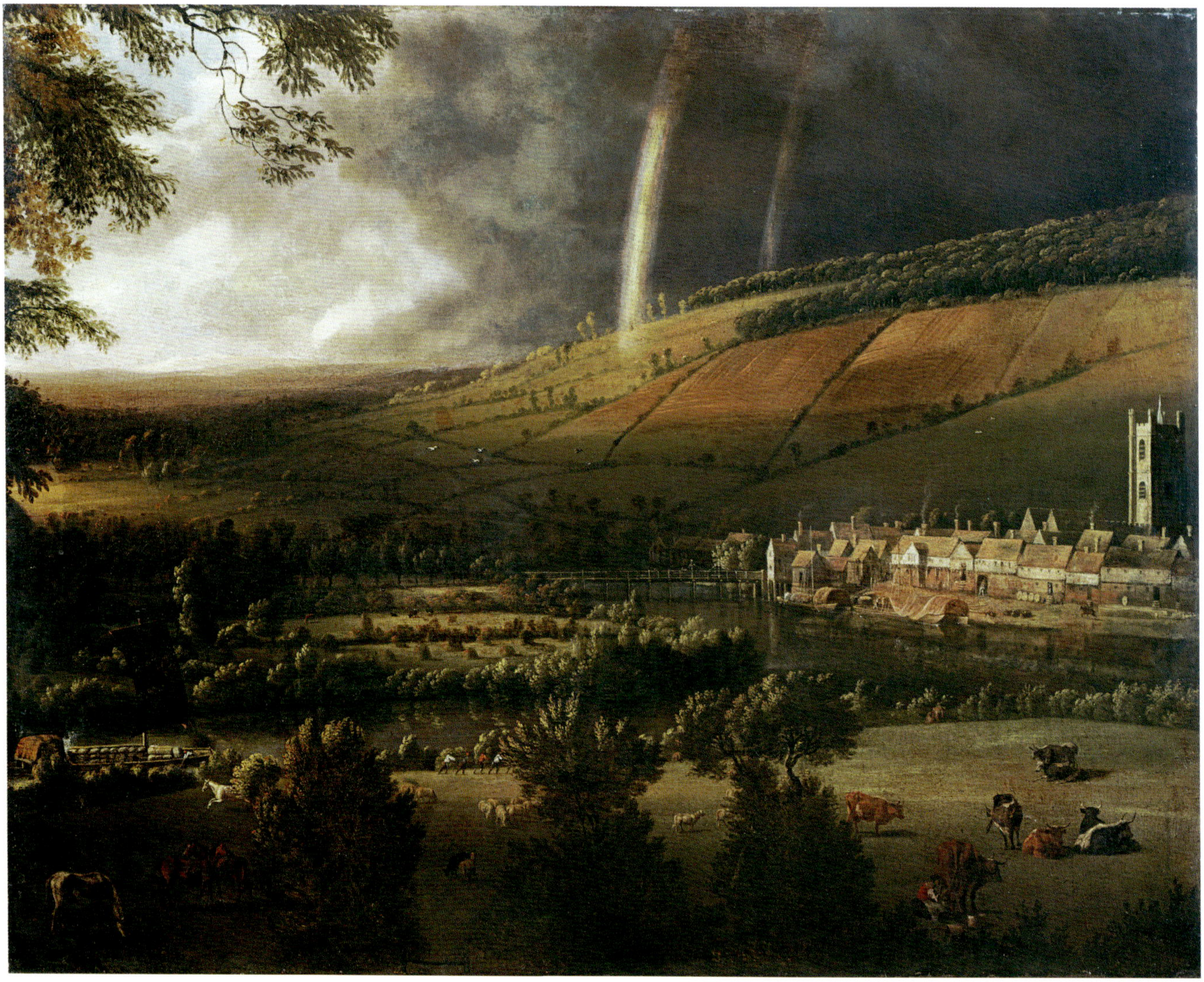

SCAPES

'For me nature is not landscape, but the dynamism of visual forces.'
Bridget Riley

From ancient times until the Middle Ages, landscapes rarely appeared in Western art and then only in idealised form, as backgrounds or in small sections of other paintings. The word landscape was not even in use in the English language before the beginning of the 17th century.

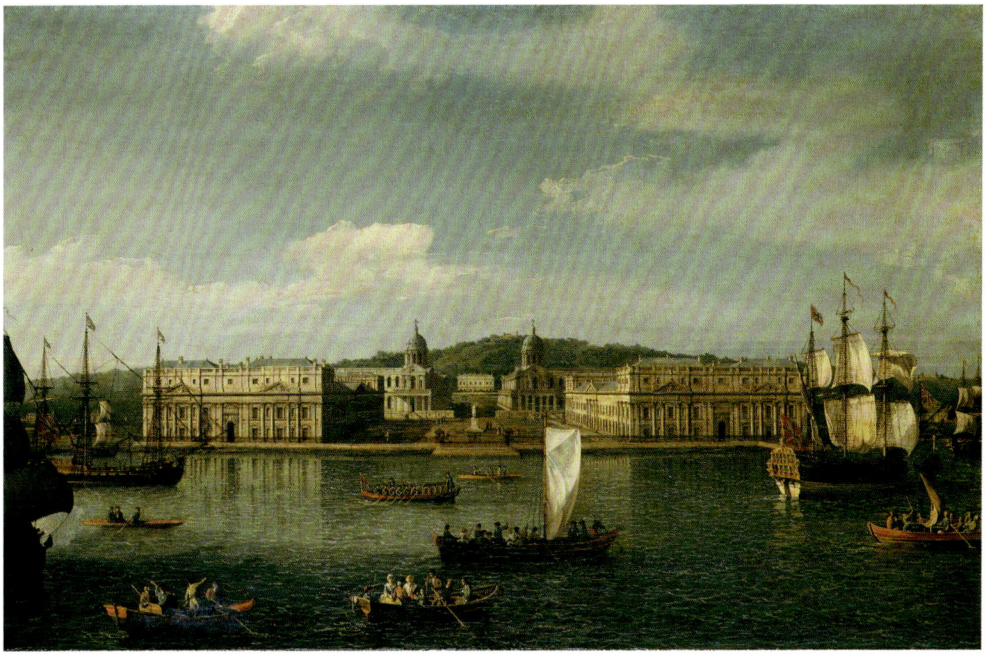

Jan Siberechts, *Landscape with Rainbow, Henley-on-Thames* c.1690, oil on canvas, 81.9 x 102.9, Tate
This is one of several views of England that Siberechts (1627–1700/3) painted in the late 17th century. Born in Antwerp, Siberechts established himself as a landscape painter in Flanders, but in his late forties he moved to England for the rest of his life. His skilful use of light and shadow and meticulous attention to detail reflect his Flemish roots, as most artists in England were not painting in such a precise style, nor was landscape for its own sake considered a significant subject. This painting features a fairly complex composition and light effects, creating a warm yet eerie atmosphere. The buildings and animals add interest and scale.

Canaletto (Giovanni Antonio Canal), *A View of Greenwich from the River* c.1750–2, oil on canvas, 59 x 94, Tate
Canaletto (1697–1768) arrived in England in 1746, already known as 'the famous painter of views of Venice'. He stayed in England for nearly a decade and helped to raise the status of landscape painting. This view shows his accurate use of perspective and the detailed depiction of buildings and nature that had made him such a successful artist.

Distant vistas

The earliest known painted landscapes are frescoes from Minoan Greece. During the first century AD to AD 79, some villas in Pompeii and Herculaneum had landscape frescoes on the walls, but landscape was not the most popular theme as the most esteemed art in the West included the human figure. Conversely, in traditional Chinese art, landscape has always been highly respected, and the period from about 907 to 1127 is known as the great age of Chinese landscape. The most skilled Chinese artists produced exotic panoramas of imaginary scenes, usually surrounded by dramatic mountains, with compositions that focused on pattern and harmony.

During the 14th century, artists such as Giotto (1266/7–1337) began including aspects of the landscape in religious images. By the end of the 15th century, Leonardo and Dürer made detailed landscape sketches from observation, but they used only parts of these as backgrounds. In the Netherlands in the 17th century, realistic-looking landscapes were painted as settings or views through windows.

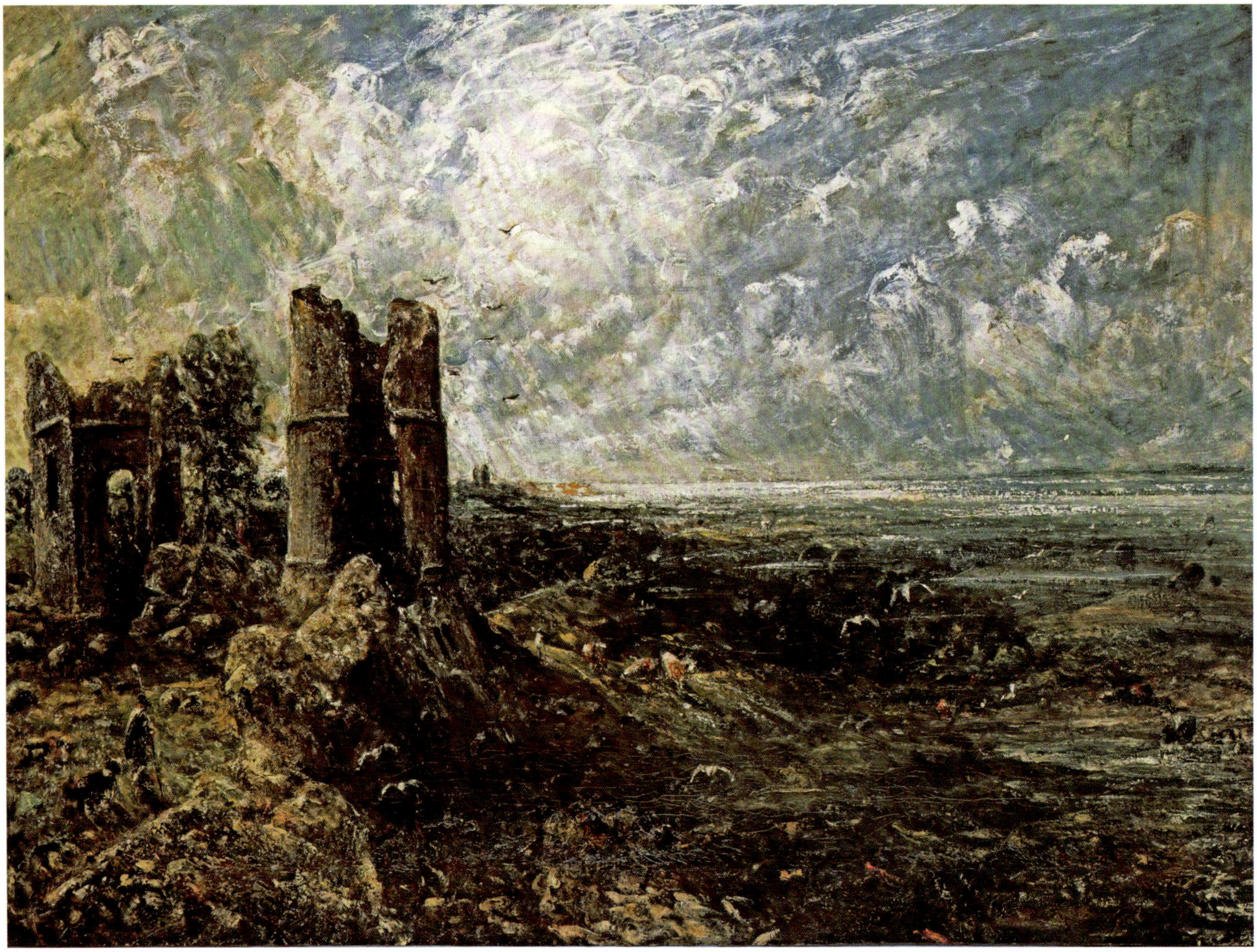

John Constable, *Sketch for Hadleigh Castle* c.1828–9, oil on canvas, 122.6 x 167.3, Tate

This is a full-size oil sketch made in preparation for a finished painting of the same subject. Constable (1776–1837) submitted the completed painting to the Royal Academy exhibition in 1829. It is one of his six-foot landscape canvases that he began in 1818. His wife Maria died in November 1828 and the desolate tone of the work seems to reflect his grief.

Light effects

The development of landscape painting in the Netherlands from the 16th century was mainly influenced by the Protestant Reformation, particularly Calvinism. Religious images were destroyed in churches and so artists had to find new subjects to paint. Portraiture, still life, genre and landscape painting flourished. These subjects also became popular as they reflected the increasing wealth of the Netherlands through the growth of overseas trade and territorial expansion. Unlike Italian Renaissance art, which had divided landscape paintings into foreground, middle ground and background, Netherlandish painters began experimenting with more interesting compositions, such as triangular or U-shaped, and more sophisticated light effects.

In the 18th century, wealthy young men toured Europe and visited places famed for their culture, art and architecture. This was the Grand Tour. While away, many travellers bought souvenirs in the form of paintings by artists such as Canaletto. His works became extremely popular, particularly his depictions of Venice. In France, Jean-Antoine Watteau (1684–1721) invented a new subject for art that became known as the *fête galante*, depictions of pastoral landscapes populated by people enjoying themselves. In Germany, Caspar David Friedrich (1774–1840) created a blend of subjective and objective elements in his landscapes. His images appear simultaneously realistic and fantastic. Friedrich was part of the Romantic movement that began in the 18th century and continued into the middle of the 19th. Generally, Romantic writers and artists celebrated nature, individuality, imagination and independent thinking.

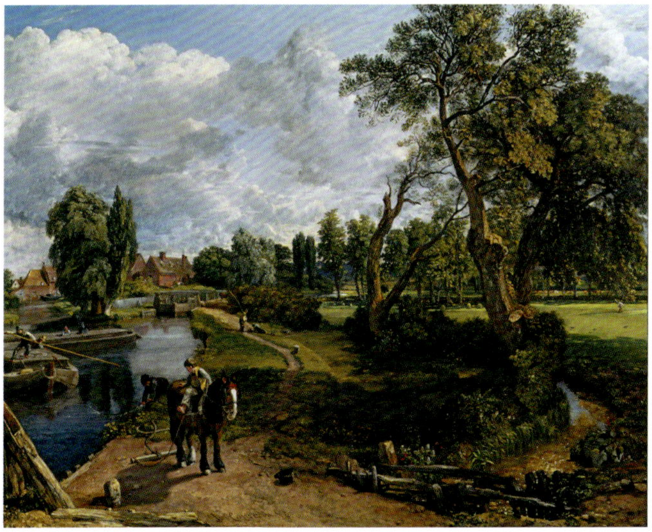

John Constable, *Flatford Mill* (*'Scene on a Navigable River'*) 1816–17, oil on canvas, 101.6 x 127, Tate
Constable began painting this mainly in the open air rather than in the studio. It was one of the last views he painted of Suffolk before moving to London. His family's business was a watermill at Flatford where they ground corn. The corn trade flourished in the early years of the 19th century, when Napoleon's continental blockade forced the country to depend on its own food supplies. Horse-drawn barges had to have their ropes disconnected to move under bridges, and here a boy unties a rope from the horse while another rides it. The French painter Eugène Delacroix (1798–1863) visited Constable in 1825 and later noted: 'Constable says that the superiority of the green in his meadows comes from it being composed of a multitude of different greens.'

Make sketches from a work such as these from *Flatford Mill* and add annotations:

- Clouds built up from observation, showing weather effects – viewers can see the wind, water gathering in the darker underparts
- Blue-grey slashing strokes underneath, white and fluffy on the top
- Abstract/simplified shapes of the trees
- Trees made up of sinuous shapes to imply trunks and branches, with small, quick dashes of paint to build up the leaves – general, not detailed
- Predominant colour is green, but lots of different shades of green
- Composition seems simple, but when a compositional sketch is made of one part of the work, it becomes clear how complex it is
- The reflections in the water pull the image together, linking colours and shapes

Plein air

In England, watercolour landscapes became a speciality. Across Britain, many artists went out to paint the scenery. In particular, Constable and Turner painted innovative landscapes, creating atmosphere and making nature a subject in its own right, even though landscape painting was still considered to be inferior by many.

In 1824, Constable's painting *The Hay Wain* 1821 was awarded a gold medal at the Salon, the official annual exhibition in Paris. He was one of the first landscape painters to make oil sketches in the open air, many of them huge, and some with no final work in mind. He intended them not as preparatory sketches for paintings he would make later in the studio, but as finished works in their own right. He applied colour in various ways – rich impasto, translucent glazes, small touches of pure white, quick strokes, and dappled dry-brush effects. Although he gained relatively little acclaim in Britain, Constable's work inspired several young French artists to rebel against the traditional art academy teaching. They began painting in the village of

New inventions

Some 19th-century inventions made it easier for artists to paint outside, away from their studios. Originally, artists had made their own paint by grinding and mixing pigments with egg (tempera) or linseed oil. The first ready-made paint was sold in pigs' bladders from the end of the 18th century. The paint was squeezed through a tiny hole in the bladder, which was then sealed with a tack, but it was messy and the paint often dried up. In 1841, the first collapsible metal tube containing ready-mixed paint was produced, making painting outside more convenient. Soon, folding easels and then folding palettes and portable paint boxes became available. The Box or Field Easel was a particularly popular 19th-century invention: a portable box with telescopic legs and a folding built-in paint box and palette. Manufacturers also produced pre-stretched canvases primed with white gesso, ready for painting. It all made painting outside extremely accessible.

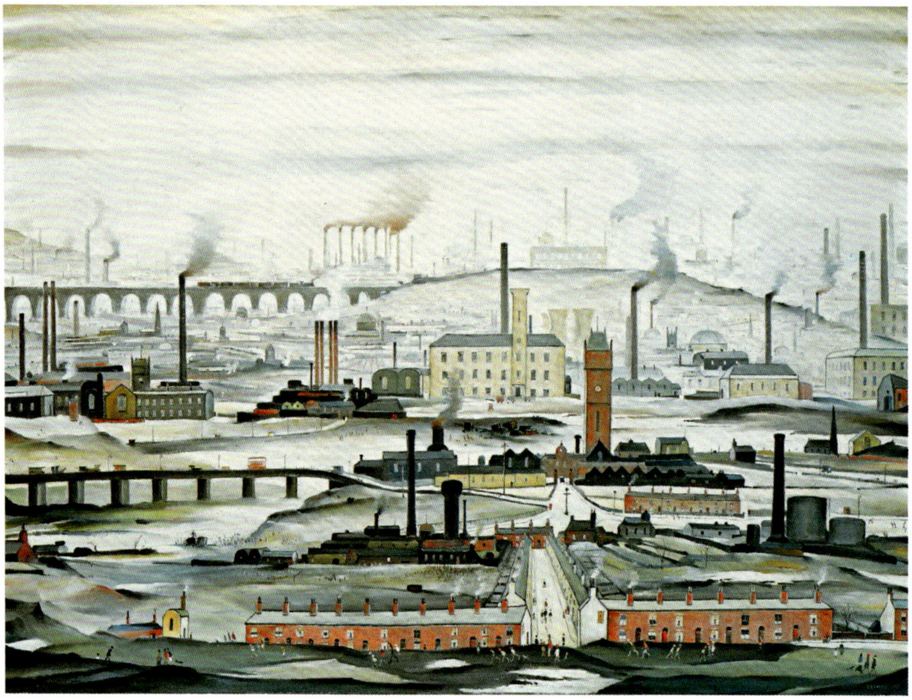

L.S. Lowry, *Industrial Landscape* 1955, oil on canvas, 114.3 x 152.4, Tate
Typical of the panoramic cityscapes that Lowry (1887–1976) painted throughout his career, this is an imaginary composition, with authentic elements taken from several northern English towns. It is a general impression of the urban environment that surrounded Lowry every day, dominated by smoking chimneys, factories, roads, bridges and industrial wasteland. In emphasising the human presence, he focuses on a small street in the foreground. Beyond this, the space is dotted with smoke and chimneys. The mood is depressing, but the people seem to accept their lives and continue with their daily business.

Barbizon near the Forest of Fontainebleau, making nature their subject. As well as painting in the open air (*en plein air*) rather than in the studio, the Barbizon painters became known for their loose brushwork, patches of unblended colour and subtle tones. Artists have painted outdoors for centuries, but it was not until the mid-19th century that entire paintings were finished there and not in the studio. At first this was considered sloppy, but soon even broader interpretations of the landscape developed, first through the Impressionists and then the Post-Impressionists.

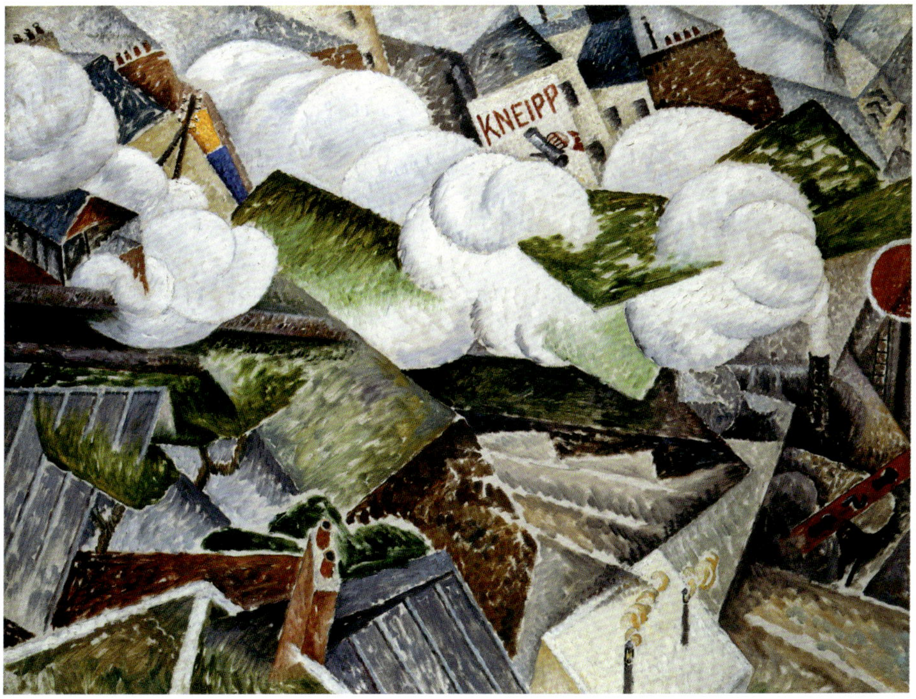

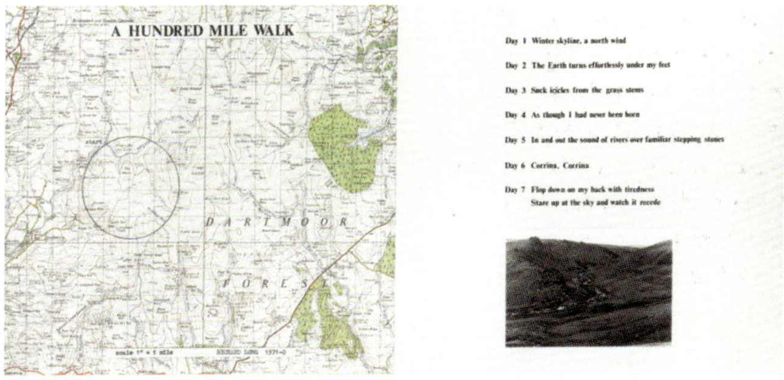

Gino Severini, *Suburban Train Arriving in Paris* 1915, oil on canvas, 88.6 x 115.6, Tate
This is a train arriving in Paris carrying munitions, soldiers and the wounded. Shown through angular lines and shapes, it emphasises machines and modernity. Severini (1883–1966) was an Italian Futurist, inspired by an idealised concept of war. In June 1915, he stayed for a while just outside Paris where he saw these trains passing close by. The word 'KNEIPP' is from an advertisement for a malted drink. How has he created a sense of movement, technology and speed in this work? How do you think the painting was received by the public when it was first produced? What is your opinion of it? Why do you think that the Futurists were so in favour of war at the time?

Richard Long, *A Hundred Mile Walk* 1971–2, graphite on map, typescript, photograph and printed labels on board, 21.6 x 48.3, Tate
This is the recording of a walk that Long (born 1945) made on Dartmoor over the New Year of 1971–2, which followed a circular route. Long recorded the sounds he heard on the walk, making a point of how they changed, emerged and disappeared as he walked. This map is his record of that solitary walk in a remote place. As can be seen, he walked round the same path in a clockwise direction about fourteen times to reach 100 miles. The photograph shows the way ahead as he walked. The work has many layers, all suggested by Long to encourage viewers to develop their own interpretations. Consider what this work reveals of our surroundings, our world, how we react to it now, long after it was made, in the light of our more recent concerns about the environment.

Perspective

Traditionally, landscape painters have aimed to make their images appear three-dimensional. In the Renaissance, artists developed a system of representing the three-dimensional world on two-dimensional surfaces. Known either as linear or aerial (atmospheric) perspective, the two systems became (and remain) standard studio practice.

Linear perspective is a mathematical method, while aerial perspective is more painterly. In Florence in the early 15th century, the artist and architect Filippo Brunelleschi (1377–1446) first demonstrated the principles of linear perspective in two panel paintings. Alberti was the first to write down the 'rules' of linear perspective for artists to follow in 1435 in his treatise *On Painting*. Linear perspective makes objects in a drawing or painting look as if they recede into the distance by appearing smaller when further away from viewers. It starts with an imaginary horizontal line, sometimes called the horizon line or eye level. Perspective (or orthogonal) lines are straight lines drawn from objects, back towards a point on the horizon line that is known as

The Hudson River School

The Hudson River School was an American art movement established by a group of landscape painters based in New York City in the mid-19th century. Influenced by Romanticism, their paintings predominantly portrayed the Hudson River Valley and surrounding areas. Artists involved included Thomas Cole (1801–48), Frederic Edwin Church (1826–1900) and Albert Bierstadt (1830–1902). Hudson River School paintings reflect three themes that predominated in America in the 19th century – discovery, exploration and settlement – and the landscapes are characterised by their detailed and sometimes idealised depictions of nature. Church particularly exploited oil sketches, which he executed both at home and on his extensive travels to Niagara Falls, Labrador, Jamaica, Mexico and the Middle East.

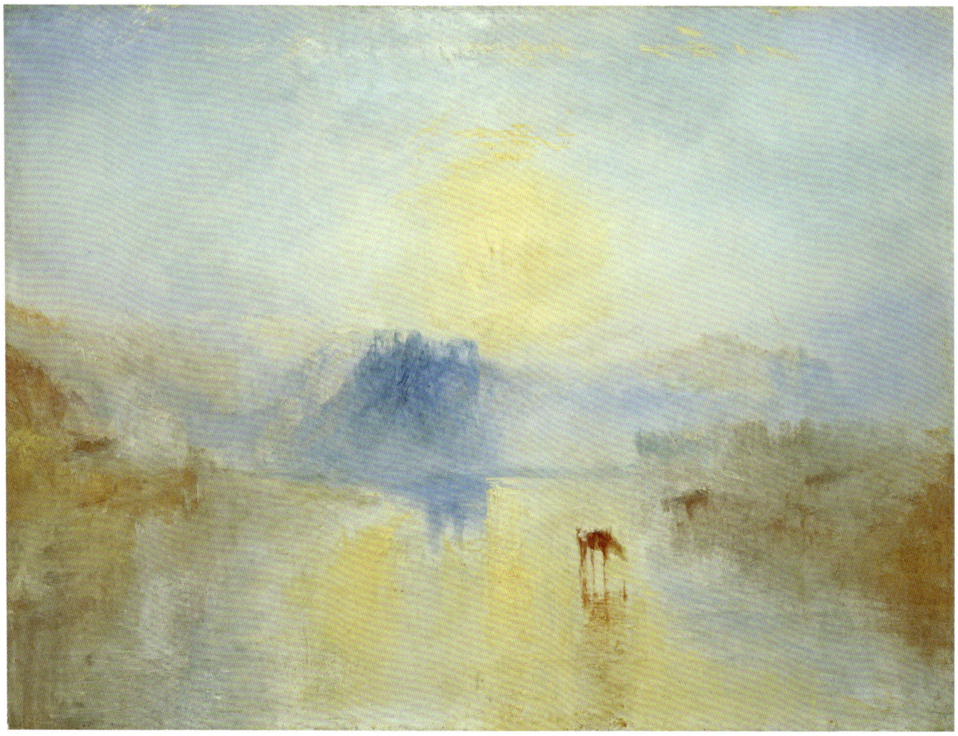

J.M.W. Turner, *Norham Castle, Sunrise* c.1845, oil on canvas, 90.8 x 121.9, Tate

Turner first saw Norham Castle on the River Tweed, on the borders of England and Scotland, in 1797 during a tour of northern Britain. He made sketches and watercolours of it and the following year he exhibited a watercolour of the castle at sunrise. This later oil painting is filled with light and atmosphere. Solid forms are treated as translucent elements of pure primary colours that merge into each other. As an unfinished work, it was not exhibited during Turner's lifetime. It might have been a sketch for a more finished picture or he might have intended to exhibit it, as he often completed his paintings on 'varnishing days', just before the opening of an exhibition.

the vanishing point. The closer objects are to the vanishing point, the smaller they become, until they become so small that they seem to disappear completely. The closer objects are to the viewer, the larger and more foreshortened they appear. A number of different instruments were developed to help artists perfect their application of linear perspective, including Dürer's grid and the camera obscura.

Aerial or atmospheric perspective refers to the effect the atmosphere has on the appearance of things when viewed from a distance. As the distance between an object and a viewer increases, the viewer's perception of details decrease and the colours of objects become less bright, usually bluer. The earliest use of aerial perspective was in Pompeii as early as 30 BC, but it appears more regularly in paintings from the Netherlands in the 15th century, with explanations of its effects written soon after in Italy by Alberti and Leonardo.

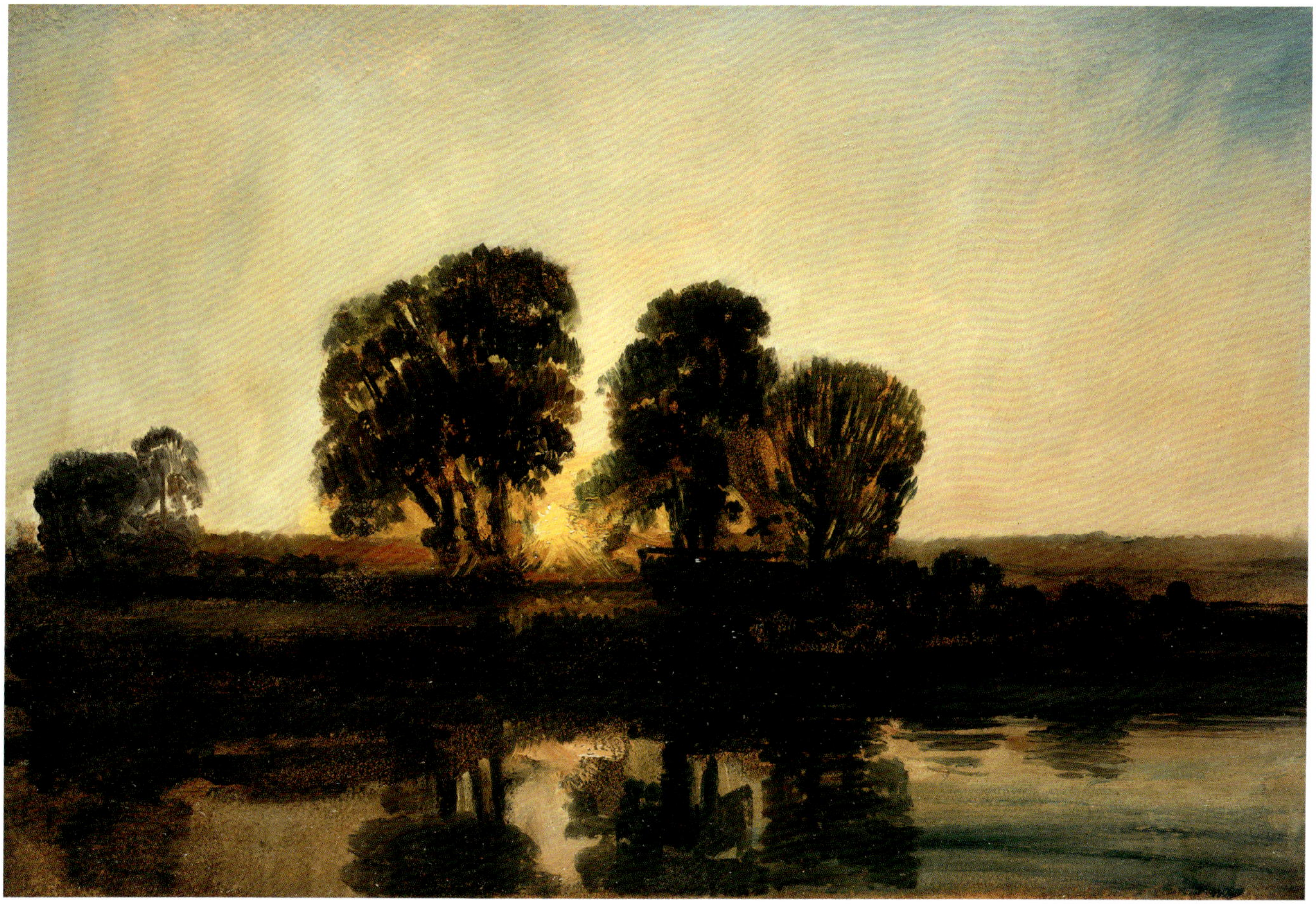

Peter De Wint, *River Scene at Sunset* c.1810, oil on paper mounted onto cardboard, 30.7 x 46, Tate
De Wint (1784–1849) painted in oils and watercolour and often painted *en plein air.* This oil sketch was made in the open air. The sky, which takes up almost two-thirds of the composition, is the most highly finished area. Sweeping brushstrokes create solid patches of colour, and paint has been applied both thinly and in thick impasto. Look how the artist has depicted the sun setting. Consider which colours he has used, and how he has portrayed distance, highlights, dark tones and atmosphere.

Composition

There are several ways that artists have traditionally created compositions to lead viewers' eyes around their images, or to create certain effects. One method is the 'rule of thirds', which was developed during the Renaissance, when artists realised that the eye does not settle naturally on the centre of any painting and that compositions with the main subject (the focal point) in the centre were not aesthetically pleasing. They developed a grid system, dividing images into thirds, both horizontally and vertically. The theory is that if the main element of the painting is on one of these lines or at any intersecting points of these lines, a balanced composition is achieved and viewers interact with the image more naturally. Negative space around and between objects is often used to give viewers a 'breathing space', while lines, such as in paths or rivers, lead viewers' eyes into or out of the picture, particularly towards the focal point. Some artists feature more than one focal point to create added interest and dynamism.

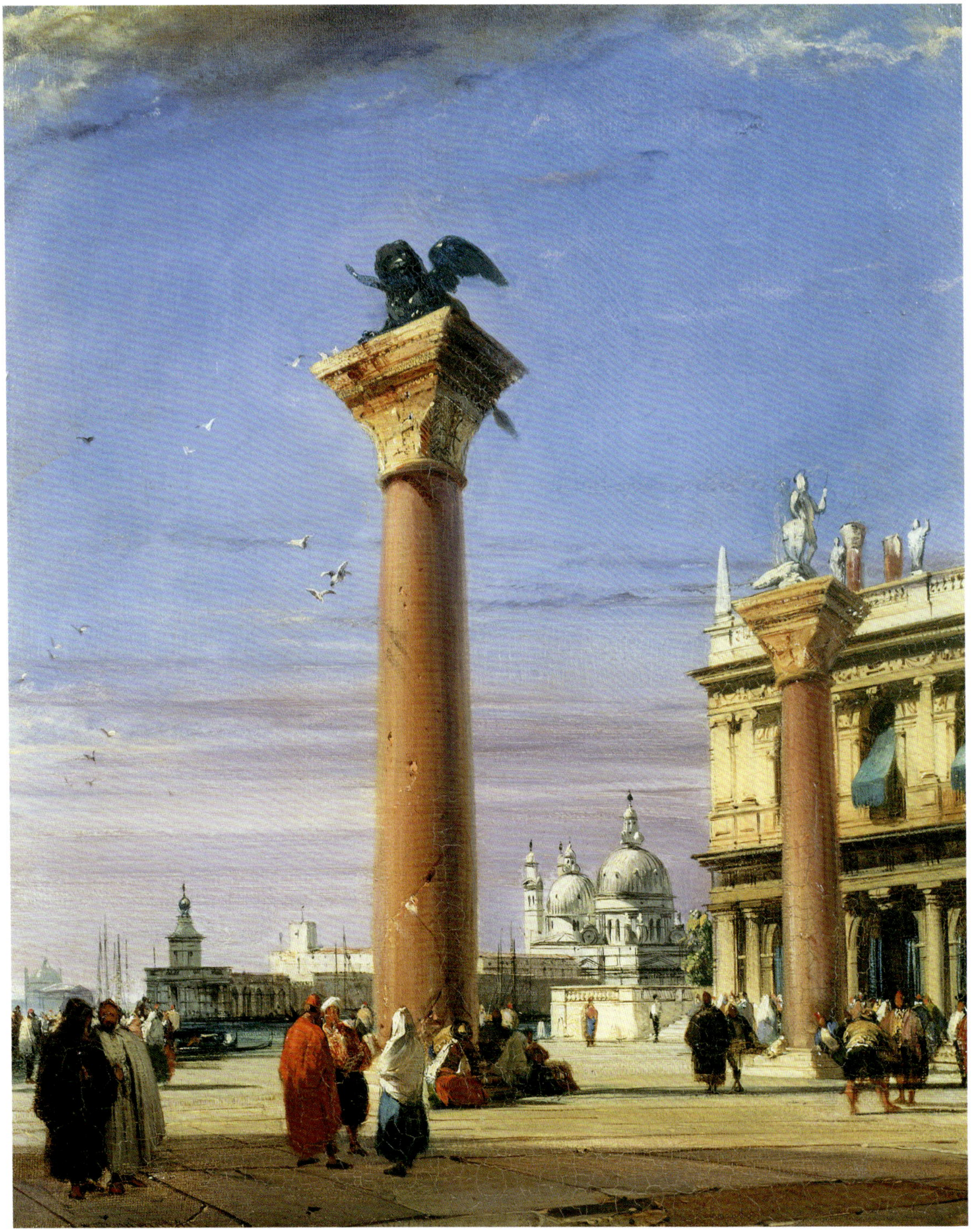

Under the weather

In 1868, a French journalist from Le Havre reported that he had seen Monet painting at his easel in the snow, looking frozen. Monet was not the only painter to be fascinated by the weather. Fifty years before, in England, Turner had made weather and atmospheric effects his trademark (see pages 4, 17, 18, 66 and 70). Influenced by Claude Lorrain (c.1600–82), he travelled extensively in Europe to find scenes to paint and he invented new techniques to express different weather conditions. After Turner, the Impressionists painted the effects of fog, snow, sun, wind and rain as subjects in their own right. Other artists have since used the weather as their central theme, such as the Danish-Icelandic artist Olafur Eliasson (born 1967), whose sculpture and large-scale installation art explores light, water and air temperature. In 2003, he installed *The Weather Project* in the Turbine Hall of Tate Modern in London (see page 71). It was an exploration of ideas about the weather, how we bring it into our everyday conversations and how artists have represented it. For the work, Eliasson created giant representations of the sun and sky and filtered a fine mist around the space. Throughout the day, the mist developed into faint, cloud-like formations and then dispersed into the air. As the mist dissipated, the ceiling above was replaced by a reflection of the space below. Through mono-frequency lamps in his re-creation of the huge sun, colours other than yellow and black became imperceptible. The work, in its size and effects, completely surrounded viewers, who became part of it. There are many ways that artists have projected the effects of weather convincingly. Look out for sources of light in sunny scenes, including the sun, sky and reflected light from objects. The brightest light will always be the sun, while other sources will be less intense. In cloudy scenes, light is diffused fairly evenly without dramatic contrasts of light and shade. Colours and tones project overall atmosphere and light. Look, too, for angles, lines and shapes of such things as clouds, shadows, paint marks and waves, as these all add to the effects.

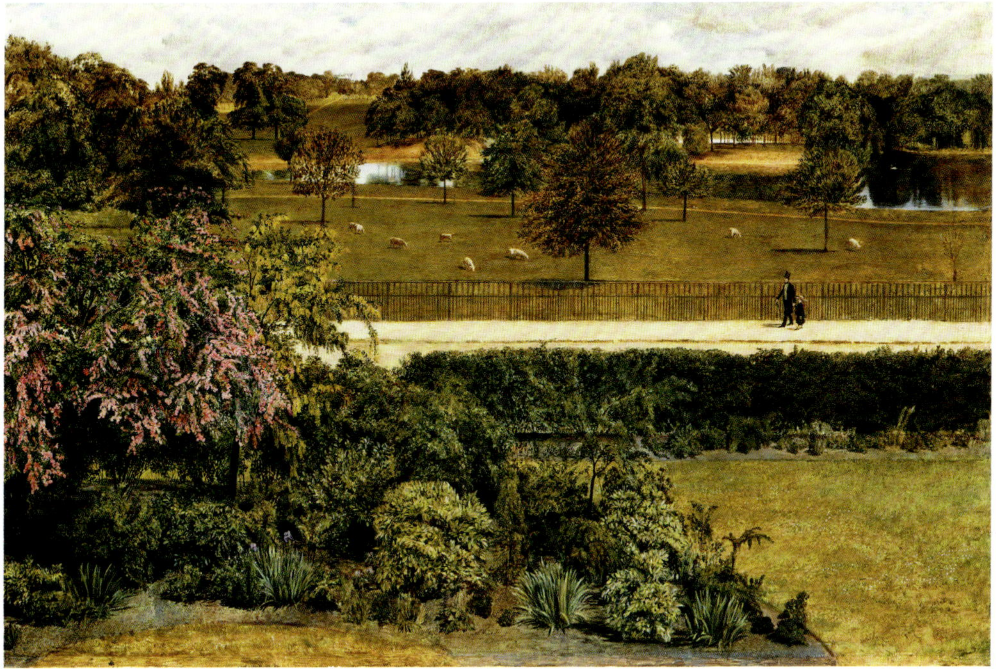

Richard Parkes Bonington, *View of the Piazzetta near the Square of St Mark, Venice* 1827, oil on canvas, 45.7 x 37.5, Tate

Bonington (1802–28) produced many *plein air* sketches and also copied works of the great masters in the Louvre, Paris. In the spring of 1826 he visited Venice, travelling there via Paris, Milan and Verona. He stayed in in the city for about a month and made many pencil and oil sketches on the spot. *View of the Piazzetta* is painted from a dramatic viewpoint, dominated by the column of St Mark in the centre, with the column of St Theodore to the right. The fresh palette and long shadows emphasise the linear and aerial perspective. What do you think of the viewpoint Bonington has chosen? What about his depiction of light? What effect is made by the buildings and shadows being cut off at the edges of the canvas?

Charles Allston Collins, *May, in the Regent's Park* 1851, oil on canvas, 44.5 x 69.2, Tate

This is a view across Regent's Park in London. The painting has been arranged following the rule of thirds, including the diagonal details in the bottom left-hand corner. What do you think of the composition, with minimal spatial depth and hardly any sky? It was criticised when first exhibited in 1852 for its lack of space and emphasis on meticulous details. Collins (1828–73) retained his precise painting style, closely following the ideas of the Pre-Raphaelites, but he was not accepted by them as a member, and by 1860 he had abandoned painting to concentrate on writing.

Skies and water

Water and sky have always been popular with landscape painters. Sometimes they have been used to represent artists' feelings, such as Constable's dark clouds signifying sadness or longing, or Turner's or Monet's dramatic seascapes that reflect their passion for the elements. Here are some questions to ask yourself when looking at such paintings:

- How important is the sky/water in your chosen artist's work?
- How has water been represented? Look at brushwork, colours, tone, lines and shapes and how they dominate the composition (or not).
- How much do you think the artist has drawn from his or her imagination and how much from direct observation?
- What are the main colours of the work? Count them – you may be surprised at how many or how few the artist has used. What effect does this have on the work's appearance?

Some notes on developing your own creative work in response to these paintings:

1. Skies and water in one scene generally share the same colours, although the water is usually slightly darker except where the sun (or moon) shines on it directly.
2. Ocean waves in motion change colours and value as they gain height. As waves rise, they become translucent and often turn greenish. In some places, they can pick up the colour of the sand beneath.
3. Still, calm lakes and ponds are filled with reflections from above. Reflections can be built up with solid shapes or broken slabs of colour.

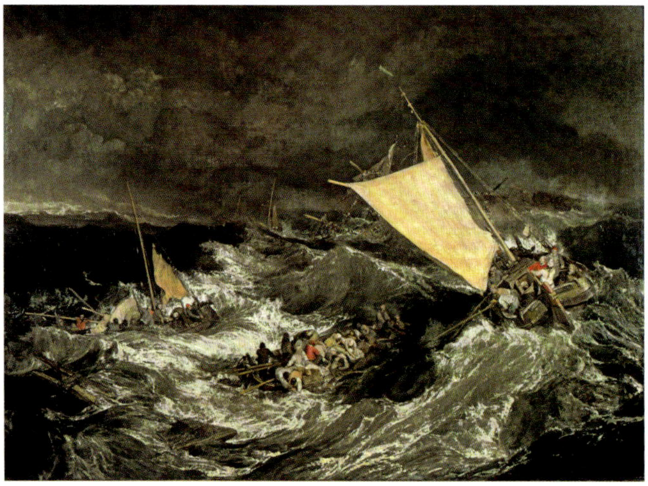

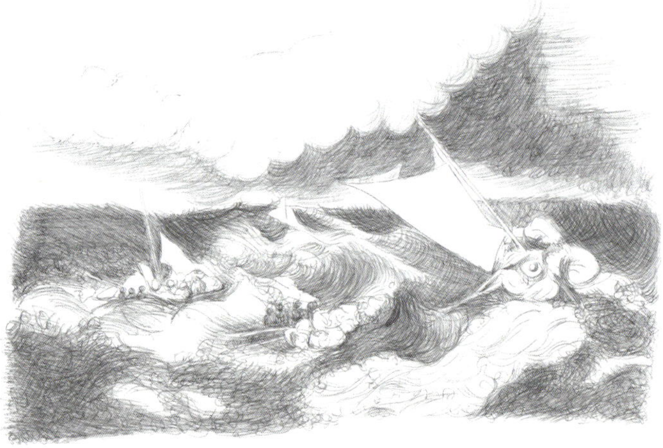

J.M.W. Turner, *The Shipwreck*, exhibited 1805, oil on canvas, 170.5 x 241.6, Tate
During the Romantic period, the shipwreck became a popular subject for artists, offering the possibility of a dramatic and dynamic exploration of the insignificance of man in the face of nature. In portraying the power of the elements and the horror of such a disaster, Turner defines the experience through colours, tones, brushstrokes and a complex composition.

The dark tones contrast dramatically with the white crests and whirls of the waves. Light brushstrokes create an impression of dynamic movement, while the composition follows the rule of thirds (see page 68). Overall, the colours are subdued, with the brightest element being the yellow-cream storm-tossed sail.

A response to Turner's *The Shipwreck*, pencil on paper

- Directional marks representing wind of storm – powerful, strong, overlapping
- Swirls of white, curving lines to suggest the foam on the tops of waves
- Strong contrasts of waves dark and light
- Darkest area of sky
- Light in the distance – symbolising hope?
- Tiny figures tossed at dramatic angles by overpowering sea, almost lost in the huge waves
- Darkness as far and beyond horizon
- Contrast of brushmarks for sky and sea
- Overwhelmingly dark, but the light sail shines out against the dark
- Hatching, cross-hatching, swirls and twisted marks describe the textures

Mood and atmosphere

Many artists have expressed moods through their landscapes, some through abstraction or completely abstract works rather than realistic-looking views. Some have conveyed their own feelings, while others have been more focused on generating feelings in viewers observing the work. Choose two landscape paintings, such as *Nocturne: Blue and Silver – Chelsea* 1871 by Whistler and *Totes Meer (Dead Sea)* 1940–1 by Paul Nash (1889–1946), and compare them.

- What are your first reactions to the works? They are both about landscape, but in what other ways are they similar – or different? What moods do they convey? List words to describe this.
- Is either of the works realistic? What themes are being explored and what messages are being communicated? Do the titles convey more about the works than you can see? Have any parts been exaggerated or distorted? If so, why? Is this effective?
- What colours have been used? Why? How is the colour organised?
- What shapes, marks or textures can you see and how does this affect your opinion of the works?
- What materials and tools have been used? How have the works been made?
- When were the works made? Where were they made? Who made them? What do you know about the artists?
- What else was going on in the world when these artworks were being made? How might that have influenced the artists?
- What else can you find out about the works or the artists? Does any of your research change your views? Why and how?
- How do people view the artworks today and how is this different from the way they were received when first made? How and why has opinion changed?

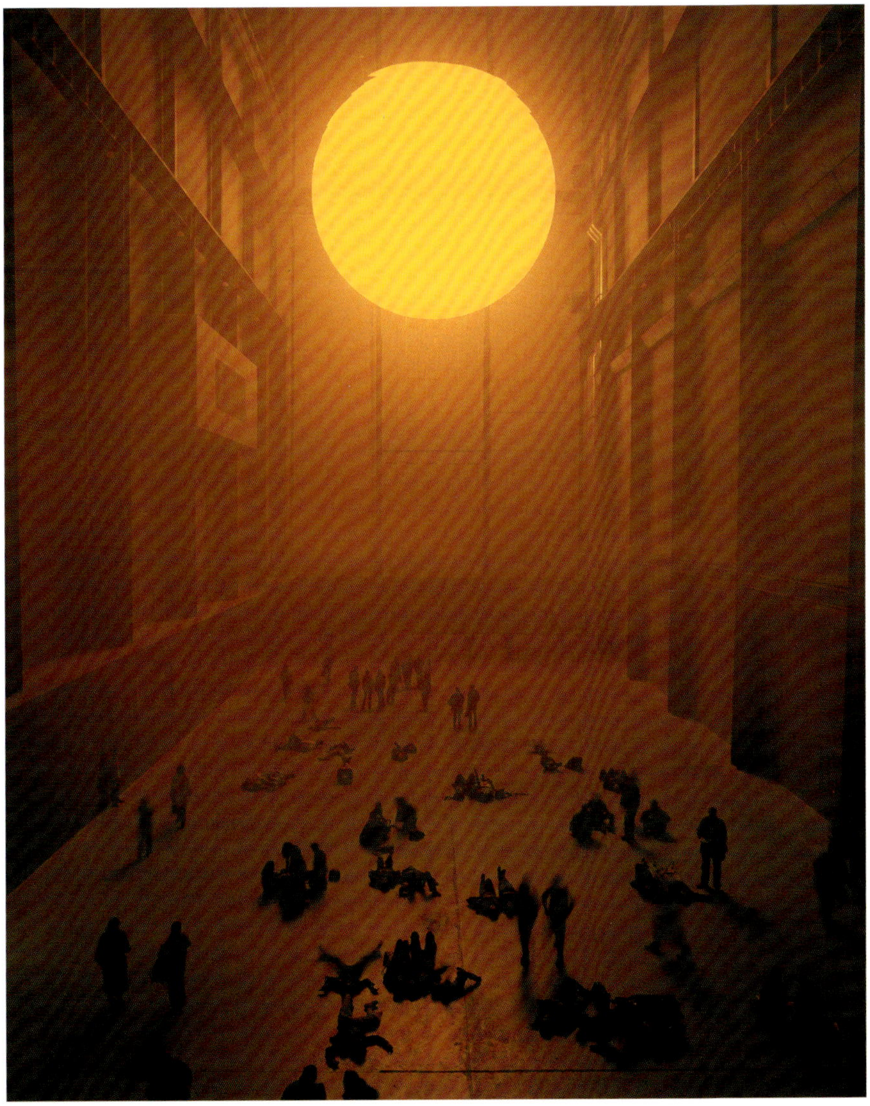

Olafur Eliasson, *The weather project* 2003, installation view at Tate Modern, London 2003
For this installation, Eliasson created different light conditions, investigating the effects of weather on a city. He also questioned how museum visitors are offered information before they see a work of art, which affects their experience. This aimed to reflect the weather's unpredictability, an aspect of life that remains beyond human control.

The environment

Since the 20th century, landscape art has expanded enormously. Land or Earth art and Environmental art all link with the actual landscape. The works frequently exist outside, far from civilisation, using the landscape rather than traditional artists' materials. The artists of these works use the land to draw attention to the natural world for various reasons and usually leave their work to be eroded by the elements. The works are often a protest against materialism, and the artists who produce them tend to record their work in photos and videos. Although they often shun traditional gallery settings, many participate in exhibitions in order to be seen. Land art, emerging in the late 1960s, was inspired by Minimalism, Conceptualism and Arte Povera, using materials generally regarded as rubbish. Artists such as Richard Long, Andy Goldsworthy (born 1956) and Robert Smithson (1938–73) are well-known practitioners of Land and Environmental art. Smithson wrote that his work was a reaction to contemporary social issues, and Long's work emphasises his respect for nature.

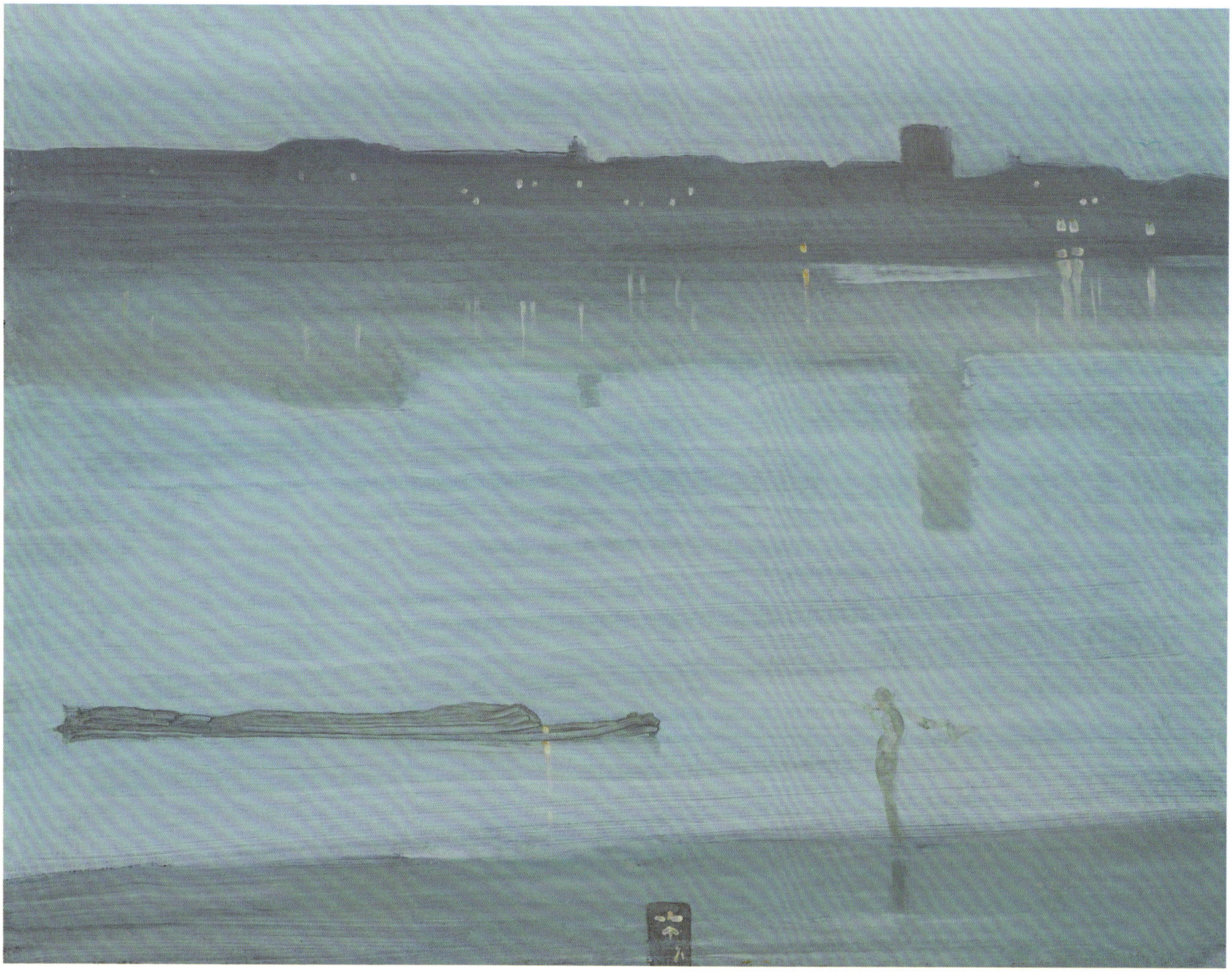

James Abbot McNeill Whistler, *Nocturne: Blue and Silver – Chelsea* 1871, oil on wood, 50.2 x 60.8, Tate
This is the first of the moonlit scenes that Whistler called 'Nocturnes', in which he aimed to convey the tranquillity and beauty of the River Thames by night, contrasting with its bustling activity during the day. The title disconnects the work from any tangible subject, reminding us that the painting is more about feelings and atmosphere than objects or places, rather like a piece of music. Whistler explained: 'A nocturne is an arrangement of line, form and colour first.' He said he had been inspired one August evening by a view of the river 'in a glow of rare transparency, an hour before sunset.' This is a view from the south of the river, looking across to Chelsea. The work is built up with thin, flat layers of paint, the mood is calm and quiet, pattern is more important than objects, and landmarks have become murky shapes. The influence of Japanese art can be seen in the restricted palette, simple composition, economy of line and Whistler's own butterfly signature.

The urban landscape

Many artists have painted urban landscapes, with architecture complementing the natural elements, or taking their place. In 1997 a large aerial view of a city was found in the Baths of Trajan in Rome, dating from the first century AD. During the early Renaissance, views of distant cities or towns appeared alongside landscape backgrounds as settings for portraits and biblical themes. Panoramic vistas of the built environment became even more popular from the 16th to the 18th centuries, often using bird's-eye viewpoints to give map-like overviews of towns and cities. Along with landscape, cityscapes became increasingly popular in thriving 17th-century Netherlands cities such as Amsterdam, Haarlem and The Hague. The subject gained in appeal across Europe, and by the 19th century even more artists were producing architectural scenes and cityscapes as paintings in their own right. As well as capturing nature, the Impressionists were keen to depict modern life around them in their views of buildings, streets, bridges and railways. This continued into the 20th century and beyond.

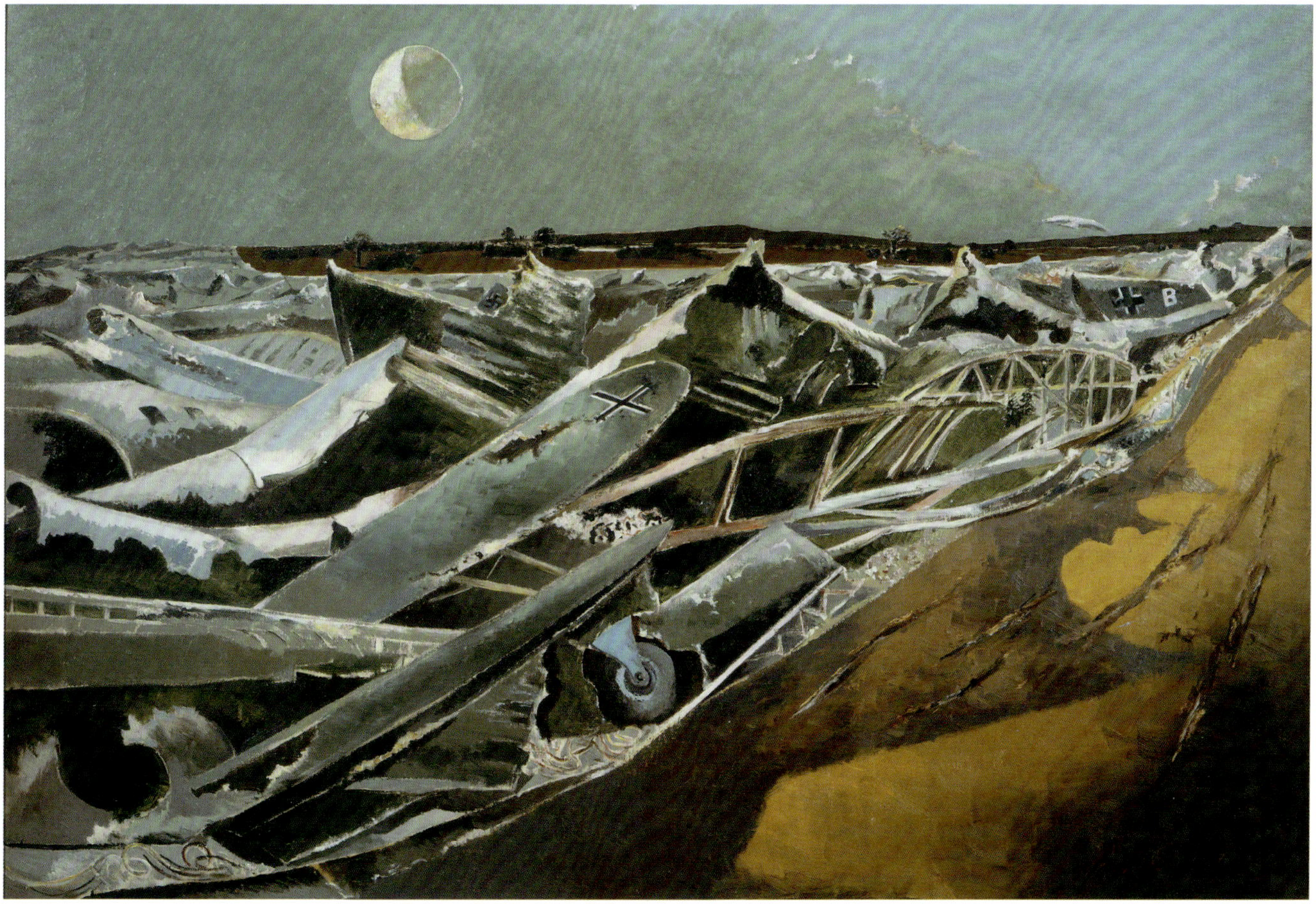

Paul Nash, *Totes Meer (Dead Sea)* 1940–1, oil on canvas, 101.6 x 152.4, Tate

Totes meer is German for 'dead sea'. During the Second World War, Nash saw a dump of wrecked German bombers and fighters that had been shot down in the Battle of Britain. He based this painting on photographs he took at the site, which he described in detail: 'The thing looked to me suddenly, like a great inundating sea ... the breakers rearing up and crashing on the plain. And then ... nothing moves, it is not water or even ice, it is something static and dead ... The only moving creature is the white owl flying low.' Nash served as a war artist in both the First and Second World Wars. Here he has expressed his own observations, but also the feelings of the people, with compassion towards both sides – for the German airmen who were killed in their machines as much as for the fighting men of his own country.

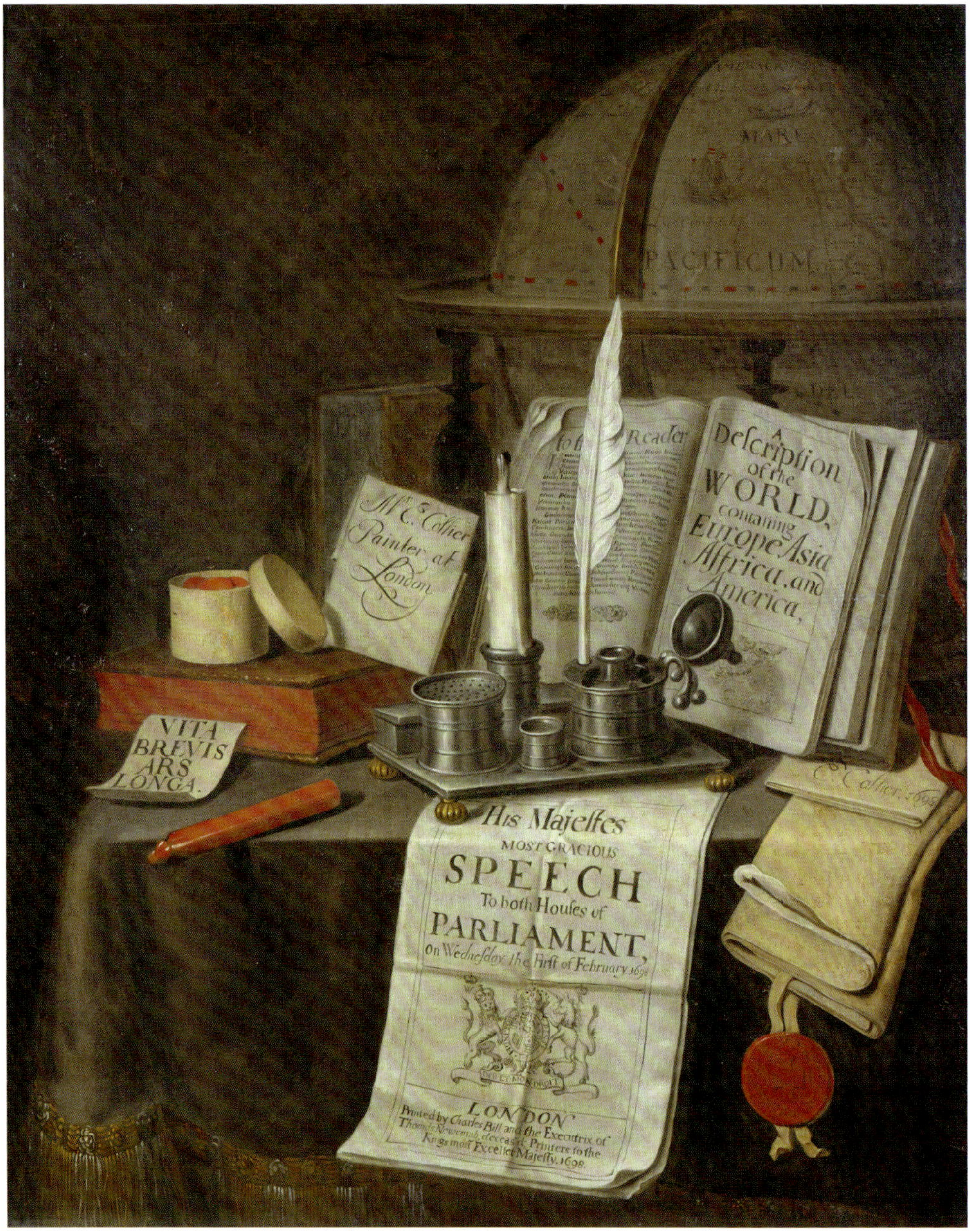

Edward Collier, *Still Life* 1699, oil on canvas, 76.2 x 63.5, Tate

Most still-life paintings bought in Britain during the 17th century came from the Netherlands. Collier (active 1662–1708) was Dutch and specialised in painting still lifes for both the Dutch and English markets. This one was intended for a British buyer as the manuscripts and texts featured are in English. The letter propped up above the tray of writing equipment is inscribed 'Mr E. Collier, Painter at London', confirming that the artist was active there at that time. The globe, circular box of seals and other writing equipment and books indicate the painting was commissioned by a wealthy and well-educated person. The globe and atlas also symbolise the wider world beyond the frame. Politics is brought into the picture with the transcript of a speech delivered by William III to Parliament about the disbanding of the British army. A stick of partly used sealing wax hangs over the edge of a piece of cloth, near to a slip of paper protruding from a book. The Latin text on this translates as 'Life is short, but art endures', a phrase reminding viewers of the transience of life. The partially consumed wax-stick and candle are also symbols of the impermanence of life. There are several more symbols in this painting, which Collier's contemporaries would have enjoyed deciphering.

STILL LIFE

'I will astonish Paris with an apple!'
Paul Cézanne

The earliest surviving still lifes in Western art have been found in – you guessed it – frescoes in Pompeian homes from the first century AD. In the 15th century, initially in the Netherlands, oil paint gained popularity, eventually becoming painters' main medium because of its smoothness and malleability. It enabled Dutch artists to paint ultra realistic-looking arrangements of objects. From about 1650, paintings of objects became called *still-leven*, meaning 'motionless nature', or the French term *natures mortes*.

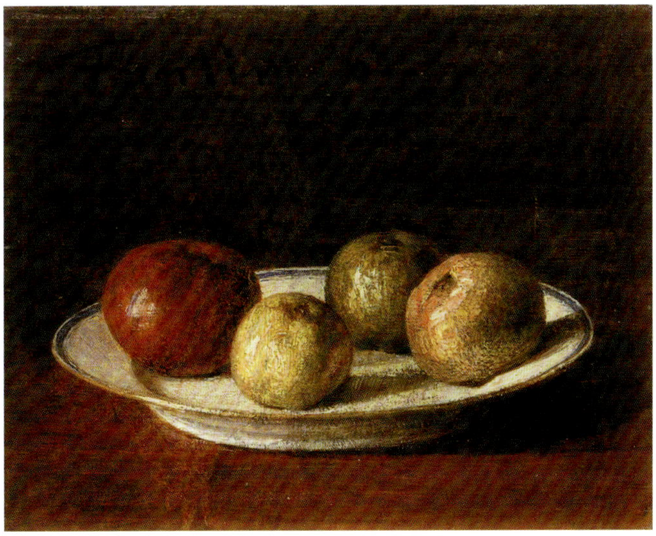

Henri Fantin-Latour, *A Still Life with Apples* 1861, oil on canvas, 21 x 26.4, Tate
Although he was French, the many still-life paintings made by Fantin-Latour (1836–1904) were more popular in England than in France, and he made a good living from them. This tiny work was painted just before the Impressionists emerged as a group, but you can see by the thickness of the paint and obvious brushmarks that conventions were changing in the art world. The bright colours and strong contrasts were popular with many middle-class buyers.

Vanitas and *bodegóns*

During the early 17th century, a certain type of still-life painting became highly valued in the Calvinist Netherlands. These were known as 'vanitas' or 'memento mori'. They included objects that show decay or the brevity and futility of worldly life, such as skulls, candles, half-peeled fruit, broken vessels, butterflies and other reminders of the shortness of life, the inevitability of death and the transience of earthly pleasures. In Spain, *bodegóns* became popular soon after this. The term *bodega* in Spanish can be translated as 'cupboard', 'tavern' or 'wine bar', and these paintings were still lifes of items from the larder, such as food, drink and cooking utensils. Occasionally, *bodegóns* also contain human figures.

Along with landscape and portraiture, still-life painting in the Netherlands reached a peak by the mid-17th century and continued as one of the most popular styles of art there for almost two centuries. The paintings celebrated the newly acquired Dutch wealth that came from their expanding trading empire, and also filled the creative

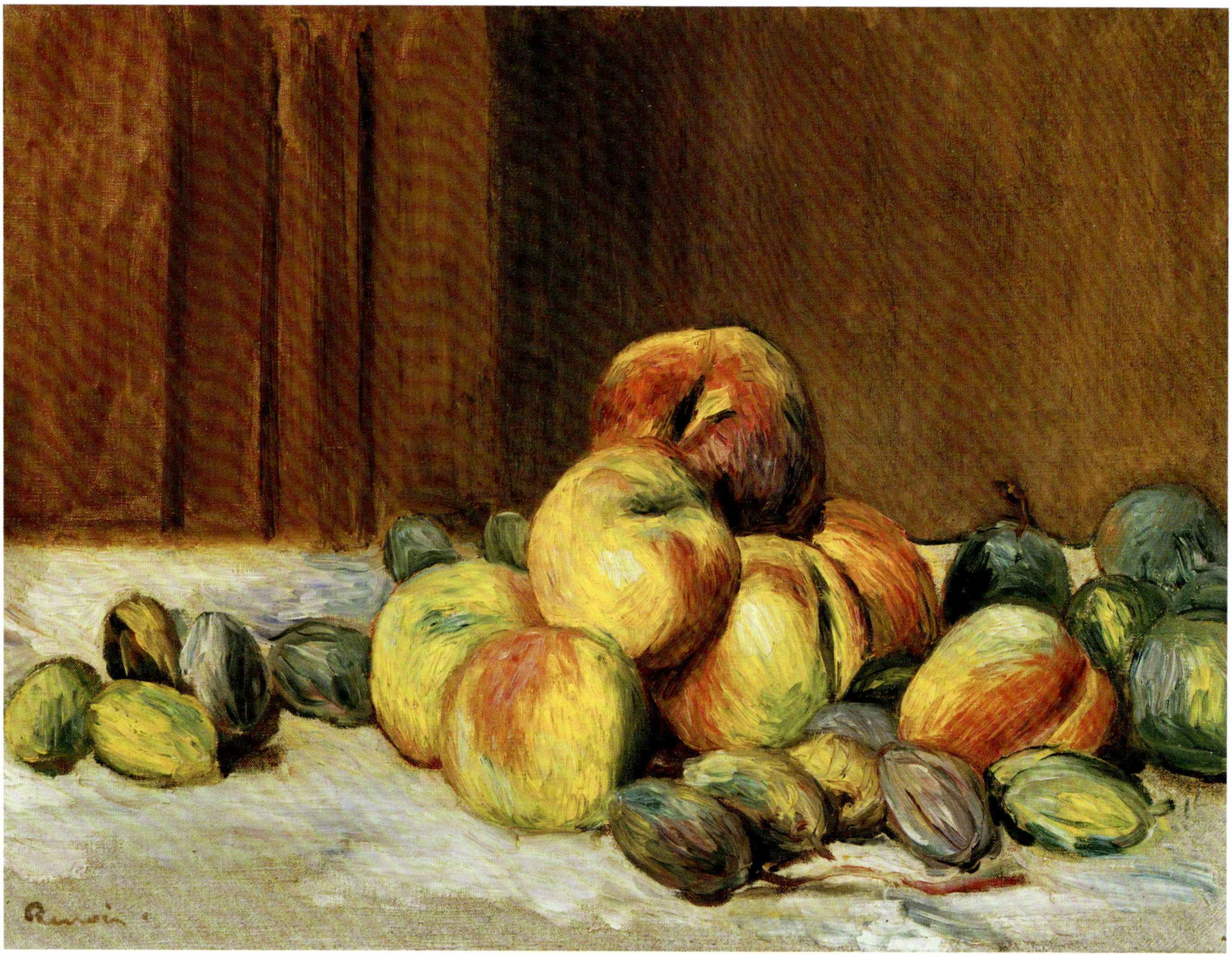

Pierre-Auguste Renoir, *Peaches and Almonds* 1901, oil on canvas, 31 x 41.3 Tate

By this point in his career, Renoir (1841–1919) was well known and prosperous. He had always painted for middle-class art buyers, however, and this market only increased as the rest of the world began to notice his work favourably. Making use of bright, clear colours he painted quickly, capturing the fruit in front of him and nothing more. The Impressionists' paintings contained no hidden meanings; they were simply images of moments in time. What do you think of the composition and contrast in the colours of the fruit and background? What about Renoir's brushstrokes, do you think they enhance the work, or detract from it? What makes you think this?

void that Calvinism had precipitated: while religious art predominated in most countries, Calvinism in northern Europe forbade overtly religious painting. So, to earn a living, many Dutch artists relied on painting secular subjects for private patrons. These were often the new middle classes who bought works in abundance to adorn their homes. Still life emphasised and displayed the goods these newly wealthy citizens could buy, and the artists' astonishingly illusionistic styles were greatly admired.

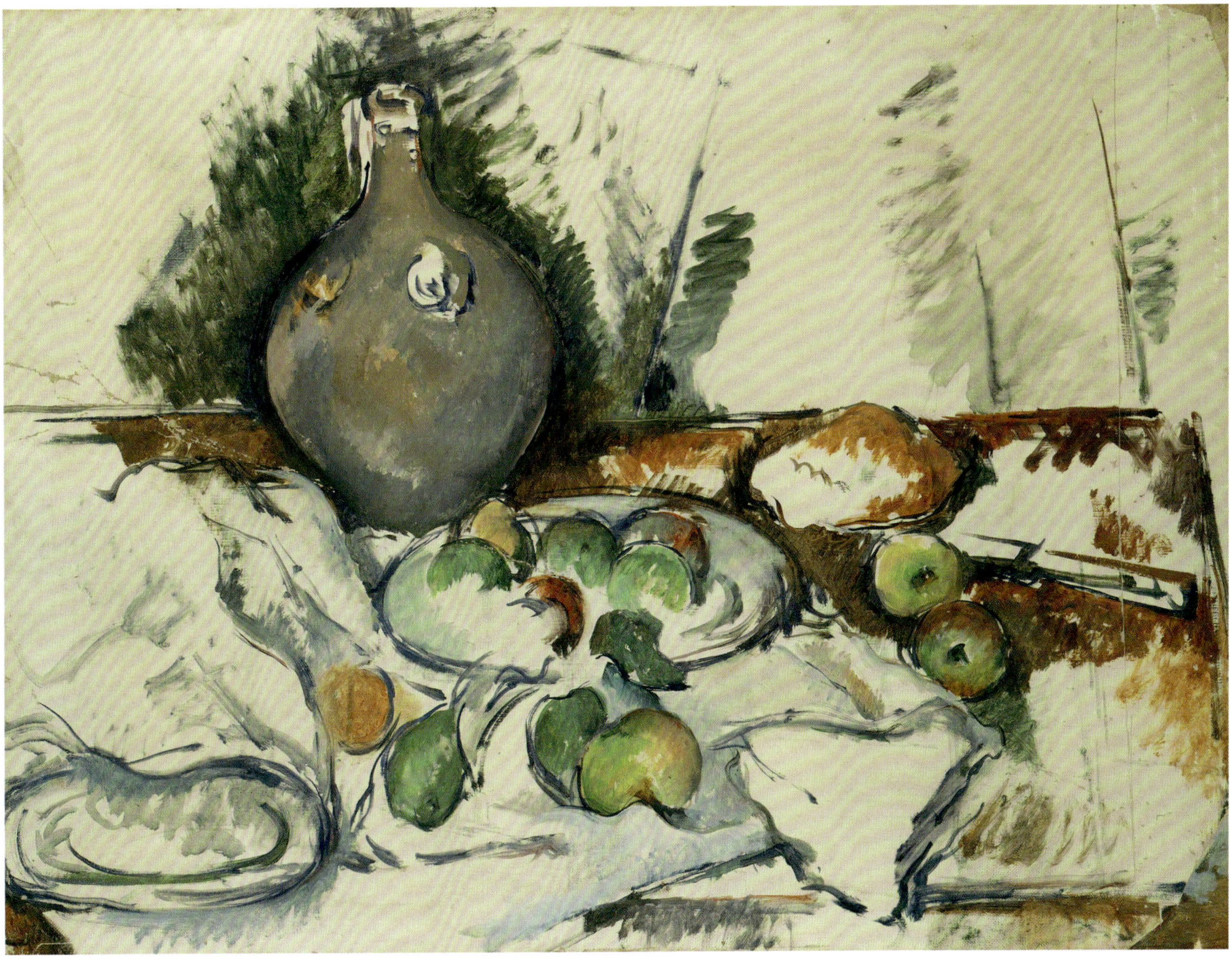

Paul Cézanne, *Still Life with Water Jug* c.1892–3, oil on canvas, 53 x 71, Tate
Cézanne (1839–1906) used still life to explore his ideas about painting and painted the same objects repeatedly in different arrangements. As the items were very familiar to him, he didn't have to concentrate so much on what they looked like, but could focus more on portraying visual sensations. He believed that the ways that artists had conventionally depicted perspective, with a single viewpoint, did not accurately show how we observe things, so he combined several viewpoints on one flat painting surface, as in this unfinished work. His ideas had a profound effect on many artists who came after him.

Art dealers

In Paris, Rome and London, still life remained the lowest-rated genre of the official academies. Artists in those cities were encouraged to promote patriotism and piety. You may wonder why any artist painted still lifes at all in those countries. At the annual Salon in Paris, history paintings were displayed in prominent locations, while landscape and still lifes were in less conspicuous places. During the 18th and early 19th centuries, annual exhibitions held by official academies were almost the only places where artists could attract buyers, so relatively small still-life paintings were often overlooked. Towards the end of the 19th century, however, a radical development occurred in the way art was marketed and sold.

The Industrial Revolution's technological improvements, particularly in printing, made the distribution of words and images faster and easier than ever before. By the mid-19th century, art auctions and art dealing also began expanding as ways for artists to sell their work all year round. Art dealers set up galleries, promoting artists' work in return

New middle-class collectors

Until the 18th century, most private art collectors were aristocrats, but by the 19th century, across Europe and North America, the middle classes were expanding and had become significant art buyers. They bought art from auctions, exhibitions and dealers. Their choice of art was 'safe'; it usually conformed to fashionable tastes. So artists who wanted to make a living had to adhere to certain requirements to reflect buyers' conventional attitudes. Popular subjects included simple mythology, landscapes, portraits and still life.

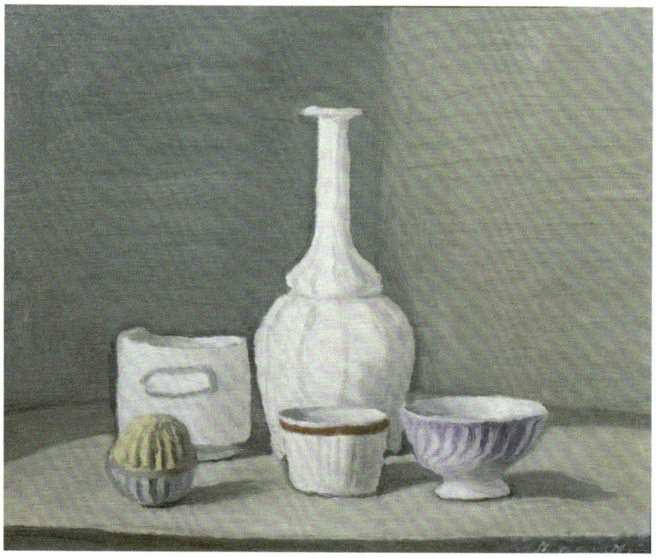

Giorgio Morandi, *Still Life* 1946, oil on canvas, 37.5 x 45.7, Tate

Morandi (1890–1964) was an Italian painter and printmaker specialising in still life, mainly of vases, bottles and bowls. Inspired after seeing work by Renoir, Monet and Cézanne at exhibitions in Venice and Rome, he particularly followed Cézanne's ideas. Briefly involved with the Futurists and Cubists, he later worked in a metaphysical style. How has Cézanne's influence affected this work?

for a percentage of the art's selling price. Soon, several art dealers became essential links between artists and buyers. Among the first works of art sold by art dealers were those produced by the Impressionists, such as Monet and Renoir. Their transactions with Paul Durand-Ruel (1831–1922) helped to make them famous. About thirty years later, dealer Daniel-Henry Kahnweiler (1884–1979) championed, among others, Picasso and Braque.

By the late 19th and early 20th centuries, still life became more sought after as the new art-buying middle classes found that these colourful, undemanding works complemented their homes. In September 1907, a major retrospective was held of Cézanne's art in Paris. Because he had painted so many still lifes, the exhibition generated an even greater interest in the genre. Picasso and Braque in particular focused their attention on his ideas with their Cubist experiments that followed.

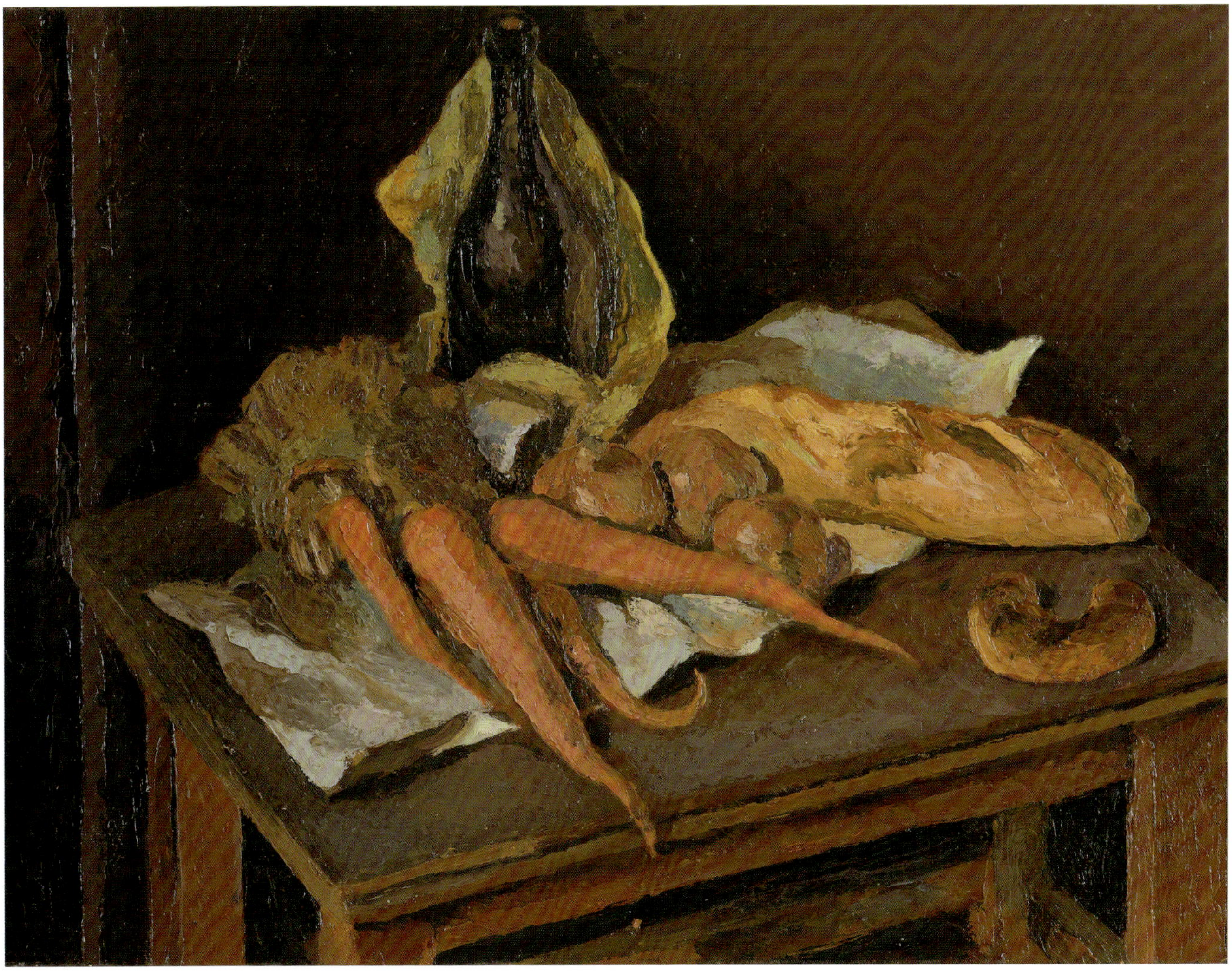

Duncan Grant, *Still life with Carrots* c.1921, oil on canvas, 50.8 x 68.6 cm, Tate
Known as one of the Bloomsbury Group of artists and writers, Grant (1885–1978), who grew up in India, developed a bold, vivid painting style after meeting Matisse in 1909 and seeing a large Post-Impressionist exhibition in London in 1910. He was also influenced by visits to Italy, Greece and Paris. As well as painting, he designed theatrical sets and costumes. This subject, with its harmonious range of colours, creates a unified image, although the objects seem to have been simply thrown down. In fact the objects were carefully arranged and it was intended to be a dynamic image.

Cubism

Although Cézanne exhibited with the Impressionists, he is usually described as a Post-Impressionist. He was concerned not with fleeting moments as the Impressionists were, but with solidity and structure. His many still-life paintings show his efforts to describe inner forms and structure, rather than momentary impressions. He painted familiar things over and again, exploring the boundaries between reality and illusion. Building on his ideas, Picasso and Braque distorted and fragmented images, aiming to show more than one perspective as Cézanne had done, but pushing his ideas further and more literally. They painted nudes, portraits and landscapes, but Cubism lent itself particularly to still life, as objects could be depicted relatively easily from several angles at once. In breaking up viewpoints, Picasso and Braque were attempting to free painting from the restrictions of perspective that had been used by artists since the Renaissance. They inspired several other artists, including Fernand Léger (1881–1955), Juan Gris (1887–1927) and Robert Delaunay (1885–1941).

Found objects

When Picasso pasted a printed image of chair caning onto his painting *Still Life with Chair Caning* in 1912, he was the first well-known artist to use an object that is not normally considered to be an art material for a work of art. Marcel Duchamp (1887–1968) continued the notion with his 'readymades' soon after. His most famous example is *Fountain* 1917 (see page 103), a standard urinal from a shop, that he displayed on its back on a pedestal. Artists began to use found objects increasingly after this. They were making the point that it's not the objects but the way in which the artist chooses to display them that makes them art. The idea shocked the art world and the public, but over the decades, the notion has become less revolutionary and more predictable. Using found objects in works of art is intended to stimulate viewers' philosophical reflection. Found objects have been particularly popular with the Surrealists, the Fluxus movement, Arte Povera, Conceptualism and in Pop art.

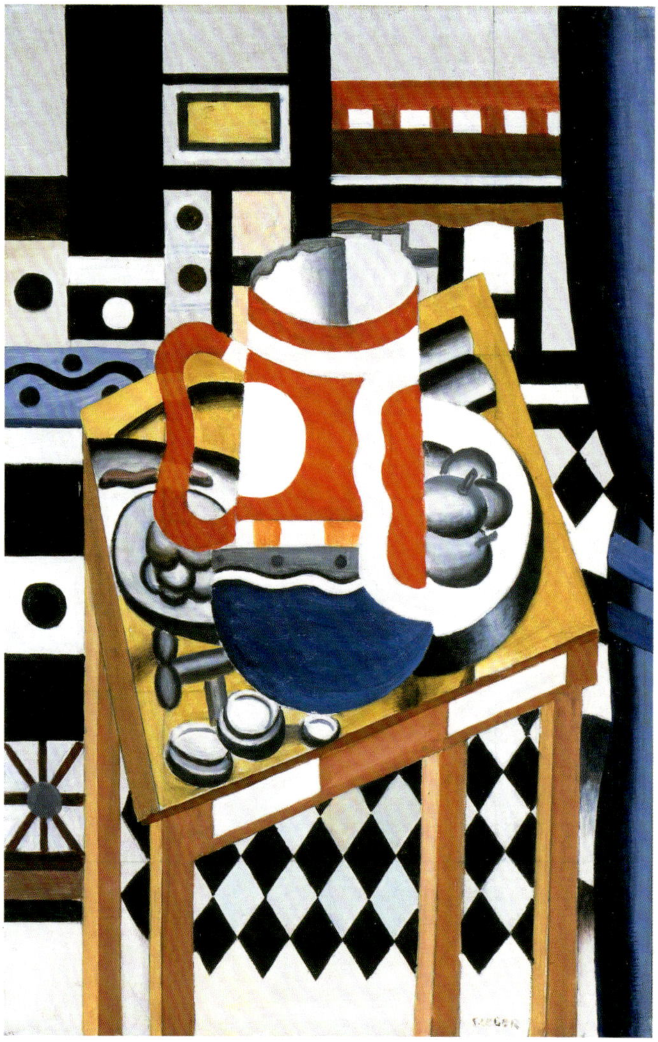

Fernand Léger, *Still Life with a Beer Mug* 1921–2, oil on canvas, 92 x 60, Tate
Léger was influenced by Picasso and Braque's experiments, as well as by his own horrific experiences in the First World War. His work became a blend of real objects, usually distorted, focusing on geometric shapes and smooth tonal contrasts. The theme here is a workman's lunch on a table, painted in bright colours plus black and white. The geometric grid-like background represents the patterned floor, the wall and kitchen window frame; the table and beer mug are represented without the constraints of traditional linear perspective. All the elements form dynamic patterns. This was Léger's personal, original response to Cubism. From 1920, he became more influenced by the Dutch movement De Stijl and the French Purist group.

Georges Braque, *Glass on a Table* 1909–10, oil on canvas, 33 x 37.2, Tate
Cubism was a nickname, used to describe Picasso and Braque's paintings that fragmented the objects they portrayed, rather than showing the single viewpoint of traditional linear perspective. Here, Braque's still life of a glass and pears on a circular wooden table looks like a series of broken geometric shapes and planes. Braque – and Picasso – believed that by breaking up the picture plane they were presenting a true depiction of the objects, but in actual fact, Cubism can be quite difficult to decipher and you need to hunt for clues! Because their Cubist works were so complex, Picasso and Braque reduced their palettes. Here, Braque used yellows, browns and black with accents of blue, touches of red and green, plus highlights of grey and white.

Symbols and tricks

As well as the early vanitas still-life paintings, many still-life artists have depicted objects for their symbolism, while many more have simply illustrated objects to show off their descriptive skills. Whether the artists intended it or not, many still lifes are interpreted allegorically anyway. As the middle classes made them fashionable, the upper classes also began commissioning still-life paintings, usually of valuable items to emphasise their wealth and grandeur. These patrons chose to disregard the moralistic and somewhat depressing vanitas messages of their Dutch forerunners, but often also liked some hidden, alternative meanings in their still lifes.

The expression *trompe-l'oeil* – or 'fool the eye' – was introduced in the 17th century to describe paintings that looked convincingly real, for example murals of subjects such as landscapes that appeared to show places beyond the walls they were painted on, but it was also used to describe exceptionally realistic-looking still-life paintings.

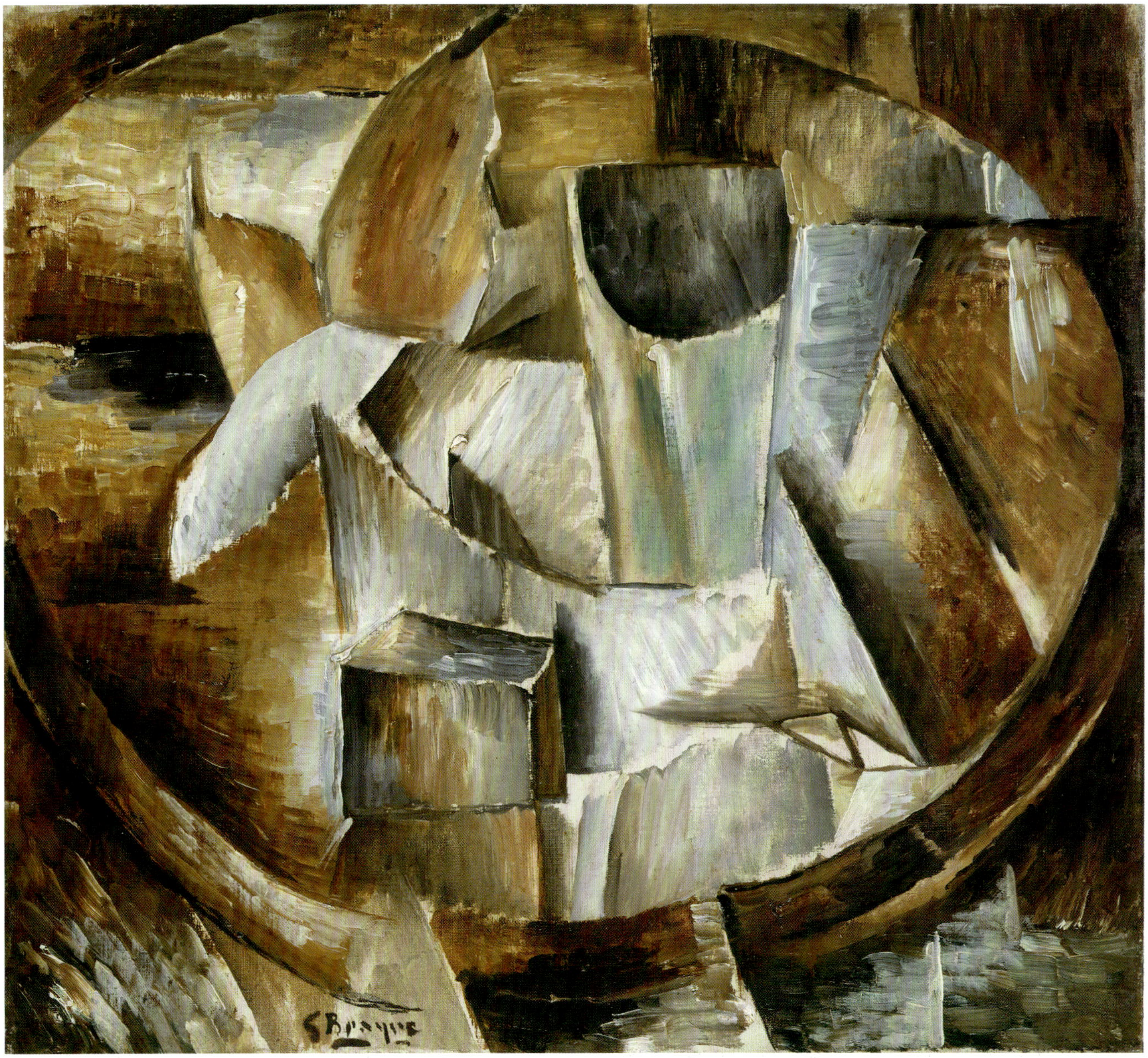

Changing expectations

So how do you analyse or respond to a still life? Should the approach be different from other types of art? What significance does still life have in the context of art? Although not all artists produce still lifes, most of them originally learned their craft by drawing objects from observation. Several modern artists continue to create still lifes, not always by drawing or painting objects, but often by arranging actual objects to provoke reactions and thoughts. Once placed in a specific arrangement and then captured in paint, ink, pastel or whatever medium is preferred, still-life objects can take on new meanings. For instance, Morandi painted several groups of familiar items over and again (see page 78). Just as when you repeat a word over and again it loses its meaning, so in Morandi's paintings, by his repetition, the objects lose their original domestic purpose, seem to become distorted, and eventually appear simply as timeless, purposeless objects, inviting contemplation.

In 1962 Andy Warhol (1928–87), who came from a commercial art background, made numerous screenprints of an everyday object that most people living in America bought regularly – a Campbell's soup can. His treatment of the subject made the image of the can far more important than it had been. Rather than being a cheap item you might see every day in a shop or kitchen, Warhol turned the soup cans into icons, encouraging introspection and reflection, provoking viewers' consideration of their personal, cultural, religious or philosophical significance. Through the 1960s Warhol continued his concept by making prints of other familiar consumer items, such as Coca-Cola bottles or Brillo boxes. He used art as a vehicle for expressing social commentary and, in doing so, he challenged what people expected art to be. Classed as a Pop artist, Warhol belonged to an art movement that emerged almost simultaneously in London and New York in the late 1950s. It aimed to bring an end to the snobbishness of art, to enable anyone to enjoy it, and he completely changed what we expect art to be.

Andy Warhol, *Black Bean Soup* 1968, silkscreen, 89.2 x 59.1, Tate
In 1962 Warhol created thirty-two prints that each looked like a different can of Campbell's soup. In an exhibition, he lined the prints along a shelf like tins of soup in a supermarket. This focus on everyday images was at the heart of Pop art, as was the silkscreen, which was not customarily used for traditional artwork. Screenprinting creates images that look flat, and more like something mass-produced and bought in a shop than an individual painting produced by an artist's hand, but Warhol displayed his screenprints on gallery walls to make a point: they were art because he said they were. Screenprinting simulated the mechanical effects used in making the label on the soup can. Yet the obvious flatness, enlargement of scale and fine black outline make the works different from actual soup cans, and the way Warhol presented them made them no longer commercial products but art objects for viewers to contemplate. He was purposely posing radical questions about the value of art and the way it is perceived and marketed. All that from a simple soup can!

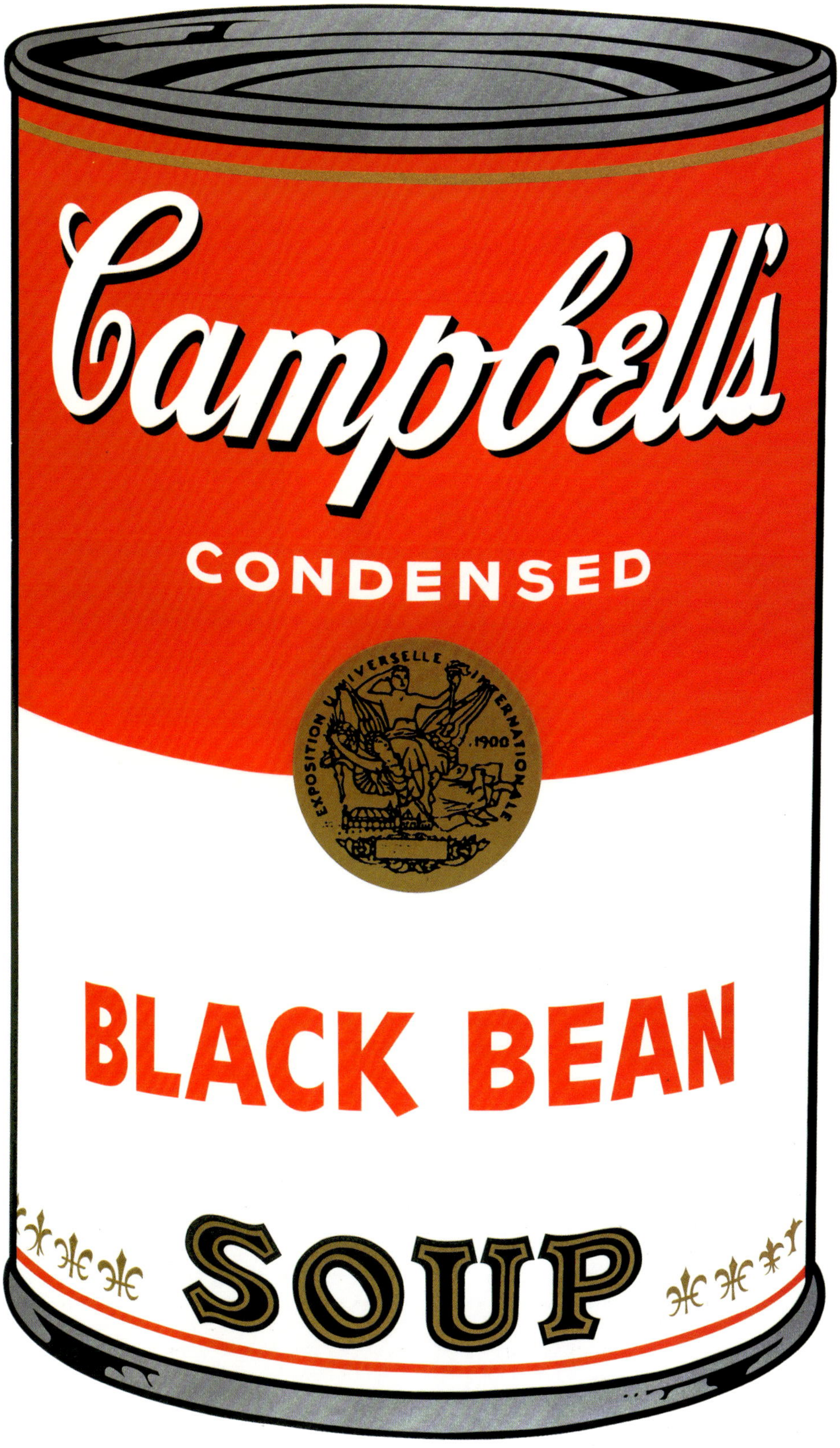
Campbell's
CONDENSED
BLACK BEAN
SOUP

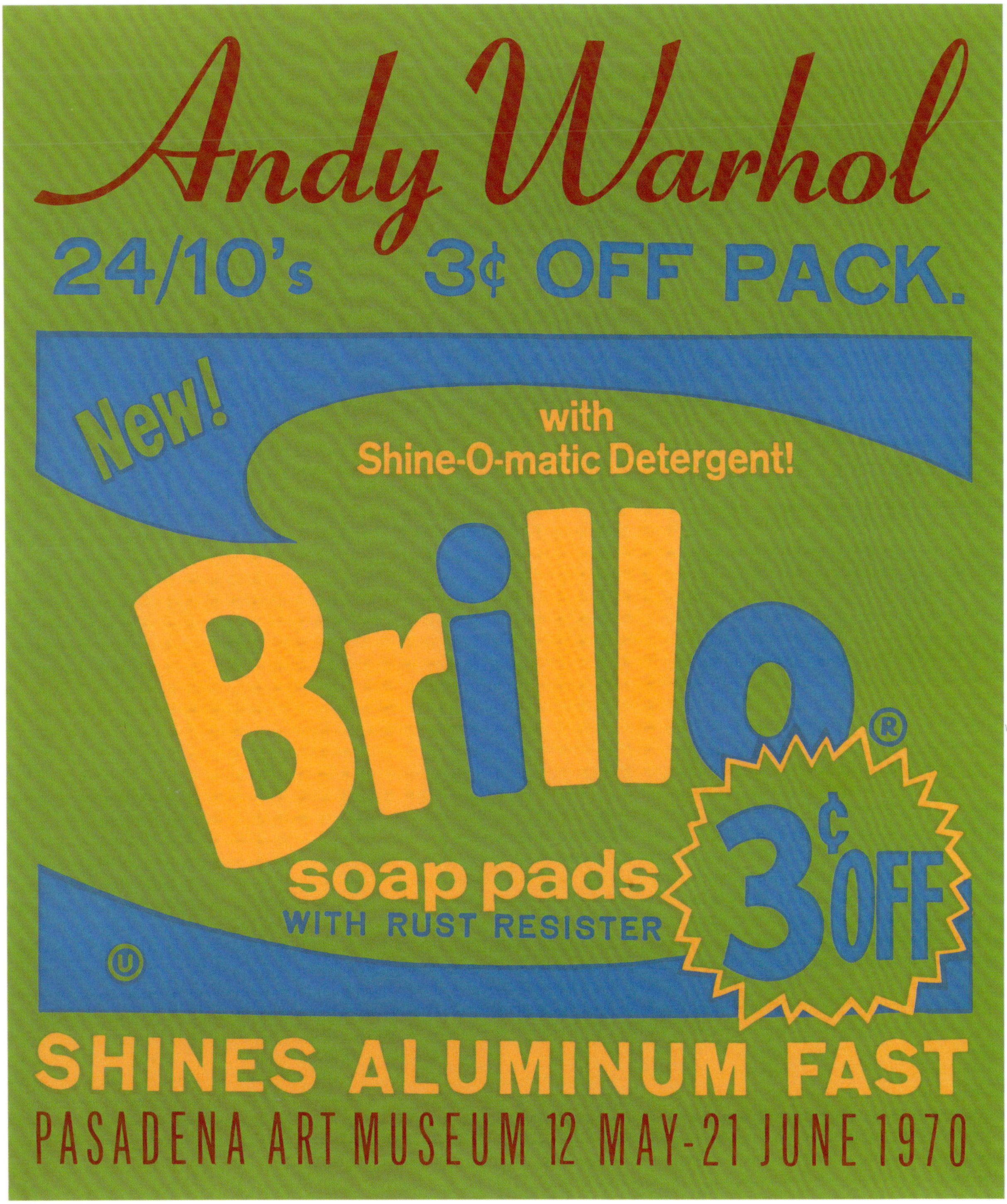
Andy Warhol
24/10's 3¢ OFF PACK.
New!
with
Shine-O-matic Detergent!
Brillo®
soap pads
WITH RUST RESISTER
3¢ OFF
SHINES ALUMINUM FAST
PASADENA ART MUSEUM 12 MAY-21 JUNE 1970

Pop art

In the 1950s, Britain struggled to counter the hardships that persisted after the Second World War, while, simultaneously, the United States was experiencing increasing wealth. In the UK, rationing of some foods continued until 1954, nine years after the end of the war. People were weary of restrictions and hungry for new, exciting things to buy, while in America consumers were being almost overwhelmed by the goods available to them. Both experiences led to consumerism, or people being overly interested in the idea of buying things. At the same time, a number of artists were bored by what they perceived as the arrogance that surrounded art, meaning that many 'ordinary' people would not go to art galleries in case they did not understand what they saw and so were made to feel foolish or ignorant. These artists decided to make art that everyone understood and could relate to.

Logos and labels

Pop artists challenged the traditions of fine art by including in their work imagery from popular culture, such as advertising, magazines or comics, or from popular goods – things that everyone was familiar with. In a similar way, many Pop artists rejected traditional artists' methods and materials, and instead used commercial art materials and techniques. They particularly embraced modern graphic design, such as comic art, labels or logos.

Andy Warhol, *Brillo Boxes* date unknown, screenprinted poster on paper, 75.8 x 65.8, Tate

This poster advertised a retrospective exhibition of Warhol's work in Pasadena, USA, in 1970. The white, red and blue original colours of Brillo boxes has been changed to green, blue and yellow for the poster. The Brillo boxes followed on from Warhol's Campbell's soup cans, but rather than being flat, screenprinted images, actual boxes were manufactured out of plywood and then screenprinted with the package design. Continuing to play with the culture of consumerism, Warhol was fascinated by commercial designs and the effects that their repeating patterns make. Yet at the same time, he was posing questions to postwar consumers, including: what effect do advertisements – and packaging – have on us? Do they make us want to buy products, or do we stop paying attention? Can objects from everyday life also be art?

Viewing still life

When viewing a still life, you need to take several things into account, as you would do with any other type of art, such as your first impressions, and when and where the work was made. What movement was the artist a part of, if any? Then, you can ask more specific questions, such as: is the subject a random collection of items, or did the artist have a particular intention when choosing them? Do the objects have anything in common with each other and, if so, what? Why has the artist grouped them together? Have any parts been exaggerated or distorted? If so, why? Remember that nearly every choice an artist makes is a conscious one. What about the ways in which the objects are presented? Are there colours in the tones and shadows?

Although many still-life paintings consciously use perspective, they rarely attempt to create an impression of movement. Most compositions, therefore, are fairly static. Think about how the artist has arranged the objects and to what effect. How does the artist make your eye move around the work? Is there one place where your

Content, style, context

1. *Content.* A still life can present man-made or natural objects, or a mixture of both. Study your artist's depiction. Why have the objects been chosen? Look for any second meanings and make notes about why you think this artist included them.
2. *Style.* An artist can show objects clearly and boldly, with sharp light, colours and textures, or from obscure angles in dull light. What kind of light has your artist portrayed and why?
3. *Context.* The objects represented may have strong associations for you, or you may not recognise them. Is the work significant to you? Does it evoke memories or feelings? Can you determine whether the objects have significance for the artist – or was it made for someone else? What can you deduce about the work from its content and how the materials have been handled? Is the date it was made significant? What do you know about the artist's life?

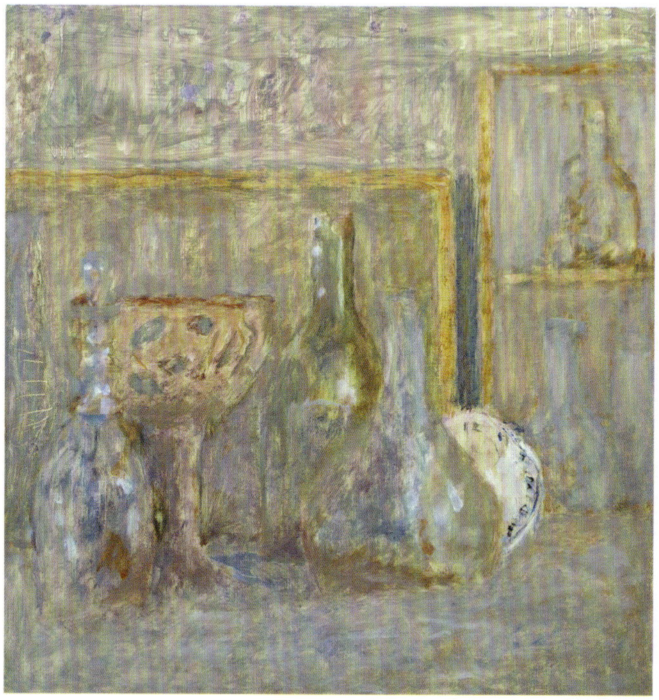

Adrian Stokes, *Still Life* 1963, oil on canvas, 45.7 x 45.7, Tate
Adrian Stokes (1902–72) wrote several books and articles about architecture, modern art and Italian Renaissance art. He was also a painter, specialising in landscape, the nude and still life. His broken brushwork, indistinct details and light effects show his admiration for Turner. Compare his still life with Hardaker's. They were both painted during the same year. Does this make a difference?

Charles Hardaker, *Still Life: Vertical Structures, Three Times Three* 1965, oil on canvas, 121.5 x 91.2, Tate
Two years after painting this picture, Hardaker (born 1934) wrote that it formed part of a series on multiple themes, which he was still developing. He said his reasons for painting this and all the others in the series were 'architectural and philosophical' and connected with symbols in Plato's *Timaeus* (c.360 BC). Clearly a thoughtful process, this should be investigated further – it is not simply an arrangement of objects, but is a much deeper process. Think about something you have been reading recently. How would you represent it as a still life? How has this artist exploited philosophical theories?

eye always ends up? Can you detect any patterns or rhythm in the arrangement? Is the work detailed and precise, or unexpected and difficult to look at? Is it realistic or like nothing you've ever seen before? What do you think the artist was trying to say through his or her style? Most of the questions or approaches that have been suggested already in this book are valid too.

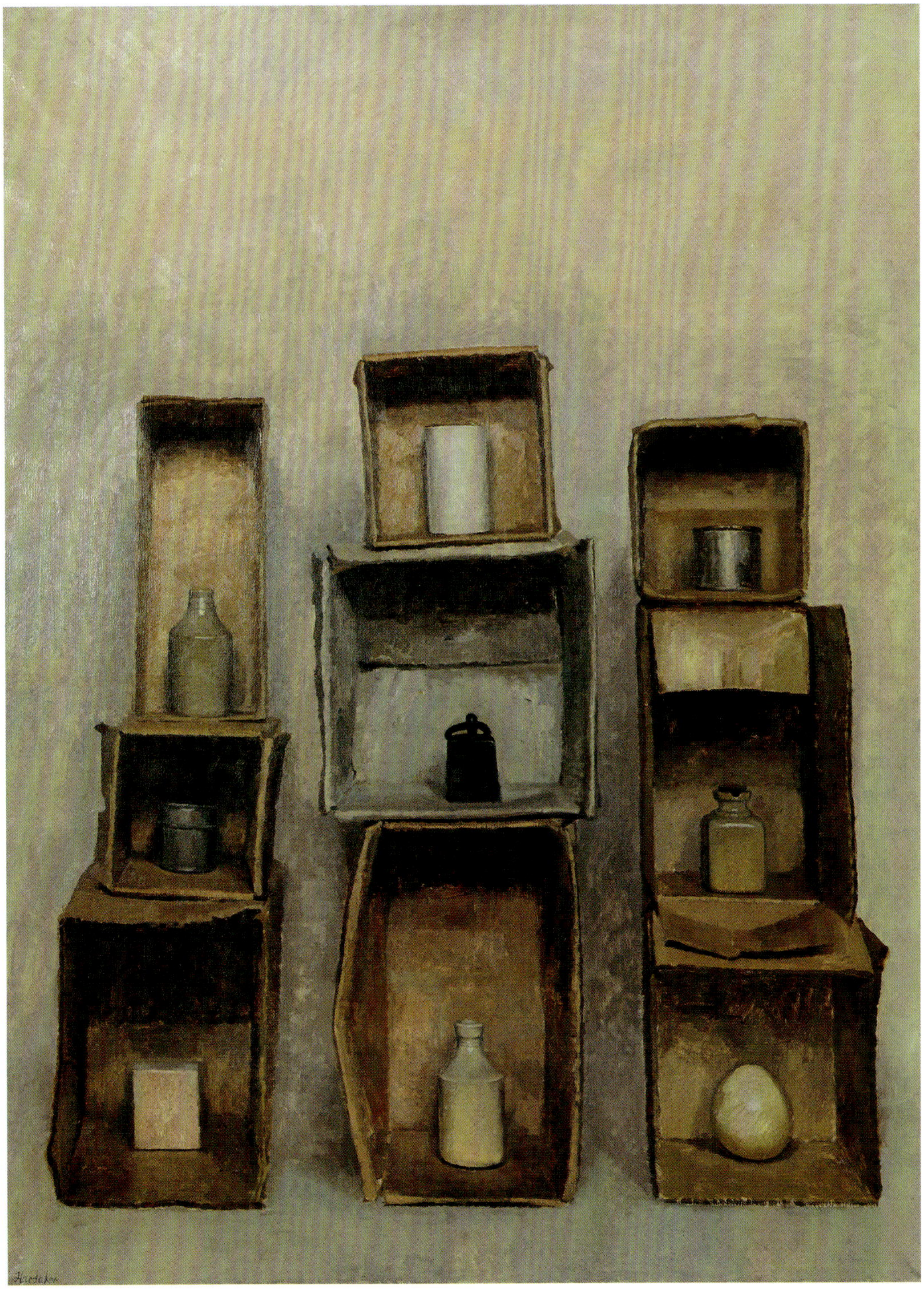

Developing ideas

Many artists have painted still lifes because the subjects can be cheap, readily available, they don't move and they can be drawn or painted whenever the artist wants to. No models to wait for, no landscapes to travel to. They have been convenient for several artists who wanted to explore new ideas. Cézanne, for instance, used familiar objects to play with perspective, space and light. Matisse created a sense of harmony with colours and shapes. Jean-Baptiste-Siméon Chardin (1699–1779), who is still considered one of the greatest masters of still life, produced balanced compositions, with softly diffused light and subtly contrasting textures. Greatly influenced by 17th-century Dutch still life, he attracted patrons among the French aristocracy and royalty. He subsequently influenced many other artists, including Manet, Cézanne, Matisse, Braque, Chaim Soutine (1893–1943) and Morandi.

Compare still-life works by any artists. Study shapes, contrasts, textures and compositions. Be objective, put your feelings aside and decide in which ways the works contradict or resemble each other. How have the artists made marks; are they subtle, energetic, or perhaps even calming? Do any shapes or patterns seem to create rhythm or structure? What decorative elements in the compositions do you notice? Are the works comparable or contrasting in size? Still life from any period in history can be interpreted on a number of levels, as many works explore the boundaries between reality, illusion and symbolism. If you are creating your own artwork in response to still life, find a painting in which you can see an obvious structure or geometry, for instance, something by Cézanne, Paul Nash, Victor Pasmore (1908–98) or Duncan Grant. Rough out a compositional plan – you may be surprised at the proportions of the painting. Next, follow these steps:

1. Make a line copy of the work – only lines.
2. Make another, reducing the lines still further so your work is just a pattern.
3. Look at your second drawing. Are you surprised by the directions of the lines? Do they help you to

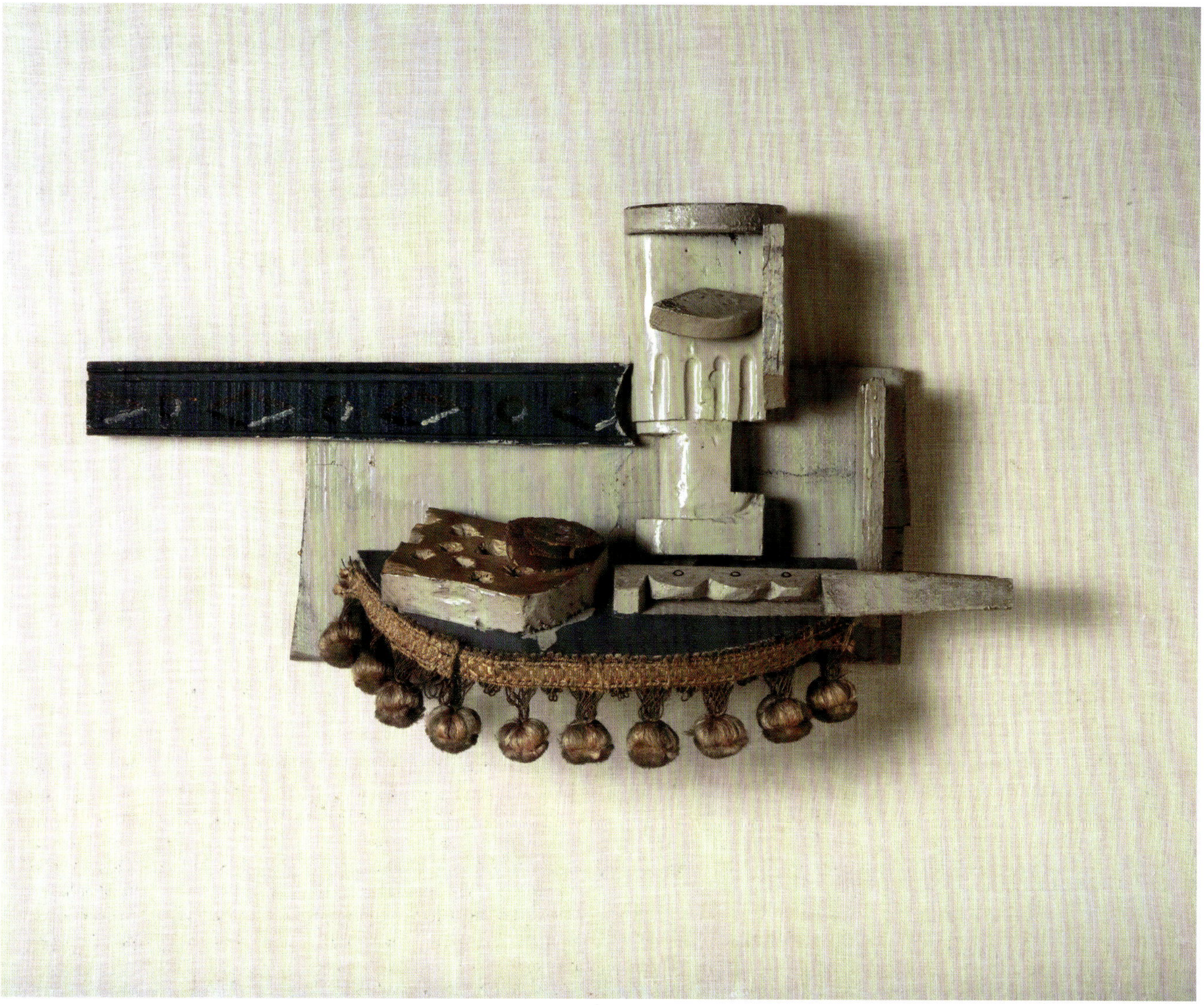

understand any intentions behind the work? For instance, do the directions and lengths of the lines seem to establish a structured or classical arrangement? Are the lines closer to one side or other of the work or do they seem to lean in one direction?

4. Take this further and make a composition with lines and geometric shapes only.
5. Now make a still life using your own objects based on the lines and shapes of your second drawing.
6. Follow the same steps as 1–4 above, only instead of lines concentrate on colour.
7. Use completely different materials to create a new still life, exploring one of the following themes:
   a) spaces between
   b) lines and directions
   c) colour and contrast
   d) pattern repeat.

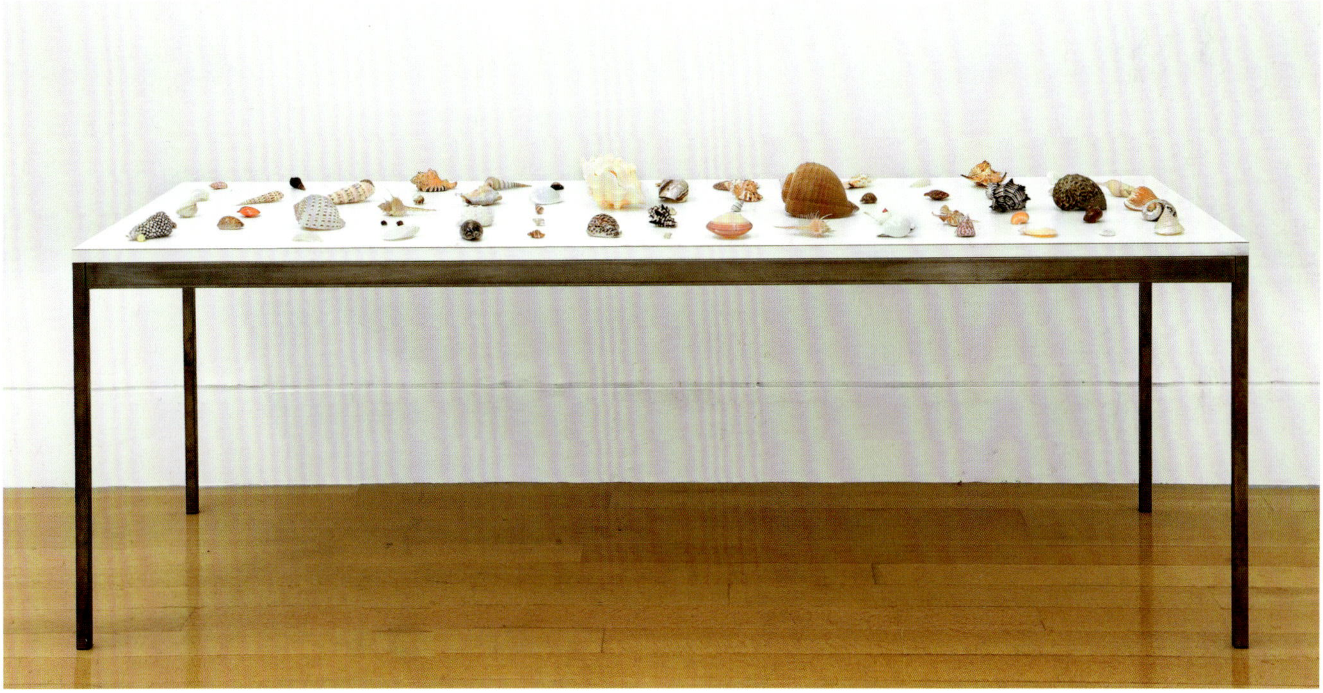

Pablo Picasso, *Still Life* 1914, painted wood and upholstery fringe, 25.4 x 45.7 x 9.2, Tate
Picasso began making relief constructions in 1912–13 as an exploration of traditional still-life painting. This composition relates to his Cubist paintings of the time. On top of a table or small sideboard are a knife, a beer glass, two slices of sausage and a slice of cheese or pâté. The work declares that paintings are objects in themselves and these found objects, including the upholstery fringe, helped to make unusual art materials less unexpected. The work is also a variation on relief sculpture. As Picasso was determined at this time to ignore conventional perspective devices, this work is made of solid, real objects presented as a work of art.

Damien Hirst, *Life without You* 1991, Formica, MDF, steel and shells, 88 x 228.6 x 84, Tate
This is an arrangement of seventy-three exotic seashells on a white Formica-topped table. It is organised in fifteen rows of five, plus a row of three, two rows of four and two rows of six. The shells vary in size from tiny to large; they are all shiny and polished (or varnished) and their colours vary, including soft, deep warm hues and shades of white. Hirst (born 1965) exhibited them as found objects, resembling a child's beach collection or tourist souvenirs. Their organic forms contrast with the plain, mass-produced table. Hirst was inspired by the work of Kurt Schwitters (1887–1948) and Joseph Cornell (1903–72) as well as Marcel Duchamp and Andy Warhol. Hirst has said that he likes shells 'because they once contained life', which is why he gave the work the title.

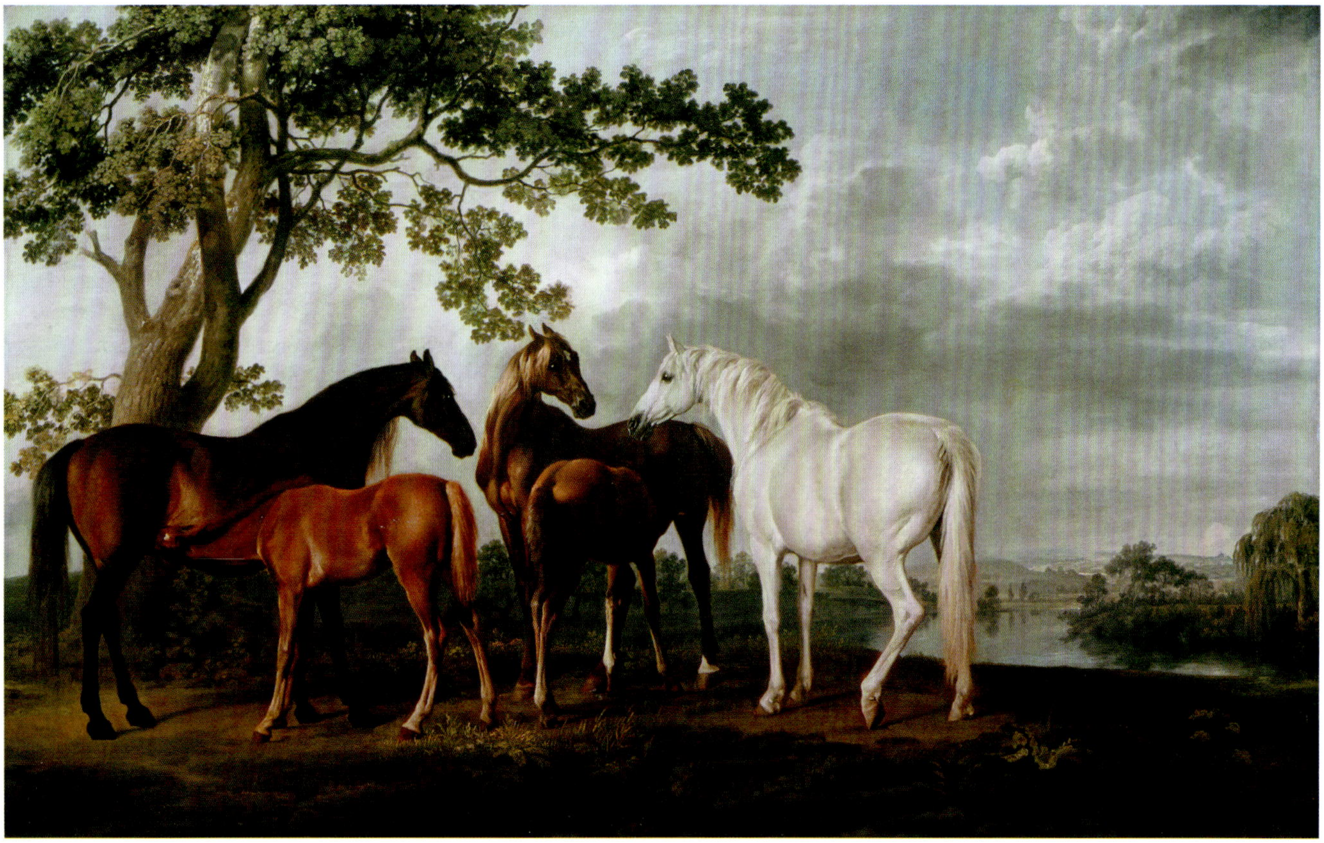

George Stubbs, *Mares and Foals in a River Landscape* c.1763–8, oil on canvas, 101.6 x 161.9, Tate
Despite animal paintings being considered less important than history paintings, at the time Stubbs (1724–1806) painted this work, horses were extremely significant animals in most Western societies. The majority of Stubbs's paintings were commissioned by aristocratic patrons who wanted accurate portraits of their best horses. The naturalism of his style derives from his close observation of living animals as well as from dissections and other anatomical studies for his book *The Anatomy of the Horse*, published in 1766. The horses are accurate portraits of mares who were famous either for their racing success or for their racing offspring. Stubbs's precisely detailed style gained him enormous success. To create this work, he first painted the horses in perfect detail on a blank background and then carefully filled in the landscape behind.

ANIMALS

'Art is about emotion; if art needs to be explained it is no longer art.'
Pierre-Auguste Renoir

From the earliest cave paintings to Egyptian symbolism, from Celtic designs to the symbolism of Franz Marc (1880–1916), or the preserved sharks, sheep and cow of Damien Hirst, animals have occupied a prominent place in the history of art. Every culture has had its own way of depicting animals and its own reasons for doing so. This has often been for symbolic purposes. Native American totem poles and some Aboriginal paintings, for instance, feature animals representing their ancestors, and in many other societies animals have signified gods, power, the supernatural, or attributes such as fidelity or courage. Like the human form, animals have appeared in art since the earliest times. Unlike the human form, however, animals have been depicted for a broader range of reasons. For instance, some ancient cave and rock paintings feature animals such as bison, horses and deer. It is believed that these works were created for magical purposes, to help to bring about success in the hunt.

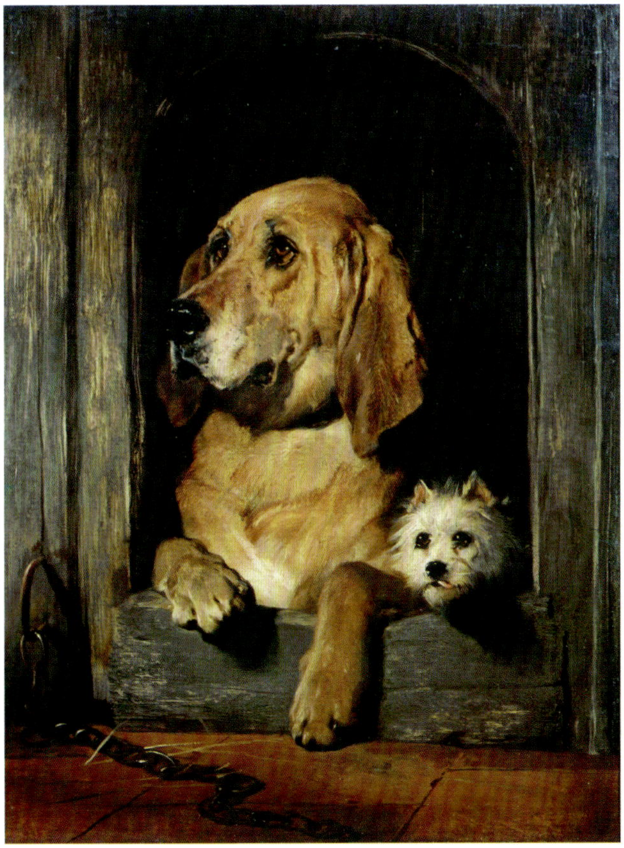

Edwin Landseer, *Dignity and Impudence* 1839, oil on canvas, 88.9 x 69.2, Tate
Landseer's dog paintings of the 1830s are among his most celebrated works and this one remains the most popular of all. You can see the human attributes he has given to the dogs. The large, dignified bloodhound (Grafton) contrasts with the small, mischievous terrier (Scratch). The dogs were both owned by Landseer's friend, Jacob Bell (1810–59), who commissioned the painting. Landseer (1802–73) parodied Dutch portrait tradition by framing the subject with a kennel and placing Grafton's paw over the edge. Grafton is painted in smooth, variegated textures, while Scratch has been expressed with a few jabbing and flicked brushstrokes to illustrate his more wiry fur.

Symbolic meanings

Many animals in ancient Egyptian art were embodiments of the gods, such as Sekhmet the lion, or Anubis the jackal. During the medieval and Renaissance periods, animals were often illustrated to represent Christian values or biblical stories. Animals depicted as real creatures or alternatively as fantastic beasts occupied a fairly important place in European medieval art and thought. Artists designed animal motifs for jewellery, illuminated manuscripts and even for functional objects such as goblets, which were often shaped into witty-looking creatures. Animal forms were universal ways for medieval craftsmen and artists to communicate, especially focusing on their symbolic meanings that even the illiterate could understand. In Christian Europe, as in many other societies, animal symbolism was generally understood. The lamb, for instance, an animal that was frequently sacrificed in ancient rituals, symbolised Jesus. The Holy Spirit is nearly always portrayed as a dove, while donkeys often represented Christ's humility. The fish, with its unblinking eyes, remains a symbol of Jesus to this day.

Art from other cultures

All art is a product of the time and place it was made. Think of Japanese woodblock prints, ancient Egyptian wall paintings or West African tribal masks, for example. Art from other cultures could be from a different continent, thousands of years old, or it could have been made in another part of your country quite recently. It's all from other cultures. To make connections with any art from a time or place that contrasts with your own, use some of the processes of investigation already suggested in this book and remain open and receptive to new ideas, materials and methods. Find out how the artist intended the work to be seen, whether the date or place it was made is significant, who made it, whether it was produced for a particular person, location or occasion, and how it links with the social, cultural or political history of the time.

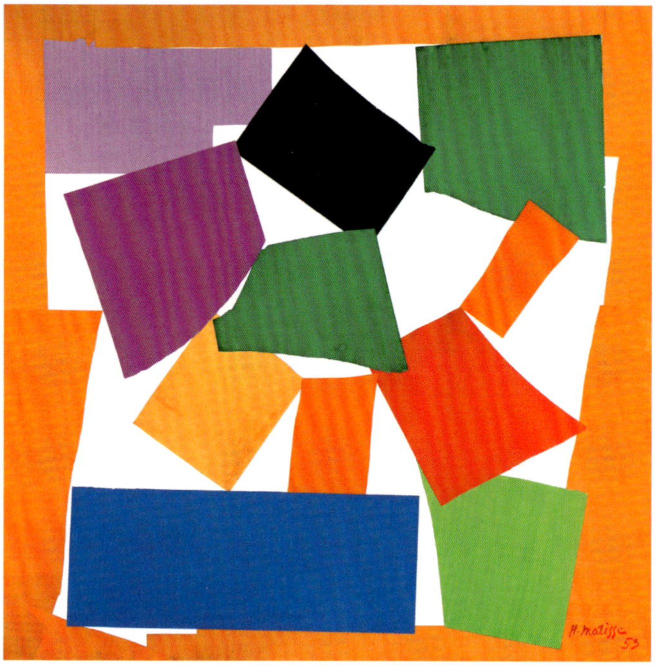

Henri Matisse, *The Snail* 1953, gouache on paper, cut and pasted on paper mounted on canvas, 286.4 x 287, Tate
This was made when Matisse was eighty-four years old and ill health prevented him from painting. Confined to bed, he produced several works that became known as *papiers découpés* (cutouts), made by cutting or tearing shapes from gouache-painted paper. The shapes were pasted down by assistants following Matisse's instructions. He had recently made many drawings of snails, which inspired this huge work that follows the spiral of a snail's shell. He said: 'I first of all drew the snail from nature...I found an image in my mind purified of the shell, then I took the scissors.' Do you think the arrangement of colours is random, or can you see reasons for their placement? What do you think the small lilac shape at the top of the work represents? Does the fact that it represents a snail enhance the image, or is an abstract pattern sufficient for a work of art?

In Greek, the phrase 'Jesus Christ, Son of God, Saviour', is '*Iesous Christos Theou Yios Soter*'. The first letters of each of these words spell 'ichthys', which corresponds with the Greek word for fish (*icqus*). The butterfly, which emerges from an apparently lifeless cocoon, symbolises the Resurrection, while the ermine, which was believed to have preferred to die than to dirty its coat, symbolises innocence and purity. Depictions of various acts of hunting were popular among wealthy patrons in medieval Europe. Falconry was a sign of nobility and an aristocratic pastime. Sons, and some daughters, of aristocrats were given their own falcons at an early age and taught to hunt with them. Stag hunts were often portrayed to symbolise the trials of life. By the 18th and 19th centuries, many paintings and sculptures aimed to realistically represent either 'man's best friend', or, conversely, the 'game' killed by gentlemen for sport.

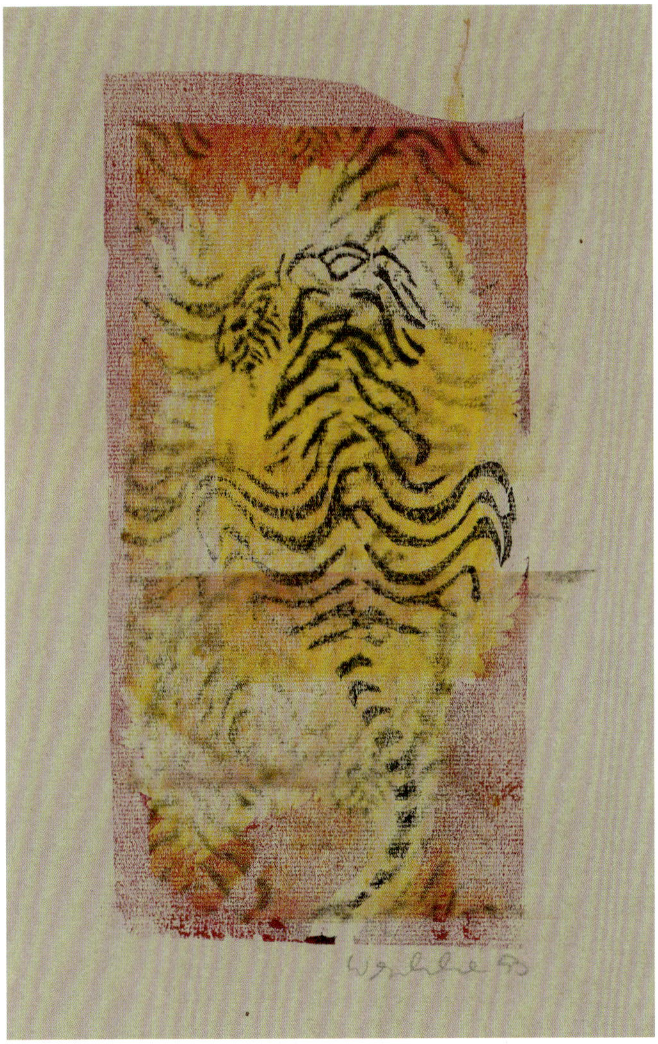

Karl Weschke, *Tiger, Tiger* 1953, woodcut on paper, 23.3 x 11.6, Tate
During the same year as Matisse made *The Snail*, German-born Weschke (1925–2005), who had arrived in Britain as a prisoner of war and remained for the rest of his life, made this small print. Weschke started his artistic career when he worked as an assistant to the lion feeder at a London circus, and he made drawings and prints of circus animals. Printed in red, yellow and black ink on grey paper, this is one of his many woodcuts. Particularly resembling oriental styling, it refers to a poem by William Blake. What strikes you first about it? Does it seem static or dynamic? Compare it with either of the other works on these two pages.

Tyger! Tyger! burning bright
In the forests of the night,
What immortal hand or eye
Could frame thy fearful symmetry?
William Blake, 1794

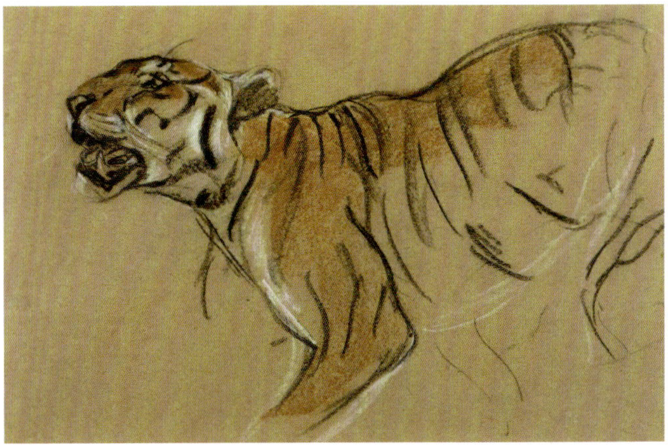

John Macallan Swan, *Head and Forepart of a Tiger* date unknown, pastel on paper, 22.2 x 34.6, Tate
Macallan (1846–1910) was an accomplished painter, draughtsman and sculptor who produced many dynamic images of large wild animals, figures and landscapes, but it was his animal art in particular that made him renowned. His style was distinguished by simple, fluid treatments with a strongly imaginative element.

The bestiary

The bestiary was a series of stories featuring strange animals in allegories that imparted moral and religious lessons. The stories developed in Europe in the 12th century and became a great source for artistic invention. Animals had been written about for centuries before the Christian era. The first known text to do this was the Greek *Physiologus*, written during the second or third century AD. The *Physiologus* was exceptionally popular and translated into the majority of the main languages of Europe and western Asia. It is believed to have been the most widely distributed book in Europe after the Bible. In the 12th century, a number of the bizarre creatures from the *Physiologus* were borrowed for the stories in the bestiary, many of which have endured: the basilisk, the king of the serpents that could kill with just one glance; the manticore, with the face of a man, the body of a lion and the tail of a scorpion; and the centaur, with the body of a horse and the upper torso of a man.

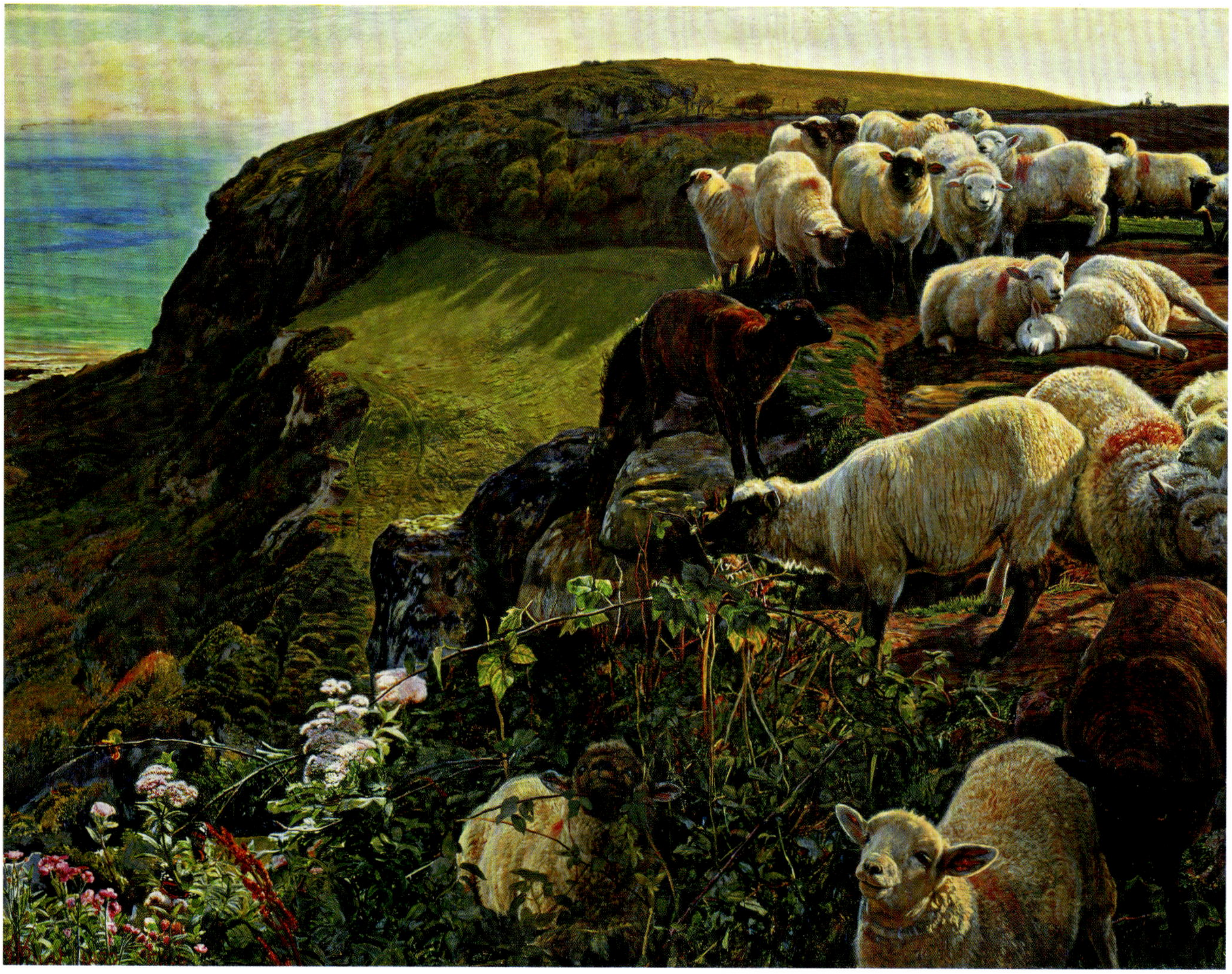

William Holman Hunt, *Our English Coasts* (also known as *Strayed Sheep*) 1852, oil on canvas, 43.2 x 58.4, Tate
The Pre-Raphaelites believed in portraying what they saw directly, with no contrived style. Holman Hunt (1827–1910) painted this in the south of England near Hastings. He paid close attention to detail, although the cliffs, sheep and parts of the foreground were painted from different viewpoints, and the butterflies were painted separately from close study. Contemporary viewers were impressed by his treatment of light, colour and tone. He worked on this for nearly four months, in all weathers, but ending up with one light-filled moment. Different textures are also implied with variegated brushmarks. How many colours can you see in the sheeps' fleeces?

Expression and emotion

From exotic to humble, wild to noble, or cherished to powerful, whenever they have been depicted, animals have nearly always shown some artist's individuality. Even when following strict rituals and rules and being instructed to remain anonymous artisans, many artists have expressed an animal's markings, texture or characteristics through various characteristic means. Textures have been rendered in short brushstrokes, grainy paint, dabs or dots, scratchings, patterns and thickness of paint. In *Fowling in the Marshes*, a wall painting from 1350 BC in ancient Egypt, for instance, birds' feathers were depicted quite freely and delicately, while a cat's fur was rendered with short, directional paint marks. In the 1891 painting of an imaginary jungle by Henri Rousseau (1844–1910), his tiger's sharp teeth, sinuous curves and large eyes imply a fierce but noble character, while Picasso's bronze *Baboon and Young* of 1951, made with a child's toy car for the head, has a humorous personality all of its own.

Landseer was one of the most popular British painters of the 19th century. Known and admired for his paintings of animals, his appeal crossed rigid class boundaries, and he was commissioned by the middle classes as well as royalty and the aristocracy. The most famous of his works, however, were not paintings but the lion sculptures in Trafalgar Square in London. Like Renaissance artists before him, Landseer learned anatomical accuracy by performing dissections. He also gave human characteristics to his animal images.

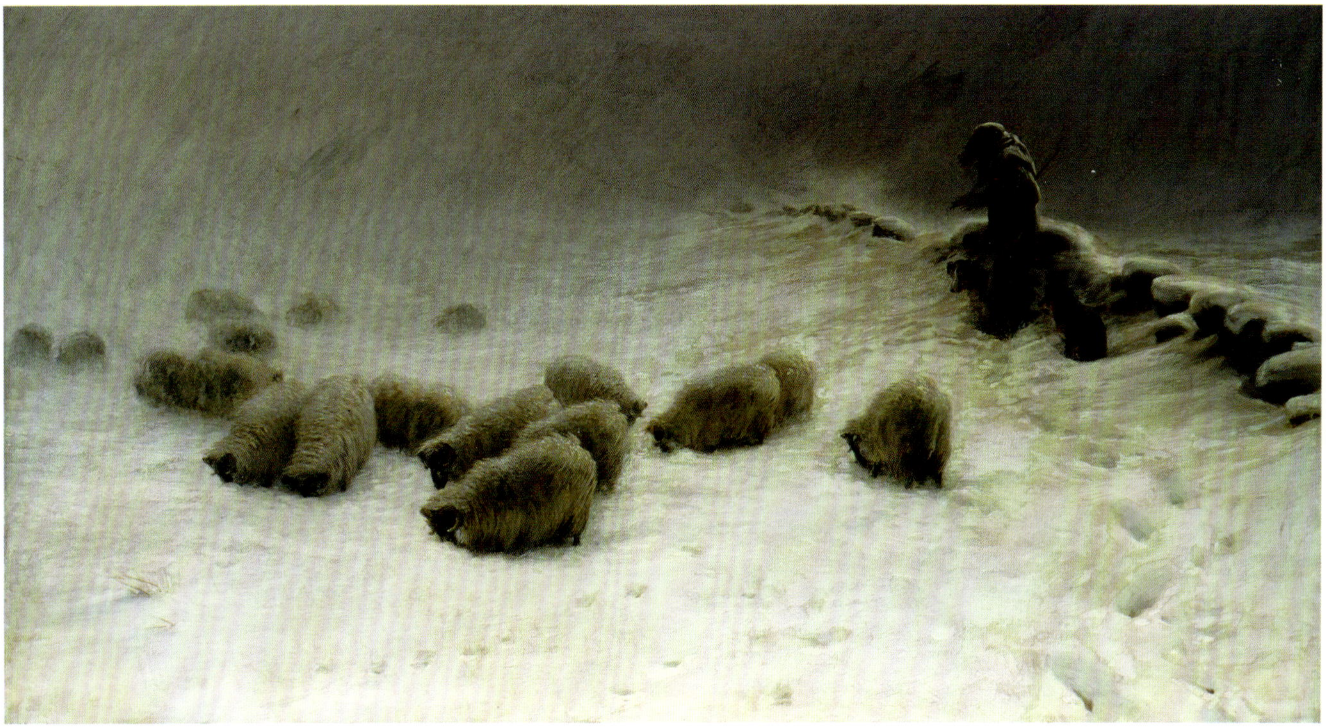

Joseph Farquharson, *The Joyless Winter Day* exhibited 1883, oil on canvas, 104.1 x 180.3, Tate
Farquharson (1847–1935) became famous for his winter landscapes, often featuring sheep and illustrating the soft and eerie light of dawn or dusk. He preferred working *en plein air* and constructed a painting hut on wheels containing a stove and a large glass window that he could put in a landscape. This work, however, was made outside in blizzard conditions. The sheep were actually imitation, made of plaster by a local sculptor. Farquharson produced so many scenes of cattle and sheep in snow that he was nicknamed 'Frozen Mutton Farquharson'. How has he depicted the cold? How has he shown light? What colours and marks has he used? How has he created atmosphere?

Methods to help your understanding

The age-old method of learning from the masters by copying all or part of an artist's work can be useful, but can also be expanded upon to develop ideas. Using whatever materials you prefer, create a work based on the work of another artist, either in your own style or resembling the original work as closely as you can, and develop from that. You could produce a set of drawings, paintings or prints that take elements from your artist's work, or make notes about your observations. It can help to research animals from primary sources before looking at an artist's work. When representing animals, consider how they move and how you can render textures, markings and underlying anatomy. Consider how your chosen artist has used materials and whether the work is stylised, realistic or distorted? What effects have been achieved? If you're copying just a section, try reproducing it several times in different materials and compare the results. If the work you are looking at is two-dimensional, you could develop your ideas in three dimensions or vice versa. Use your own

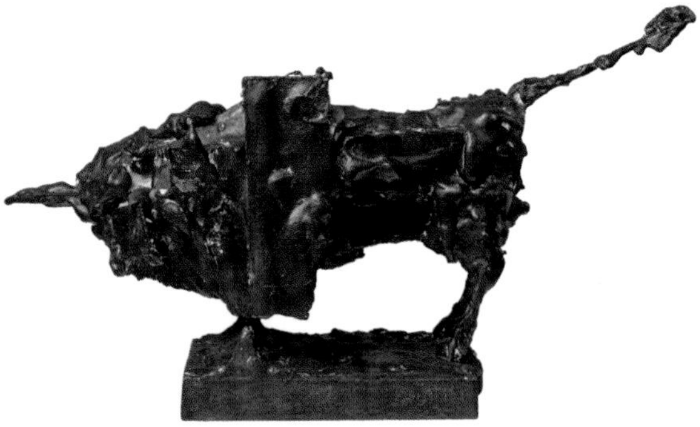

Robert Clatworthy, *Bull* 1955, bronze, 32.4 x 19 x 45.1, Tate
This textured sculpture gives the impression of having been executed quickly. Clatworthy (born 1928) said it was inspired by the sight of a bull in the field next to his Sussex studio. As one of several small versions of a life-size sculpture made in 1953, it captures the 'essence,' or spirit, of the animal. Clatworthy described the work as his attempt to discover 'an equivalent for the sheer physical power of the bull'.

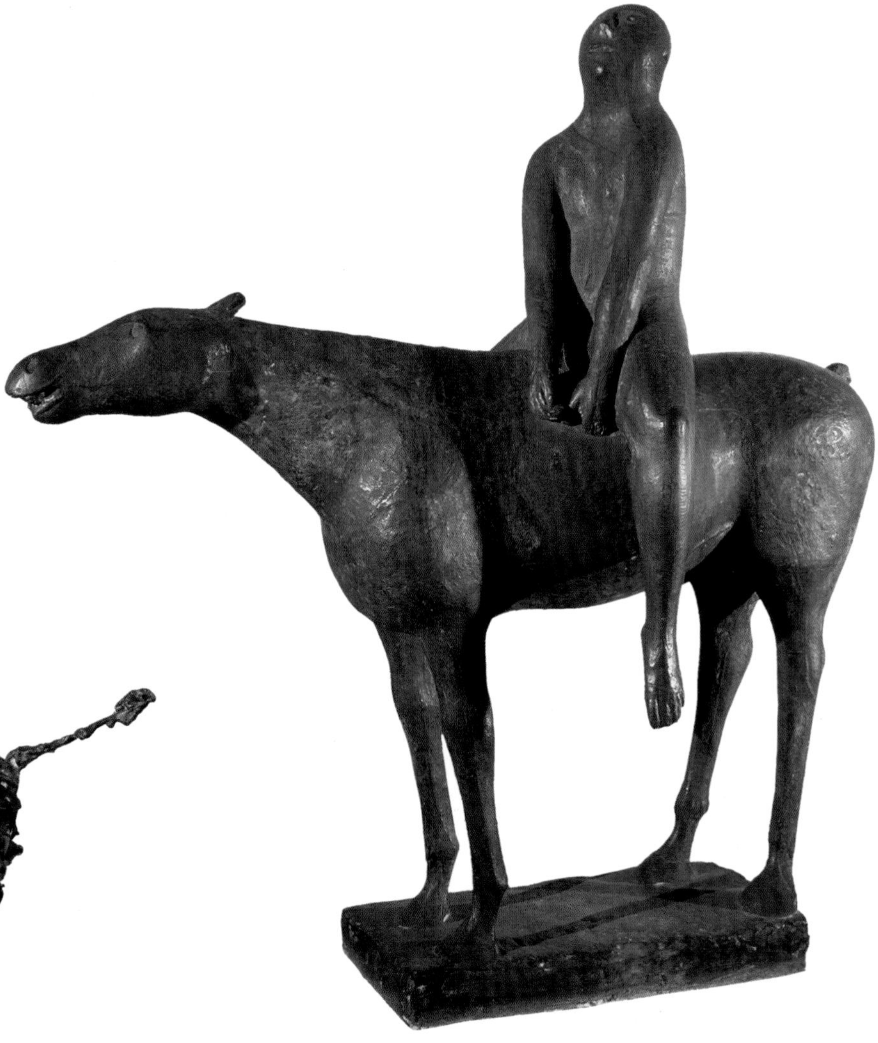

Marino Marini, *Horseman* 1947, bronze, 163.8 x 154.9 x 67.3, Tate
After seeing sculptures of medieval knights riding in Germany, Marini (1901–80) began producing equestrian works in the mid-1930s. He aimed to portray a sense of harmony between man and nature, but this work also expresses anguish, as it was made after the Second World War when Marini had seen Italian peasants fleeing bombardment on frightened horses.

strengths and preferences where you can. Even if you are transcribing another artist's work, perhaps do it in a different scale, with different materials or in different colours, for example. All these ideas will make your work more personal and unique. Keep all your experiments, whether they're successful or not. When you make notes about artists' work, mention your own insights and thoughts. Avoid 'so what' comments (where anyone reading your notes might think 'so what?'). Also avoid the blatantly obvious, such as 'I drew this dog in pencil' or 'this is a painting of a horse'. Working to a set of questions is always useful. Most of the questions suggested in other chapters of this book will also be helpful when considering animals in art. The 'personal, formal and contextual' approach in the first chapter is excellent, or try any of the following: The five Ws – who, what, where, when, why? Or 'content, form, process and mood' (see page 42). Whichever you follow, always answer in your own words. Never copy other people's work and never copy and paste. You may think it's not obvious to others, but it nearly always is!

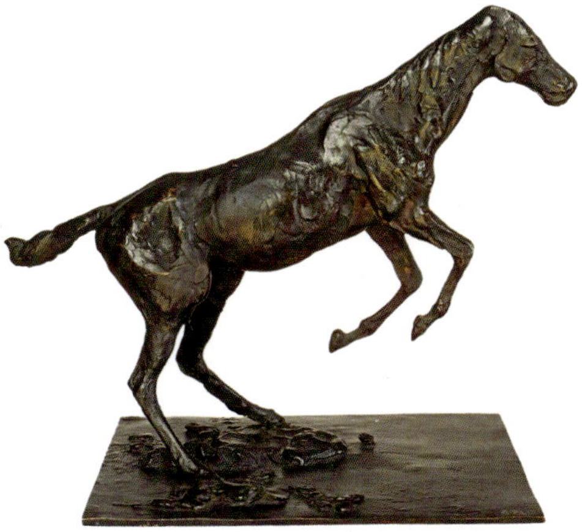

Edgar Degas, *Horse Clearing an Obstacle* c.1887–8, bronze, 30.5 x 38.7 x 24.1, Tate
Degas executed a number of works on the theme of horses. Along with several other bronzes, this is believed to have been inspired by Eadweard Muybridge's (1830–1904) photographs of horses in motion. Degas produced more sculpture after 1881 as his eyesight became too impaired for painting. This work gives an impression of spontaneity and motion.

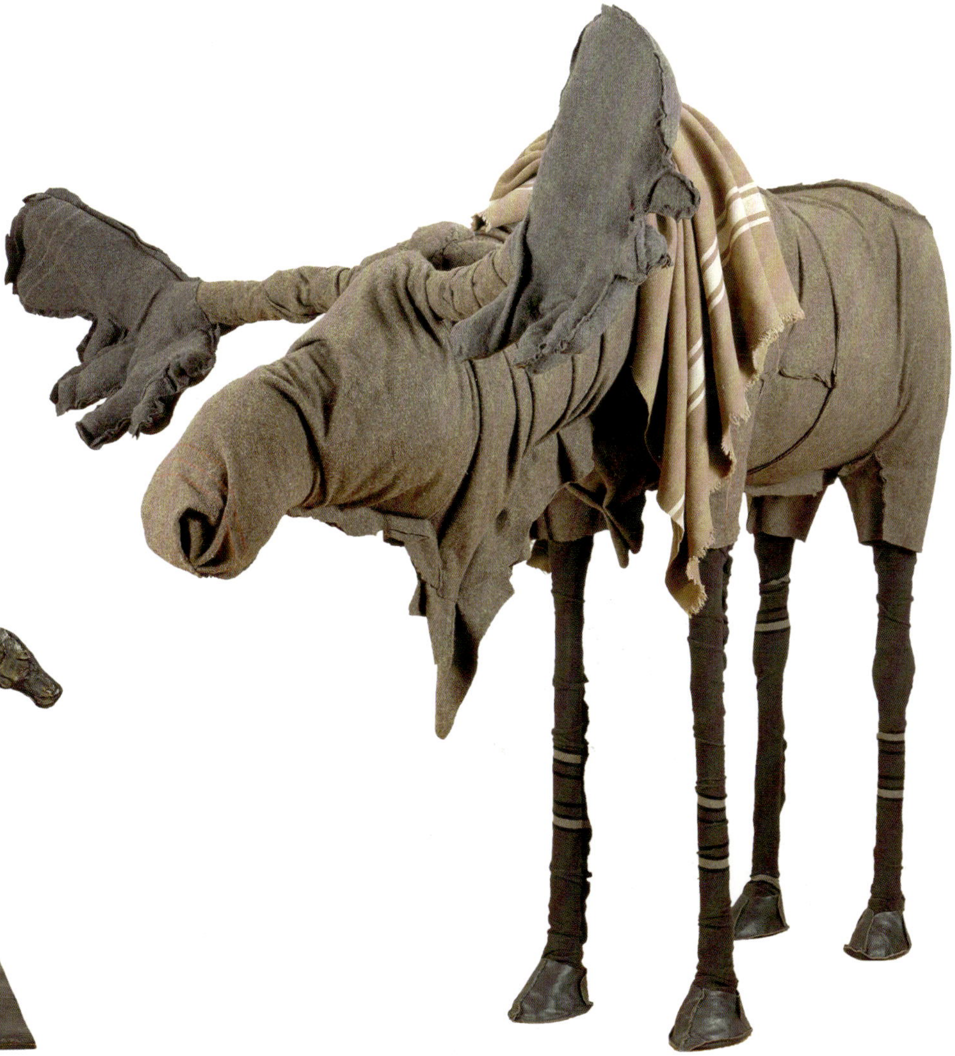

Laura Ford, *Moose* 1998, metal, plaster, wool and leather, 175 x 300 x 85, Tate
Moose is one of a series of sculptures of animals made by in the late 1990s by Ford (born 1961). It is an over-life-sized representation and symbolises Ford's childhood; she grew up on a fairground and then on an old farm, which had previously been a zoo, in Cardiff, Wales. This, like many of her sculptures of animals, is anthropomorphised. Made of an armature of various materials including scaffolding poles, chicken wire and plaster, and covered with fabric, the sculpture looks almost as if it is wearing clothes. Ford has said that her sculptures represent emotional states with a wide range of ambiguities. What do you think about the lack of eyes? What opinion do you have about the work? Do you think the moose conveys an introverted or extroverted personality?

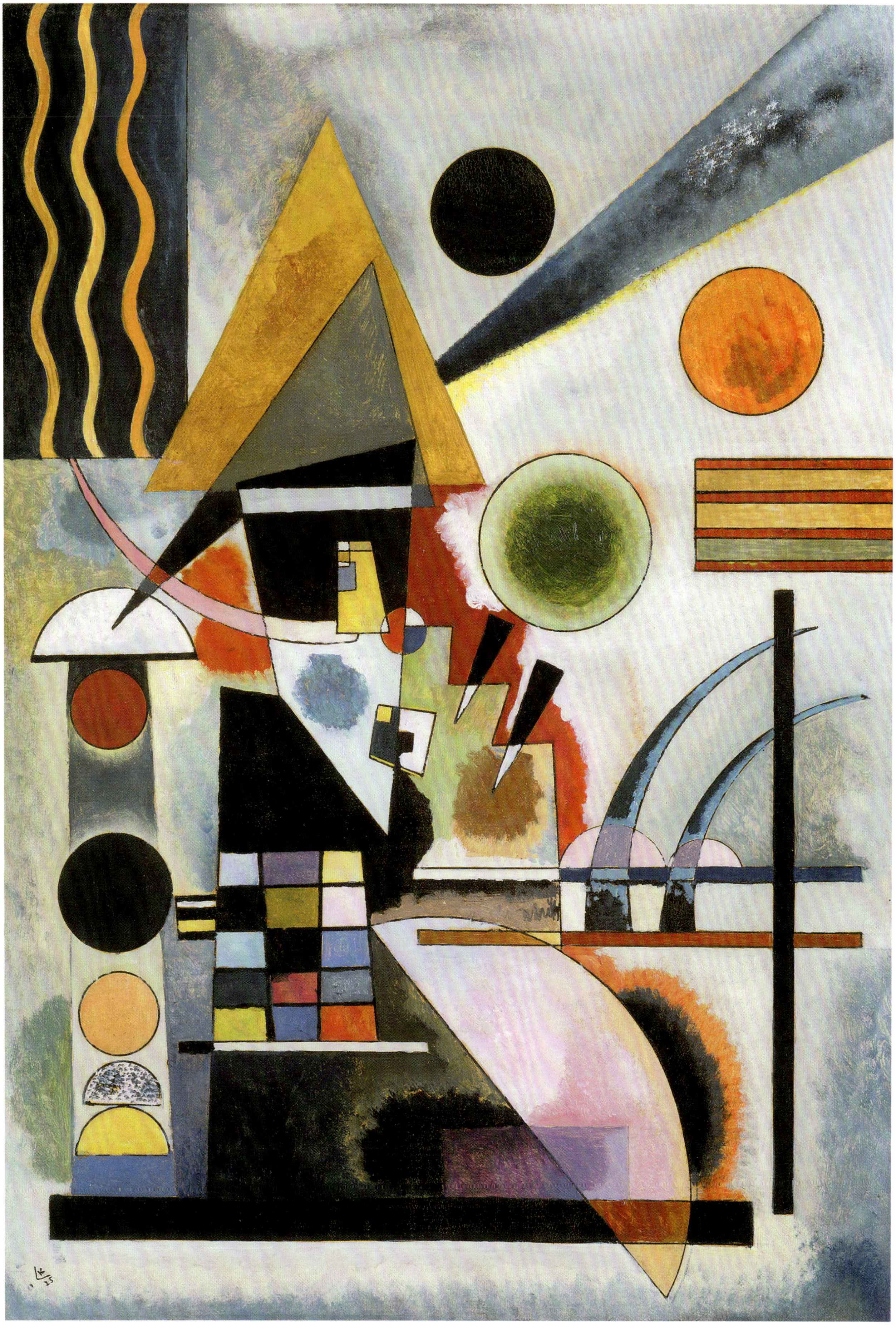

ABSTRACTION

'Lend your ears to music, open your eyes to painting, and ... stop thinking! Just ask yourself whether the work has enabled you to "walk about" into a hitherto unknown world. If the answer is yes, what more do you want?'
Wassily Kandinsky

All art involves a certain amount of abstraction. When you think about it, a painting is made of lines, colours and shapes arranged by the artist on a flat surface to signify something else. Sculptors choose what forms to shape. But it can be confusing. Figurative art (see page 53) represents things from the real world. 'Abstracted' art or an 'abstraction' is where an artist represents things from the real world, but distorts or abstracts them. Abstract art can be any art that does not depict something recognisable or representational; not a person, place or anything from the natural world.

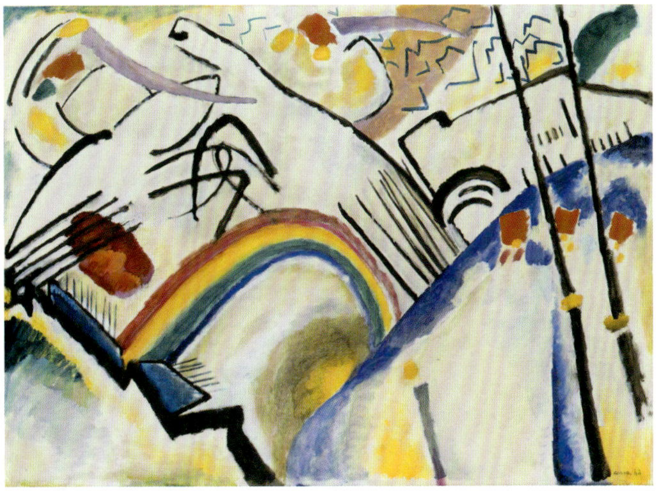

Wassily Kandinsky, *Swinging* 1925, oil on board, 70.5 x 50.2, Tate
Approximately fifteen years after painting *Cossacks* (above) Kandinsky (1866–1944) created this totally abstract work. What does it mean, do you think? Does the title help you to understand it? It was intended to suggest rhythm, the feelings we get when listening to music we enjoy. Do the colours or shapes remind you of anything? Does this affect your impression of the work?

Wassily Kandinsky, *Cossacks* 1910–11, oil on canvas, 94.6 x 130.2, Tate
What are your initial thoughts about this work? Can you see anything from the real world in it? It's not completely abstract; it includes some representational elements. The clue is in the title. *Cossacks* represents a battle in Russia. In the foreground are three Russian cossacks in tall red hats. Two hold lances and one leans on a sabre or rifle. Behind them are two hills, with many lances appearing, indicating armies marching. Birds fly in the air; there is a fortress and a rainbow. Towards the top of the picture are two more cossacks on horses fighting with sabres. The red blob represents blood and the rainbow suggests ultimate peace. In reducing recognisable elements and using vibrant colours, Kandinsky's work was unique and expressive. Does the story make a difference to your opinion of it? Why?

Some people believe that the idea of abstract art is derived from the ancient Greek philosopher Plato, who said that the highest form of beauty lies not in the forms of the real world but in geometry. Most would agree that it developed as a direct result of the invention of photography in 1839. Artists began to try to do things other than capture realistic images, which cameras could do so easily. They began to explore and exploit other ways of expressing themselves. Some artists believe that because abstract art doesn't represent the material world, it can symbolise thoughts, feelings, spirituality, or things beyond our understanding or beneath our consciousness. Some believe that it can represent virtues such as order, purity and simplicity. As photography developed, some artists began experimenting. First of all, the Impressionists challenged artistic conventions; then more artists began pushing previously accepted boundaries. Pioneers of truly abstract painting were Kandinsky, Kazimir Malevich (1879–1935) and Piet Mondrian (1872–1944) during the decade 1910–20, but they reached that point only after other artists had paved the way by distorting

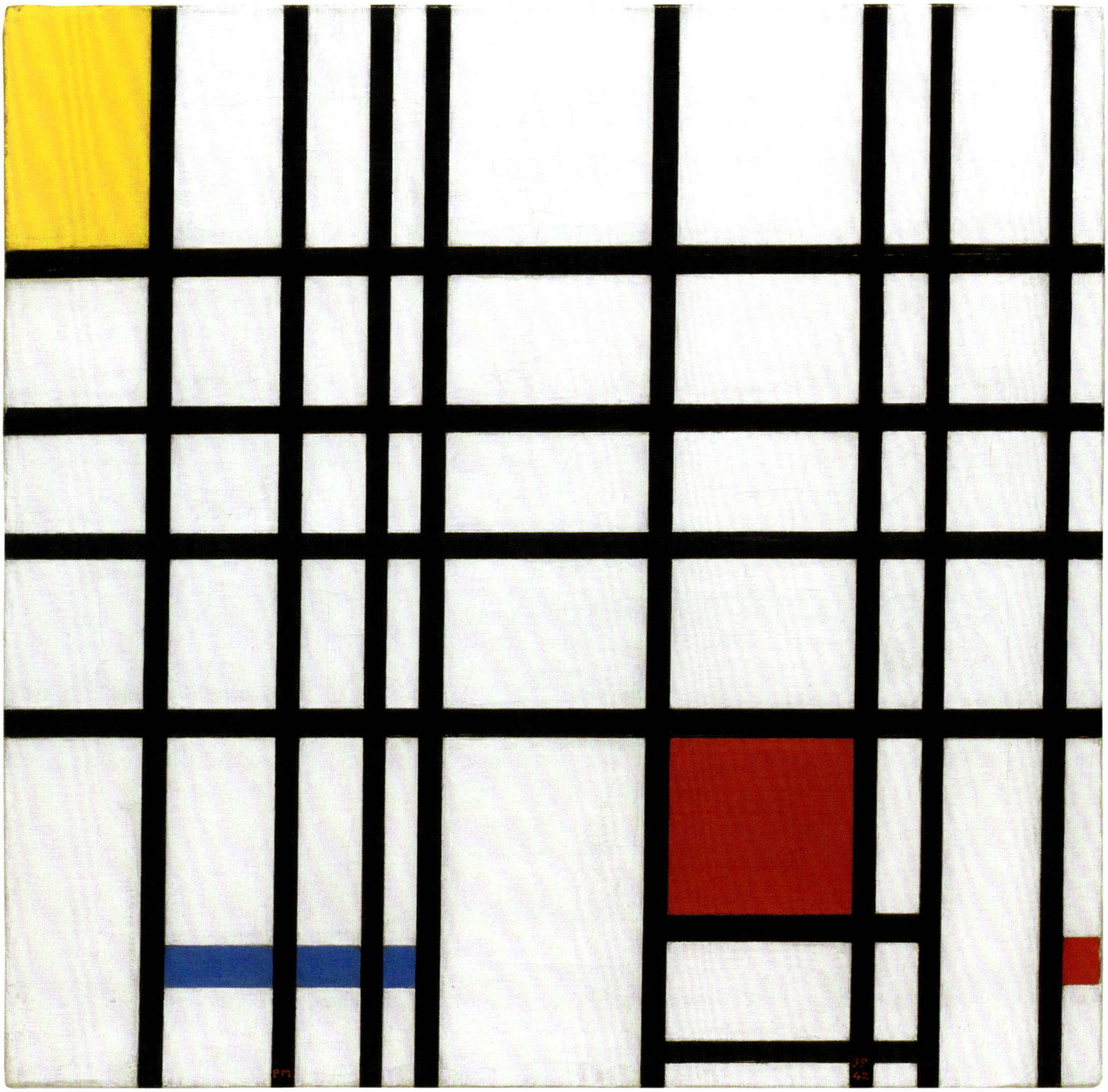

colours, shapes and other aspects of their art. These included artists such as Gauguin, Paul Signac (1863–1935), Matisse, Derain, Munch and Marc Chagall (1887–1985). A pioneer of abstract sculpture was the Russian Constructivist Naum Gabo (1890–1977). Since then, abstract art has continued to be explored in many ways.

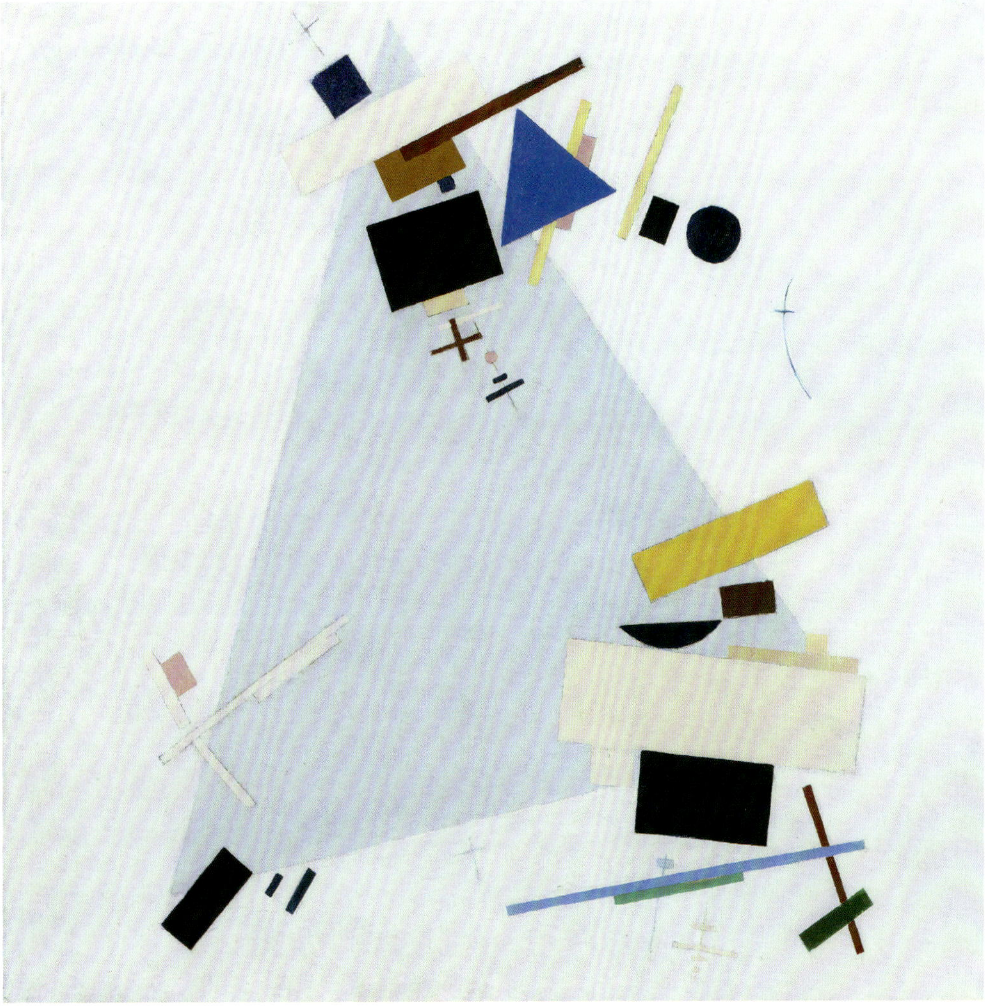

Piet Mondrian, *Composition with Yellow, Blue and Red* 1937–42, oil on canvas, 72.7 x 69.2, Tate

Mondrian started this painting in Paris and completed it in New York. He lived in Manhattan from 1940 until his death four years later. Intentionally not representing anything 'real', this contains only essential forms and colours; all natural elements have been eliminated. Yet although the work looks rigid and mechanical, in close up, many of the brushmarks are apparent. Focusing on balance and harmony (like Kandinsky, Mondrian was fascinated by theosophy), he painted black lines in an irregular grid, placing the coloured blocks judiciously and using white to give the design 'breathing space'. What do you think of the painting? Try making one with your own design. Is your work balanced? If not, why not? How has Mondrian achieved equilibrium?

Kazimir Malevich, *Dynamic Suprematism* 1915 or 1916, oil on canvas, 80.3 x 80, Tate

This work was made during the intense period just before the 1917 Russian Revolution. In 1915, Malevich abandoned representative images and began experimenting with something he called Suprematism. It involved severely reduced geometric forms to inspire meditation and reflection in observers, much like religious icons have been used in the past. In this painting, shapes appear to float, as well as pull and push against each other. This was completely original at the time; Malevich, like Kandinsky, was a pioneer of abstract art.

But is it art?

When art can be made of marble or film, paint or pillows, rocks, bricks or even rubbish, and when much of it bears no resemblance to anything we recognise, it can be easy to wonder what it has become. So what is art, what is good art – and who decides? Here are some things to think about:

1. You know it's art if it's called art, written about in an art magazine, newspaper or book, exhibited in a gallery or museum, or bought by a private collector. Anything can be called art, but it has to be accepted by the art world, which is a loose description of people involved in art every day, including curators, critics, those in charge of galleries and museums, art writers, tutors and buyers, dealers, restorers and even artists themselves.
2. A lot of modern art is not about skill, but more about philosophical or psychological ideas. If you're looking for technical skill, or for art to look realistic, you'll often be disappointed. There are no longer any rules, so try not to have a rigid idea about what art should be. There was a great fuss in the 1870s about Impressionism, then in the early 20th century about Fauvism and Cubism and in the 1940s and 1950s about Abstract Expressionism. People are upset when they see something new. After Duchamp exhibited a urinal in 1917, he paved the way for anything to be classified as art. But even so, before a work is accepted, the art world has to decide whether it's worth considering. Since the Industrial Revolution, social values in Western societies have been continuously shifting and their definitions of art have been constantly challenged. You can't compare abstract art with, say, Renaissance or Impressionist art. Life has changed, and so has art.
3. If a work of art changes your mind, your opinion or your feelings about something, then it has given you something extra. That should be enough.
4. Art is entertainment that makes you think about life.

What does it mean?

Ask yourself these questions:

- What does 'abstract' mean?
- Is abstract art the same as modern art?
- How can abstract art have a meaning?
- Should the subject of a painting or sculpture always be taken from the world around us?
- Why might an artist choose to make abstract art?
- How can we judge the skills of an abstract artist?
- How can we evaluate or judge the merits of abstract art?

You might not come up with any immediate answers, but think about these questions as they'll help you to consider abstract art in broader ways and will ultimately help you to understand it better.

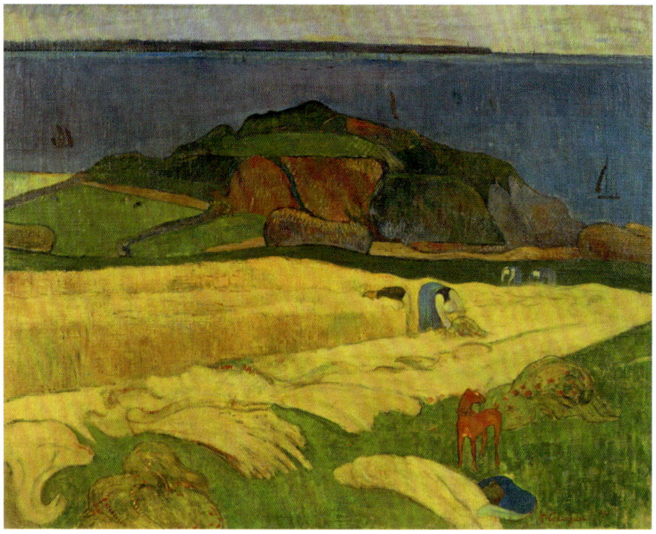

Paul Gauguin, *Harvest, Le Pouldu* 1890, oil on canvas, 73 x 92.1, Tate
Gauguin painted this work at the end of the 19th century, when he had become established as the central figure of a group of painters in Brittany, in north-west France. Influenced by folk and primitive art, he went against current fashions in painting and began to create flat areas of colour and a distorted perspective. The idea behind this was to show the essence of life beneath superficial appearances. Consider how audacious Gauguin was being; this was long before abstract art had been developed.

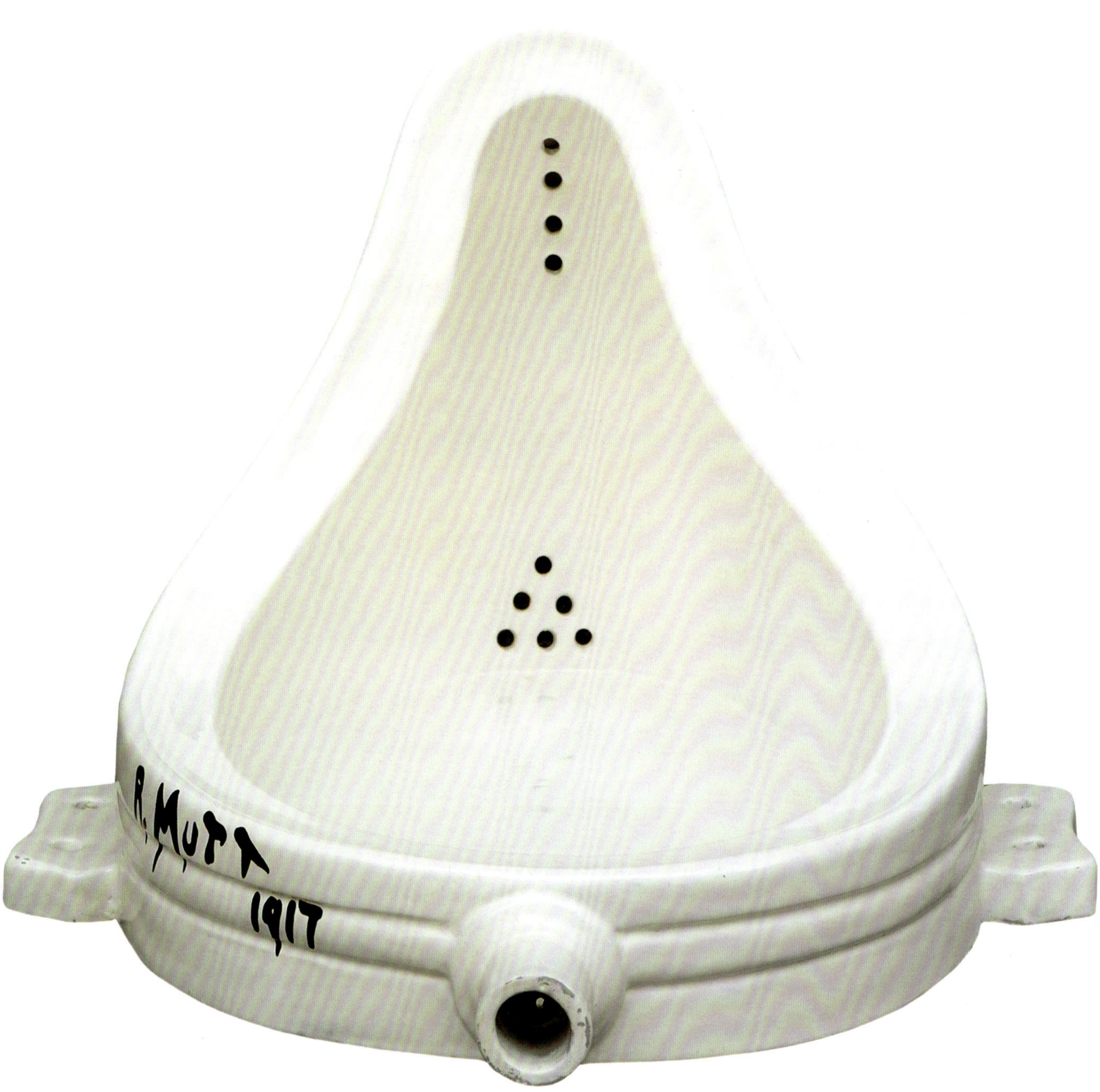

Marcel Duchamp, *Fountain* 1917, replica 1964, porcelain, 36 x 48 x 61, Tate

This is the most famous of Duchamp's 'readymades'. When he exhibited this object – an ordinary manufactured urinal – as a work of art, he flouted the accepted notions of art and changed them forever. The original object, now lost, was a standard urinal, laid on its back and signed with the pseudonym 'R. Mutt 1917'. This is one of a small number of replicas that Duchamp authorised in 1964, based on a photograph of the original. Duchamp was protesting against the inhumanities of the First World War. He considered beautiful art as being nonsensical in the context of the horrors of war. When the Society of Independent Artists refused to exhibit *Fountain*, as Duchamp called the urinal, he said: 'Mr Mutt's fountain is not immoral, that is absurd, no more than a bathtub is immoral. It is a fixture that you see every day in plumbers' shop windows. Whether Mr Mutt with his own hands made the fountain has no importance. He CHOSE it. He took an ordinary article of life, placed it so that its useful significance disappeared under the new title and point of view – created a new thought for that object.' And that was what Duchamp changed; after *Fountain*, whatever an artist chose to exhibit was art, because he or she said it was. What do you think about this – can people enjoy looking at a work of art, even if it was not originally created as one?

Abstract origins

Throughout history, a great deal of art has been abstracted. Celtic, Mexican, ancient Egyptian, African and Asian art, for example, developed abstract or semi-abstract stylised forms to convey various meanings. In the West, however, between the 15th and 19th centuries, artists usually produced illusionistic and figurative art that aimed to look as close to real life as possible. By the late 19th century, the impact of photography, scientific discovery, technological progress and the Industrial Revolution changed how people thought about the world. Artists began to search for new forms of expression. As seen on page 72, Whistler, for example, believed that painting should be simply an arrangement of abstract qualities that appealed to the senses and that it shouldn't depict stories for a social or moral purpose.

Kandinsky is widely credited with making the world's first truly abstract paintings. He aimed to evoke sound through colours and shapes and to create the painterly equivalent of a symphony. Around 1911, he abandoned all recognisable elements in his art. He probably had synaesthesia, a condition that allows a person to appreciate sounds, colours or words with two or more senses simultaneously. So when he listened to music, he 'heard' colours, and when he saw colours, he 'heard' music. The word synaesthesia is a combination of the Greek words *syn*, meaning together, and *aesthesis*, meaning sensation. Kandinsky also followed theosophy, a philosophy based on spirituality. Yet even with all these influences and inspirations, his development towards complete abstraction was gradual; he went through several stages before producing works for their colours and shapes alone.

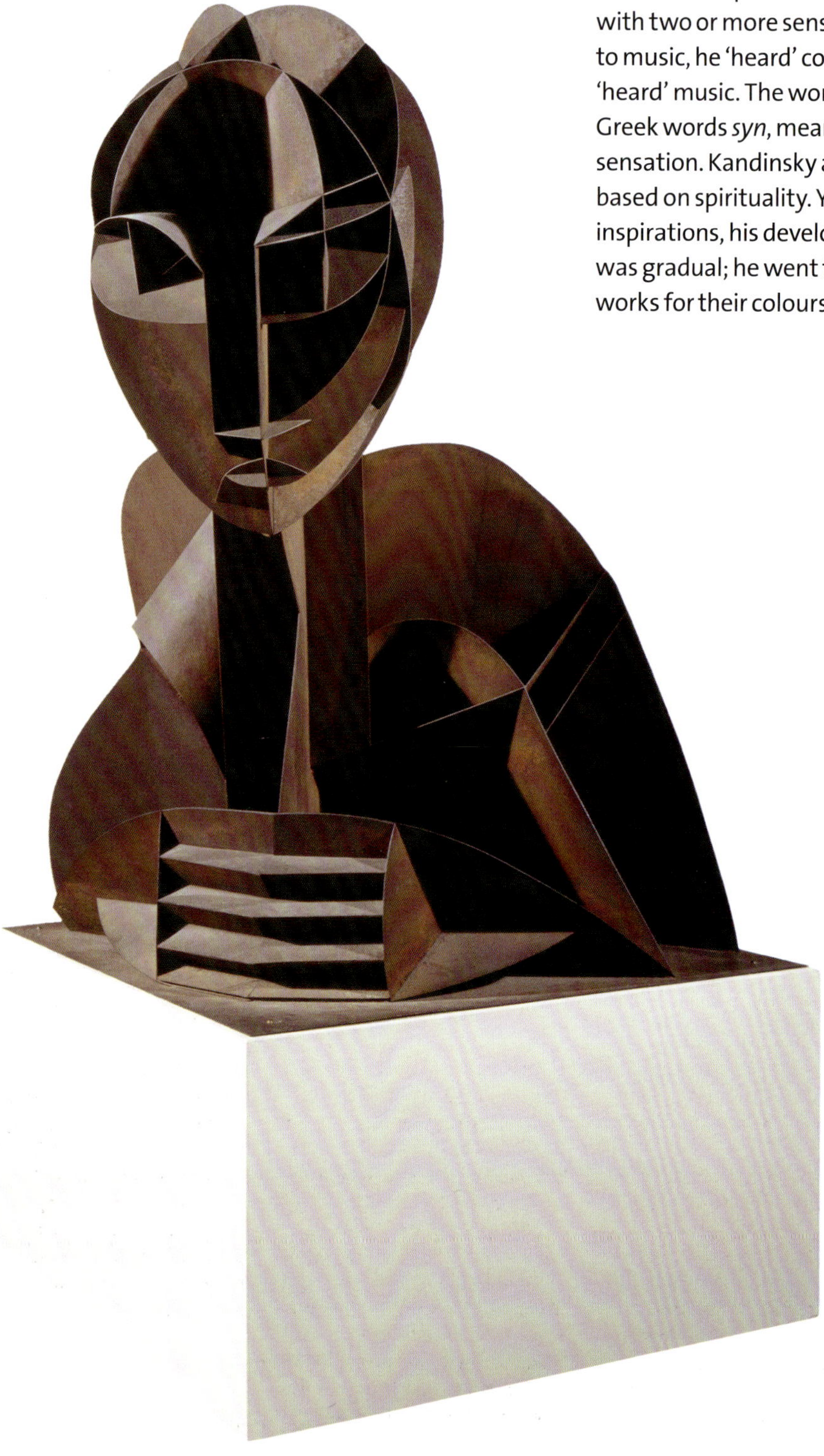

Artists of the machine age

Artists have directly expressed ideas about the changing world around them by emphasising elements other than visual reality. Many of these have been abstractions of things from the real world rather than totally abstract works. These artists include the Italian Futurists such as Umberto Boccioni (1882–1916) and Giacomo Balla (1871–1958), British Vorticists and artists like Léger and Delaunay. The Futurists, for example, wanted to express their excitement about new technologies and powerful machines. This optimism, however, was sadly tested with the First World War. The Vorticists were inspired by Cubism and rejected traditional painting styles and subjects. After the 1920s, abstract art developed in numerous ways, some of which are described on the following three pages.

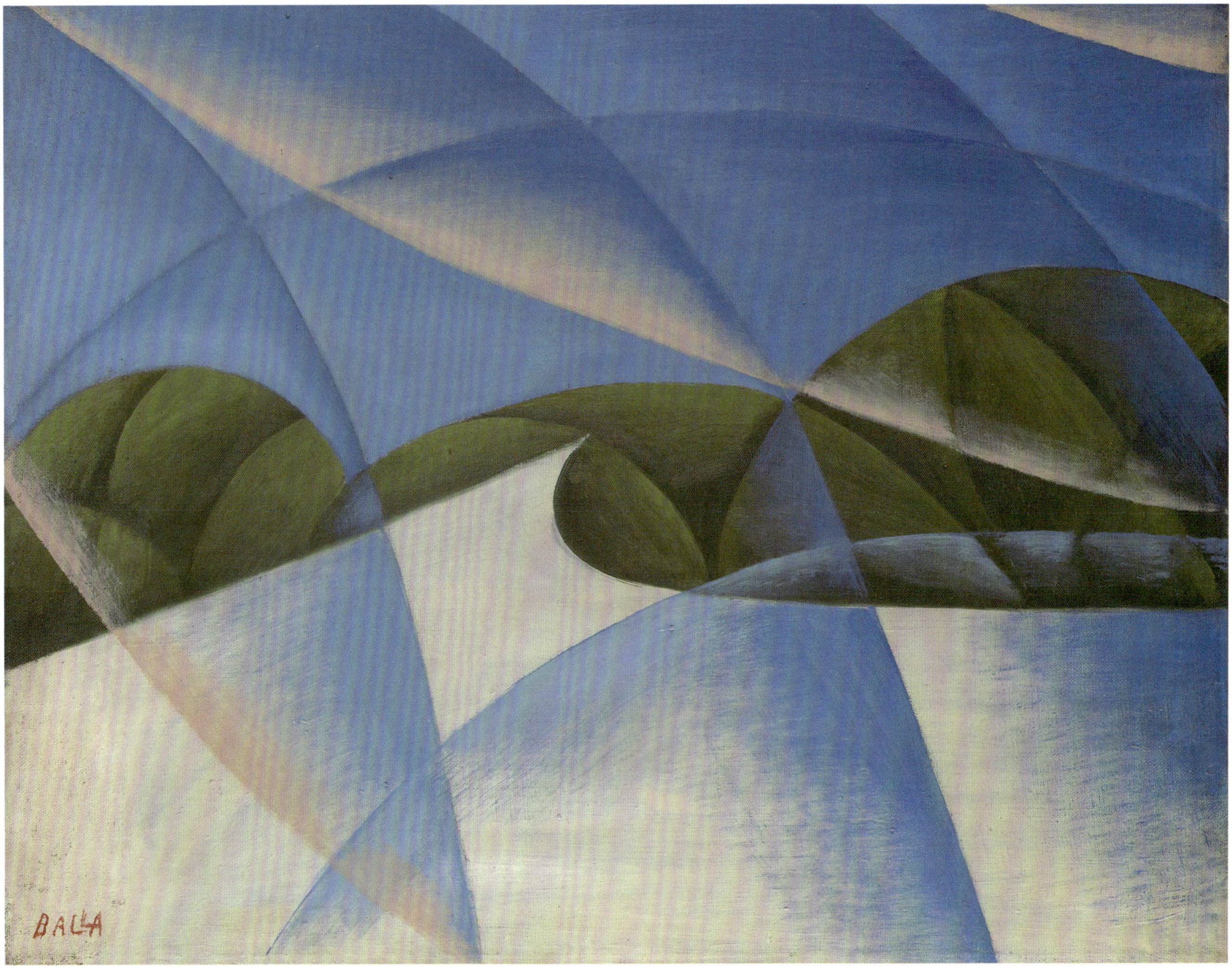

Naum Gabo, *Head No 2* 1916, steel, 175.3 x 134 x 122.6, Tate
Created in Norway a year before the Russian Revolution, this work shows the influence of Constructivism, with which Russian-born Gabo was associated at the time. The Constructivists believed that one of the outcomes of the Revolution would be an artistic renewal that embraced new scientific theories and industrial materials. Gabo returned to Russia in 1917, to join Vladimir Tatlin (1885–1953), Malevich and Kandinsky. Gabo used a method known as 'stereometric construction', in which he created 'space' rather than 'mass'. This is similar to drawing negative space rather than positive shapes. From 1915 to 1920, he used planes to construct heads and figures and this was his second head using the stereometric technique. Although not completely abstract, he applied the style later for his fully abstract works.

Giacomo Balla, *Abstract Speed, the Car has Passed* 1913, oil on canvas, 50.2 x 65.4, Tate
Balla was a leading figure in the Italian Futurist group. He believed that the power and speed of innovative machines such as cars was exciting and would improve life in general. This painting was originally the right-hand part of a triptych, showing the passage of a car along a white road, with green and blue forms either side, suggesting the earth and sky. The pinkish areas represent the exhaust fumes left by the passing car. How would you show speed on a static surface? Does this work succeed in that? Cars were relatively new when Balla painted this. Do you think he has epitomised the sense of excitement and freedom that many of his contemporaries felt about cars?

De Stijl

In 1917, Dutch artists Mondrian and Theo van Doesburg (1883–1931) founded 'De Stijl', Dutch for 'The Style'. Also known as Neoplasticism, the movement included other artists and architects and aimed to express their ideals of spiritual harmony and order. To do this, they produced purely abstract work, reducing everything to their essentials of vertical and horizontal lines, and used only primary colours plus black and white.

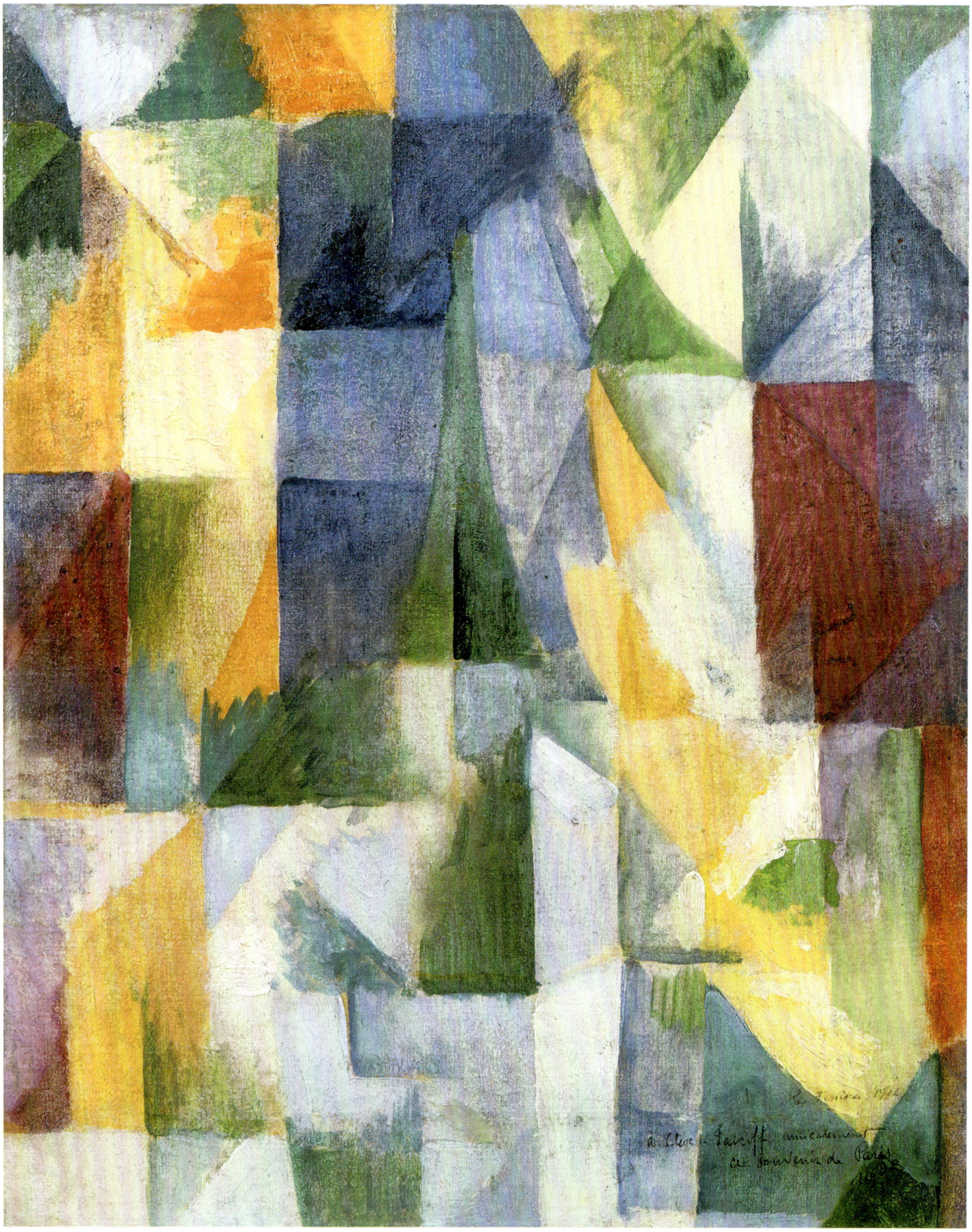

Constructivism

The Constructivists worked mainly in Russia, but also later in Germany. They were a group of artists who aimed to interpret abstract art in practical design, symbolising the values of the new Communist order after the Russian Revolution of 1917. As well as traditional painting and sculpture, the Constructivists experimented with film, photography, graphic design and architecture. Often working with industrial materials, including glass, metal and wood, and basing their work on geometrical shapes and mathematical ratios, they celebrated what they perceived as the new modern age. Constructivism profoundly influenced subsequent modern art and design movements, including the Bauhaus and De Stijl. Major Constructivists included El Lissitzky (1890–1941), Malevich, László Moholy-Nagy (1895–1946) and Gabo.

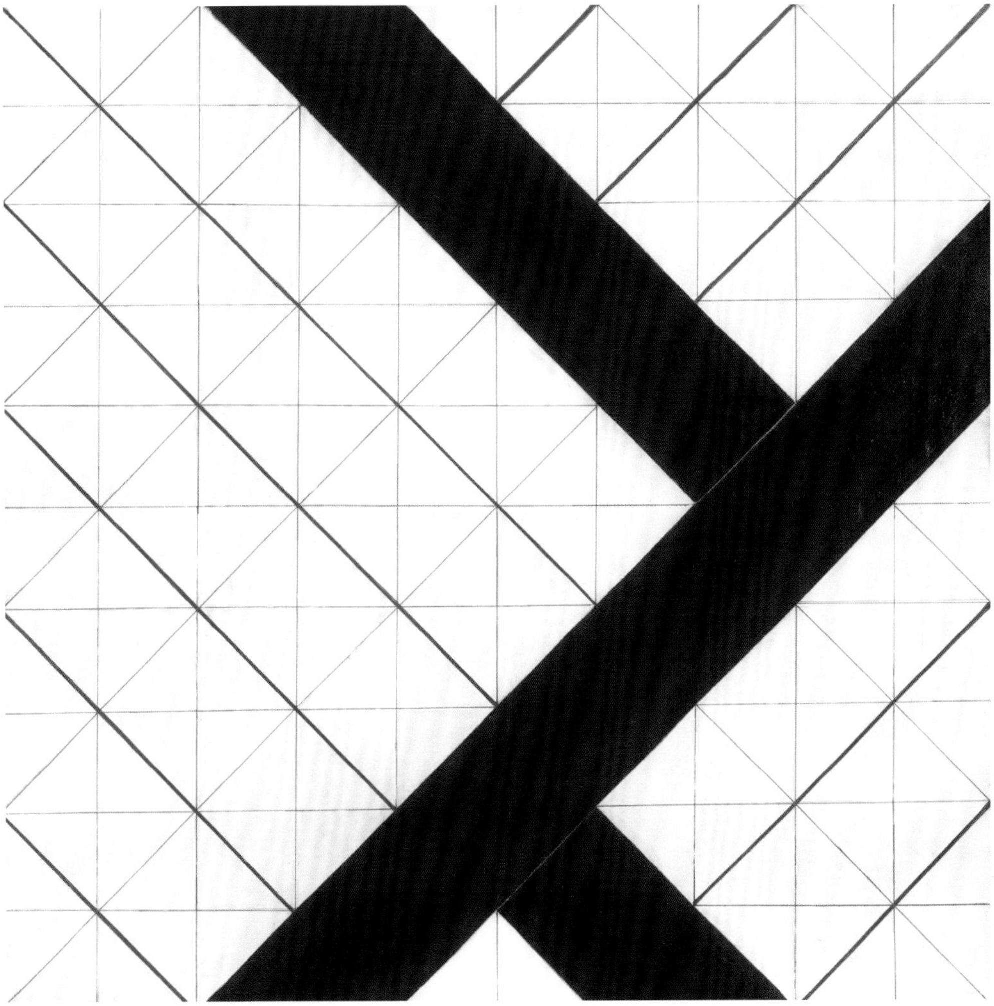

Robert Delaunay, *Windows Open Simultaneously (First Part, Third Motif)* 1912, oil on canvas, 45.7 x 37.5, Tate
Inspired by the effects of light falling on glass windows, Delaunay exploited his interest in light refraction, colour and reflection. He was particularly fascinated by the notion of 'simultaneous contrast', when two colours placed adjacently interact with each other and change our perception of them. The actual colours are not altered, but we see them differently. Like Kandinsky, with whom he was in contact, Delaunay associated art with music. His style of painting became known as Orphism after the Greek musician Orpheus. In this painting, pure bright colours evoke sunlight falling on the windows. But this was before he completely discarded representational imagery; in the centre can be seen a green silhouette of the Eiffel Tower. Interlocking, fragmented planes of colour suggest transparent, reflective glass, while the brushmarks and patches of colour are reminiscent of elements in the paintings of Cézanne and Braque.

Theo van Doesburg, *Counter-composition VI* 1925, oil on canvas, 50 x 50, Tate
In an attempt to create a universal art, in about 1916 van Doesburg began reducing his images to essential elements, abandoning subject matter and simplifying all he saw. This idea worked in any discipline, but although it appears to be calculated and mathematical, he achieved balance through intuition.

Abstract Expressionism

During the 1940s and 1950s, a group of artists in America developed painting styles that explored our unconscious feelings and the spiritual through pure abstraction. They became known as Abstract Expressionists and there were two styles within the movement. 'Gestural' painters like Jackson Pollock (1912–56) and Willem de Kooning (1904–97) applied paint spontaneously and freely. 'Colour Field' painters such as Mark Rothko (1903–70) and Clyfford Still (1904–80) saturated their canvases with large areas of colour. All the Abstract Expressionists explored the emotive effects of scale, colour and texture, and for many of these artists, the actual act of painting was a spiritual experience.

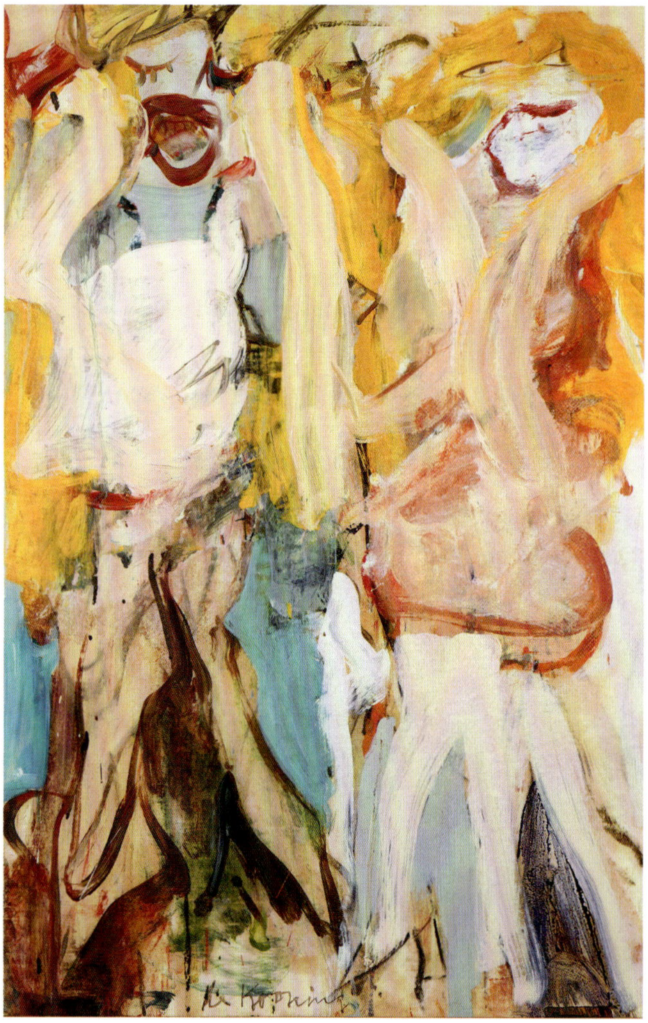

Willem de Kooning, *Women Singing II* 1966, oil on paper on canvas, 91.4 x 61, Tate
Willem de Kooning once said, 'Flesh is the reason oil paint was invented.' So although his work is often completely abstract, the female form was a theme he returned to frequently. The painting looks spontaneous, but de Kooning made numerous preliminary studies, and the painting itself is built up with energetic brushwork and a deliberately colourful palette. It is one of three paintings he based on pop singers he had seen on television. What else can you see? Now you know it was not merely instinctive, but also carefully considered, what evidence can you see of pre-planning? (Hint: look at the arrangement of colours, the types of brushmarks and the overall mood of the work.)

Jackson Pollock, *Yellow Islands* 1952, oil on canvas, 143.5 x 185.4, Tate
Pollock invented a new technique of laying his canvas on the floor and adding paint to it from all sides. He said that this helped him to be 'more a part of the painting'. He used many methods to apply paint, including flicking it from sticks and dripping it from cans. Five years before he made this work he said: 'When I am painting I am not much aware of what is taking place.' By dripping and pouring paint, he worked freely and intuitively. He began this painting by pouring black paint onto the canvas, over which he added areas of yellow and crimson with a brush. He then lifted the canvas up while the paint was still wet, allowing it to sag and the paint to run. Then he trickled more black paint over the canvas.

Moods, marks and gestures

Abstract artists have often tried to communicate emotions and ideas through their art; without anything recognisable from the world, many delve inwardly, focusing on their own and our subconscious minds. Colour and expressive mark-making are important factors, as these affect us instantly. We talk about 'seeing red' when we're angry or 'feeling blue' when we're sad. Abstract art in general portrays what an artist feels and thinks, rather than what he or she sees. To appreciate or try to understand any abstract work, it's usually best to see it on display in a gallery or museum. Focus on a small area first of all, then consider the whole work. Study the scale, colours, shapes and marks. Do any of these things seem angry, gentle, thoughtful or distracted, for example? Does the work, or any part of it, remind you of anything? How do you feel when looking at the work? Do you find it disturbing, peaceful, relaxing or sad? Analyse what qualities in the work prompted these feelings. Now look at the title. Does this give you any clues about the work? What about the time and place it was produced? What was happening there at that time?

Next, using any materials you wish, try to imitate the marks or colours in the work. Produce several versions of these experiments with different materials. Try a flat, textureless material and then do the same with thick impasto paint. Try selecting some of the most prominent elements of the work and then move them around, creating your own versions. Can you find a better combination of shapes, lines or colours than the artist did? What emotions and thoughts do you feel you've expressed in these works? Did this occur unintentionally or deliberately?

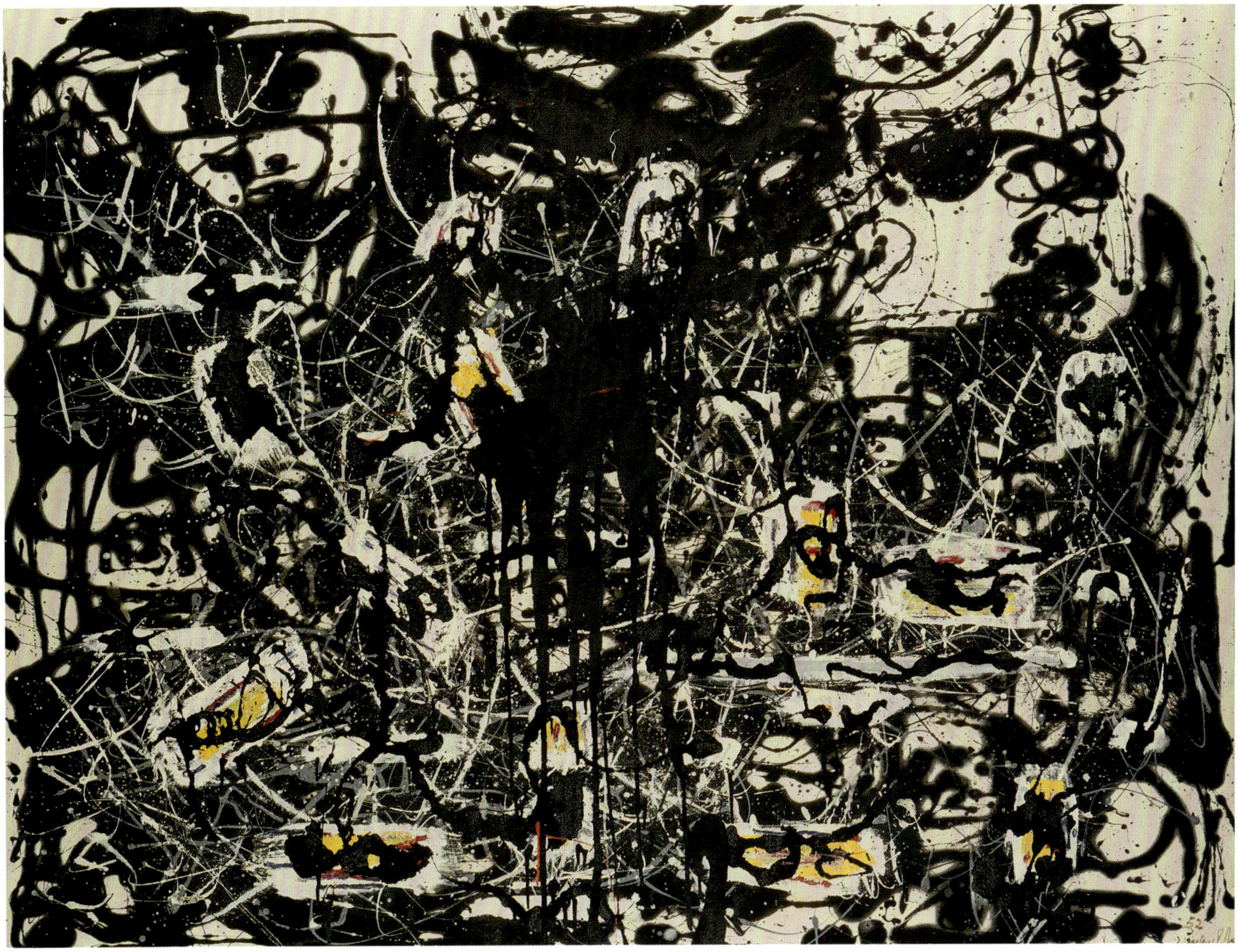

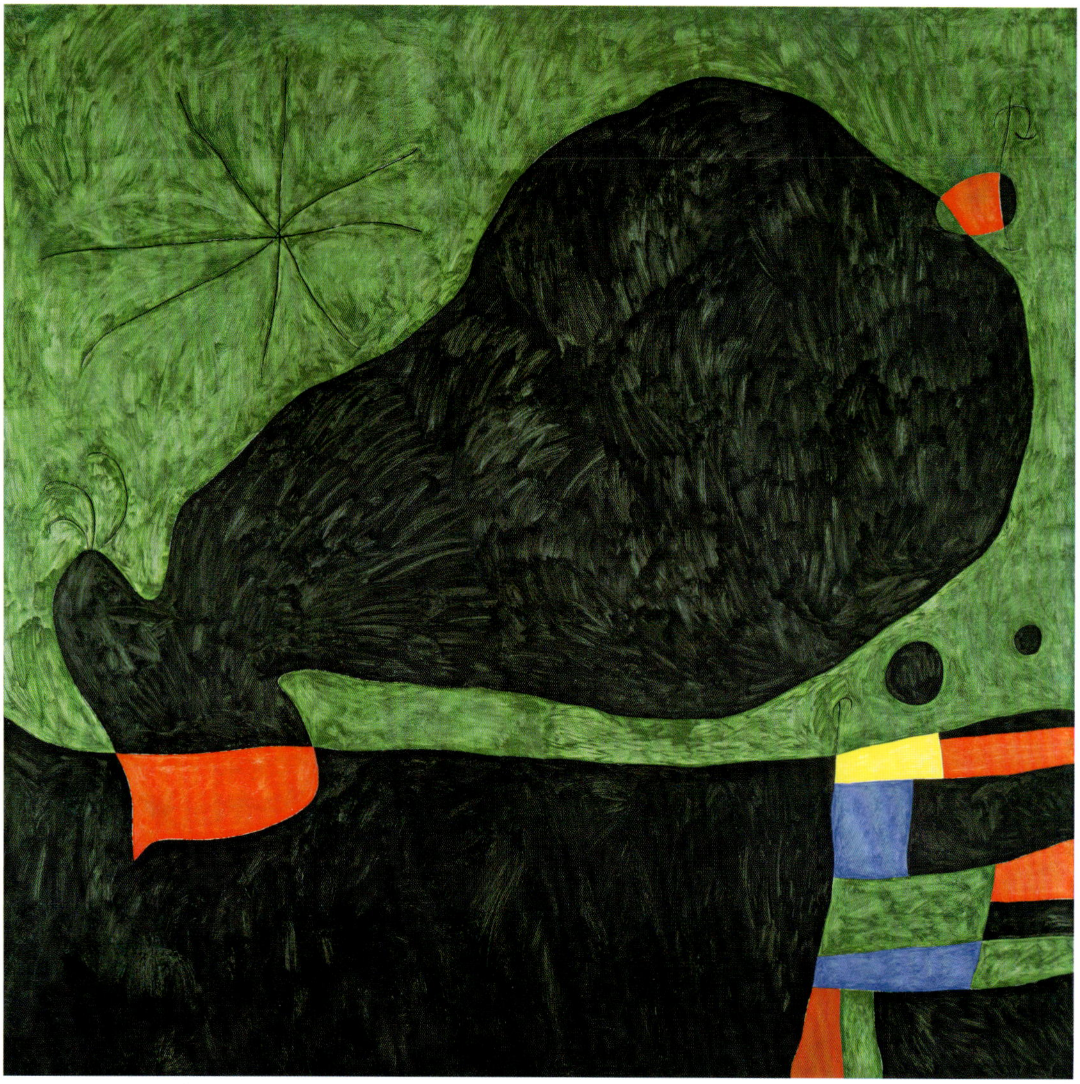

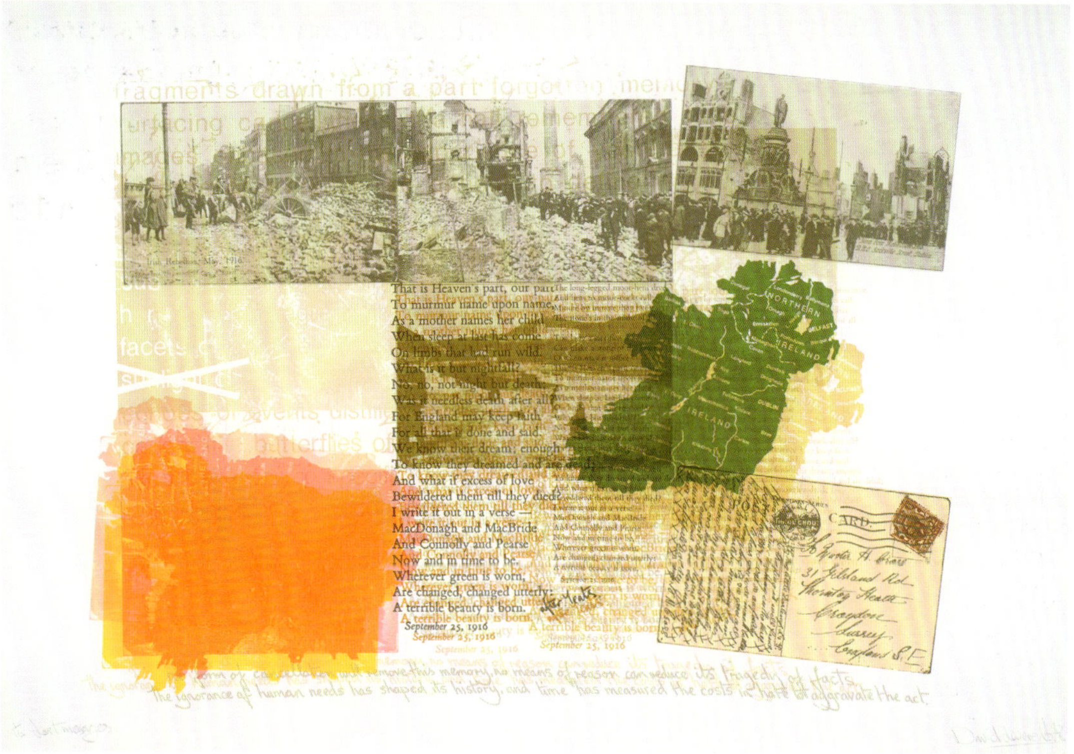
fragments drawn from a part forgotten
facets
That is Heaven's part, our part
To murmur name upon name,
As a mother names her child
And what if excess of love
Bewildered them till they died?
I write it out in a verse —
MacDonagh and MacBride
And Connolly and Pearse
Now and in time to be,
Wherever green is worn,
Are changed, changed utterly:
A terrible beauty is born.
September 25, 1916
NORTHERN
IRELAND
IRELAND
the ignorance of human needs has shaped its history, and time has measured the costs in hate to aggravate the act.

THEMES

'Different themes inevitably require different methods of expression. This does not imply either evolution or progress; it is a matter of following the idea one wants to express and the way in which one wants to express it.'
Pablo Picasso

Exploring art through themes can enhance your understanding of it. Many of the same or similar themes have featured throughout history, depicted in numerous ways by different artists, and themes can be interpreted and analysed broadly. The art already looked at in this book comprises a multitude of themes, and most of the questioning, scrutinising and responding to it already suggested can also be used for themes. For practical reasons, most art books and galleries group art chronologically, in subjects, movements or time periods. But as themes are often so diversely interpreted, according to artists' viewpoints, by investigating them you will develop greater creative and critical thinking skills.

Joan Miró, *Message from a Friend* 1964, oil on canvas, 262 x 275.5, Tate
Miró (1893–1983) believed that his work should be mysterious and elusive. He deliberately made shapes in his paintings unclear and indefinite. He never explained exactly what his paintings were about, so the title is almost the only clue here. The friend in the title refers to his fellow artist Alexander Calder (1898–1976), so the message is probably about art.

David Leverett, *Lost Messages* 1977–8, screenprint on paper, 59.5 x 82, Tate
This is one of seven prints exploring messages that flow between our subconscious selves and our outer realities. Leverett (born 1938) incorporates some of his poems. Themes that can be explored in this work include words, messages, relationships, exploration, boundaries, and perception.

Sketchbooks

Sketchbooks are great for exploring themes. Take yours to galleries and museums to engage with original artworks, draw what you see, make annotations, jot down your thoughts about artists and their work, gather information from labels and other artworks, collect and stick in postcards and leaflets from relevant places you have visited. At other times, use your sketchbook to experiment with ideas, materials and styles, make drawings and other images based on artwork you have studied, record information and ideas and invent further ideas based on what you've discovered. Sketchbooks can help you to focus your mind and unravel what you see.

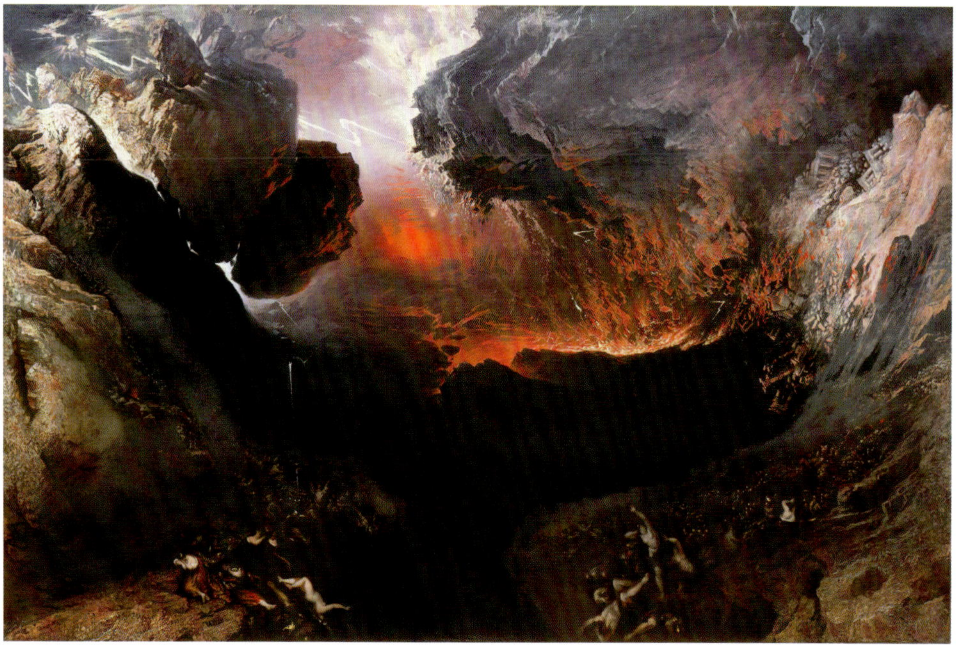

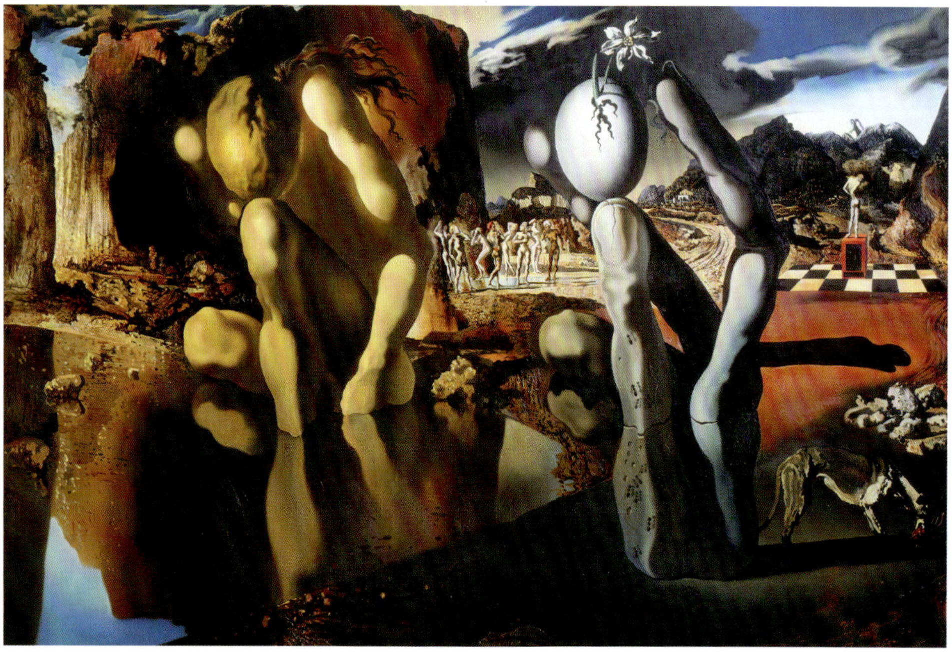

John Martin, *The Great Day of His Wrath* 1851–3, oil on canvas, 196.5 x 303.2, Tate
This is the third picture in a great triptych painted by Martin (1789–1854) and known as the Judgement series. This enormous work was inspired by an account of the Last Judgement in Revelation, the final book of the New Testament: 'There was a great earthquake and the sun became black as sackcloth of hair and the moon became as blood.' Destruction, despair, horror, allegory, nature and beliefs are all themes that could be considered with this work; Martin was focusing on all of them. Although the paintings were admired hugely at first, by the end of the 19th century their popularity had plummeted and he was nicknamed 'Mad Martin'.

Salvador Dalí, *Metamorphosis of Narcissus* 1937, oil on canvas, 51.1 x 78.1, Tate
This is Dalí's interpretation of the Greek myth of Narcissus, the beautiful youth who broke many hearts by caring for no one, then fell in love with his own reflection and died waiting for his loved one to emerge. The gods immortalised him by turning him into a flower, named the narcissus. In his meticulous technique, Dalí (1904–89) painted clever juxtapositions of figures, a hand, an egg (symbolising life cycles) and the narcissus. In the background is a group of beautiful figures surrounding Narcissus, who is admiring himself. Themes that could be connected with this work include juxtapositions, metamorphoses, pride, death, life, beauty, allegory or myth.

The name exchange

Because themes are so broad, they often overlap and many are interchangeable or transferable, which can be helpful when you're investigating them. Considering any art from a different viewpoint will give you scope for greater discernment about thoughts and processes behind the work. Here are some comparative themes:

- Discord/conflict/opposition/contest/disharmony/clash/division/imbalance
- Pattern/embellishment/decoration/arrangement/organisation/structure
- Growth/cultivation/expansion/progression/processes/energy/movement
- Courage/endurance/enterprise/adversity/ambition/strength/power/belief
- Relationships/intimacy/connections/loyalty/ancestry/attachment/fastenings/links
- Forces/energy/power/speed/regiments/compulsion/intensity/violence/war

You can do the same for any theme. Take a theme and look it up in a dictionary or thesaurus to find synonyms. You may be surprised at how many themes can be considered from the same starting point. As with any art, keep an open mind (or think 'outside the box', see pages 24–5).

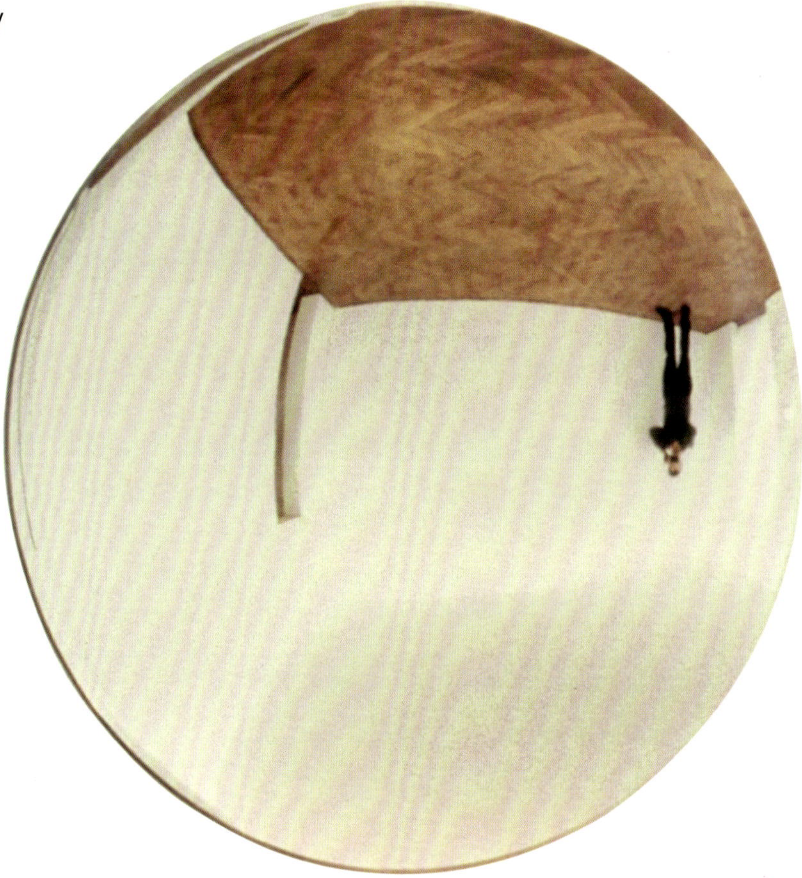

Cerith Wyn Evans, *Inverse Reverse Perverse* 1996, Perspex and acrylic, 171 x 171 x 31.5, Tate
A large concave mirror with a highly polished surface creates distorted reflections that change depending on how near or far you stand from it. From a distance, reflections are inverted; closer in, the reflection becomes larger and longer. Emphasising our subjectivity – or how we all see things differently – the unsettling nature of gigantic distorted reflections also suggests the passage of time and changing identities, perception, self-perception or even just simply reflections or viewpoints.

Discovery and exploration

So how do you find themes in art and how do you analyse or interpret them? Without a specific title, how do you know whether an artist has considered a particular theme, or whether an artwork can be linked to a theme you are considering? Don't panic! Keep open-minded, stay curious and use your imagination. For any theme, look at what the artists have actually represented, then consider the reasons and thoughts behind the work. Here are a few ideas to help:

Messages (overlapping themes: communication, information, letters or allegories). In 1977 David Leverett made seven prints called *Lost Messages*. The prints explored the relationship between our inner thoughts and beliefs, compared with outward realities. The 'messages' are lost because our thoughts do not always correspond with how others see us. In 1964, Joan Miró produced *Message from a Friend*, a deliberately ambiguous abstract painting, dominated by a whale-like shape. Miró had long practised 'automatism', or free association, working from his unconscious mind. The message he was suggesting in the work, therefore, is ambiguous. Just over a century before, in the early 1850s, John Martin painted *The Great Day of His Wrath*, *The Last Judgement* and *The Plains of Heaven*. These three huge paintings carry moral messages about God's power over humans and human frailty against nature. Similar sorts of messages can be seen in vanitas still lifes. Moral messages have traditionally been conveyed in religious works, myths and allegories. The word allegory comes from the Greek word *allegoria*, made up of *allos*, meaning 'other, different', and *agoria*, meaning 'language, speaking'. Allegories in art illustrate something in an understandable form that means something more complex. Like metaphors in words, allegories are hidden meanings or messages.

Change (which could also be: transformation, metamorphosis or adjustment). In 1996, Cerith Wyn Evans (born 1958) exhibited *Inverse Reverse Perverse*, a large concave mirror on a wall where it would reflect viewers

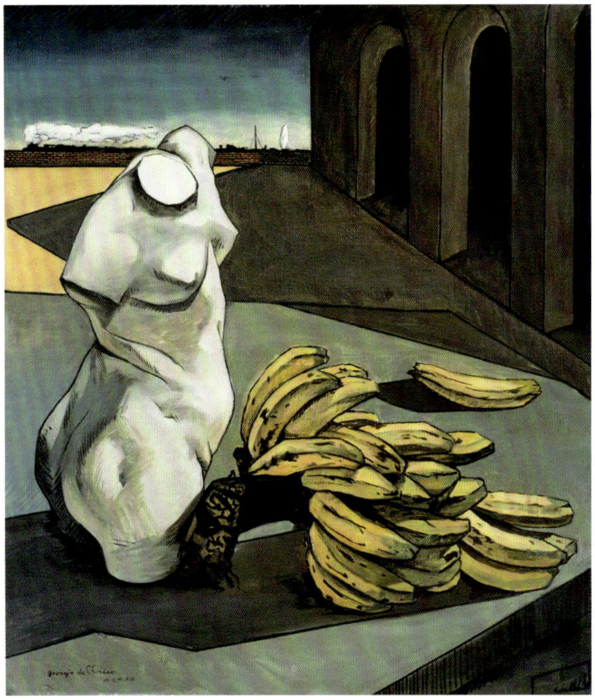

Giorgio de Chirico, *The Uncertainty of the Poet* 1913, oil on canvas, 106 x 94, Tate

A haunting square featuring classical arcades and a statue of Aphrodite. In the foreground next to the sculpture is a large bunch of bananas, and in the background a train whistles by. Distorted perspective and long shadows create an eerie atmosphere; the streets seem silent. Strange juxtapositions add to the bizarre nature of the scene, leaving many unanswered questions. From 1911 to 1915, de Chirico (1888–1978) lived in Paris and met several influential people, including the poet and writer Guillaume Apollinaire (1880–1918) and Picasso. During that time, he painted this and other works that evoked similar, dream-like architectural visions. The style became known as metaphysical painting. The word 'uncertainty' in the title helps to augment the mysterious atmosphere of the painting.

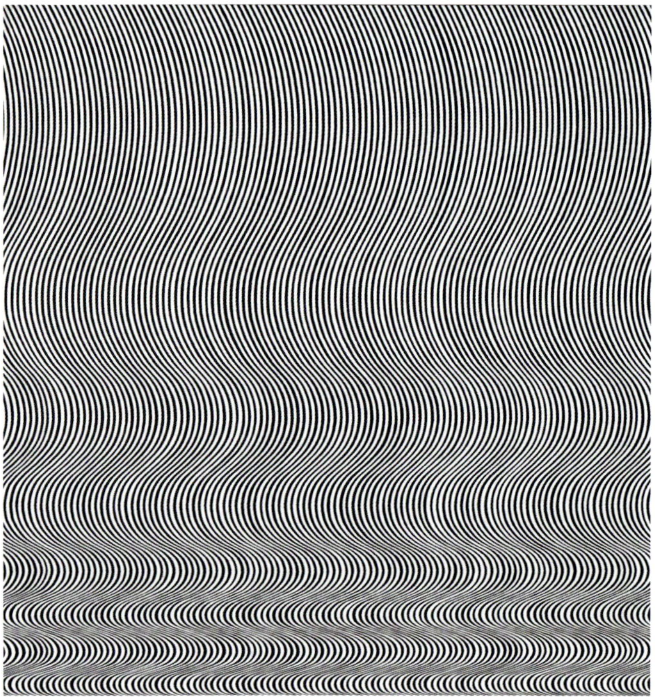

Bridget Riley, *Fall* 1963, polyvinyl acetate on hardboard, 141 x 140.3, Tate

Creating an illusion of movement, Riley's work was labelled 'Op art' in the 1960s. From 1961 to 1964 she painted in black and white, creating designs that influenced contemporary fashions. This seems to undulate and ripple; illusions of colours appear. Riley wrote: 'I try to organise a field of visual energy.' Related themes could include illusion, rhythm or perceptions.

coming into the room. Like the inside of a giant spoon, it reflected a distorted image that changed depending on how close or far away viewers stood. Wyn Evans was exploring how our viewpoints and expectations change over time. In *Metamorphosis of Narcissus* of 1937, Salvador Dalí illustrated the Greek myth of the vain youth Narcissus changing into a flower. Change, or any related themes, can be explored in a vast number of works of art. Think of changes in the weather, in creative styles, viewpoints and attitudes, changes in fashion, science and technology, life and the seasons, changes wrought through decay and destruction, ageing or growing up.

Protest (alternative themes include: dissent, revolt or confrontation). Look again at Paul Nash's *Totes Meer* on page 73, Duchamp's *Fountain* on page 103 and Picasso's *Weeping Woman* on page 43. In what ways can you see protest being expressed in those works of art? This theme can also be explored in any artwork of war, revolution, political unrest or unwelcome change, anger or disgruntlement.

Many art movements, such as Impressionism, Expressionism, Constructivism, Dada, Pop art and Abstract Expressionism, began as protests, particularly against the art world. In 1951, Boris Taslitzky (1911–2005) painted *Riposte*, a scene of protesting dockers in France in 1949 who were attacked by armed police.

Cities (comparable themes: urban life, the built environment, territory or architecture). For this theme, consider any of Canaletto's works, Lowry's *Industrial Landscape* on page 64, *Dynamic Suprematism* by Malevich on page 101 or work by the Futurists, Suprematists or other Constructivists, or artists and architects of the Bauhaus and De Stijl. At the turn of the 20th century, Jacques-Emile Blanche (1861–1942) painted several views of London, often from unusual viewpoints, while Delaunay was doing the same in Paris. In 1913, the year before the outbreak of the First World War, Wyndham Lewis (1882–1957) founded Vorticism, which extolled the virtues of the modern world. In his semi-abstract works, he celebrated the architectural rhythm of urban life.

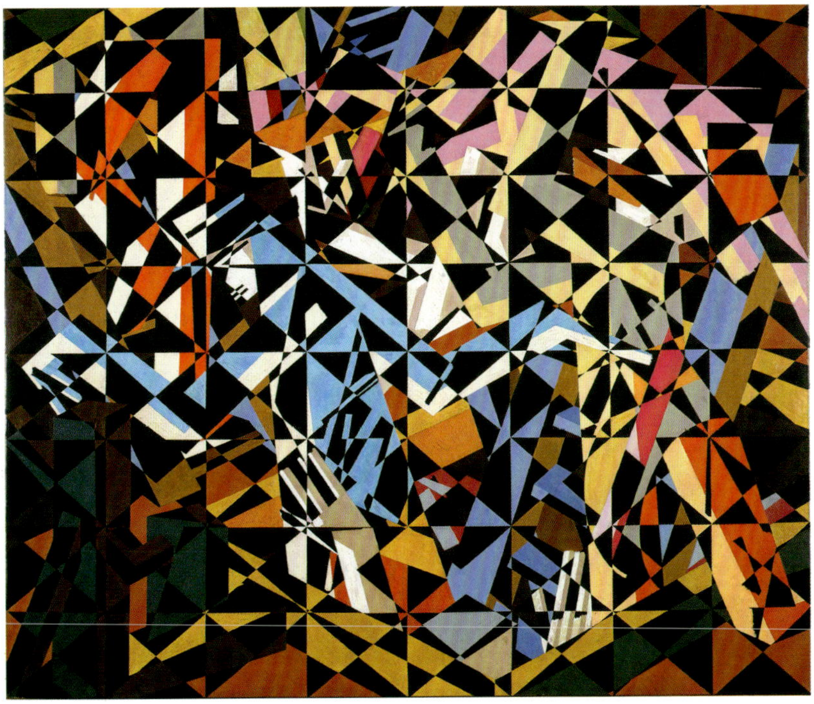

David Bomberg, *In the Hold* c.1913–14, oil on canvas, 196.2 x 231.1, Tate
You could be forgiven for thinking that this work – resembling a mosaic or a kaleidoscope – is nothing but shapes and colours. But it does include some elements from our world. The clue, as with so many works of art, is in the name. Bomberg painted dockers working in a ship's hold. Everything is fragmented into facets and planes. On the lower right, in cobalt blue, is a ladder connecting the hold with the deck. Across the centre, in lighter blue, is a docker wearing a hat. Other hands can be seen, including one holding the ladder. Coloured, geometric shapes suggest more people and objects. Although he mixed with them, Bomberg was never a member of the Vorticist movement. After the First World War, he resented the destructive power of machines and changed his style. Themes to consider with this work include broken, machines, work and fragments.

Time (which could also be: moment, passage, the seasons or duration). Look for works that show different or particular times of the day or night, the seasons, ageing, rituals, celebrations. Look again at Turner's *Moonlight, a Study at Millbank* 1797 on page 4, or how Paula Rego has depicted different stages of life in *The Dance* 1988 on page 51. Any artwork that explores the ideas of vanitas – the transience of life – time marching on, or calendars are also good starting points. Richard Long's *A Hundred Mile Walk* of 1971–2 on page 65 can be considered in the light of this theme, as can many other works of Land or Environmental art.

Perspectives (corresponding themes: viewpoints, panorama, attitude, illusion, vista or outlook). All themes are broad, but almost any work of art can be examined under this theme. You could consider how viewers perceive certain works of art, whether this is from actual positions, or attitudes and opinions about the work. Again, you can be literal and focus on works of art that exploit linear or

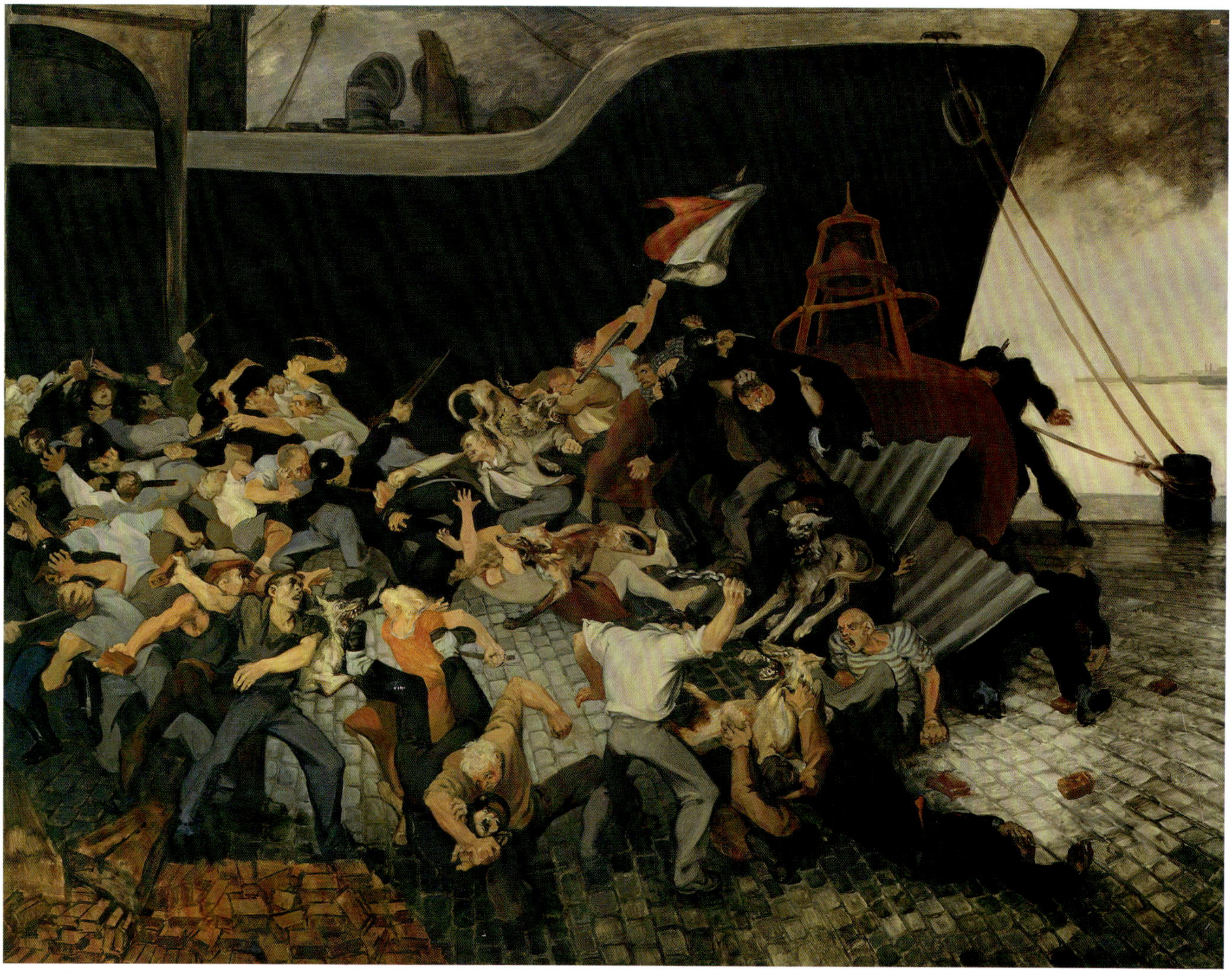

Boris Taslitzky, *Riposte* 1951, oil on canvas, 210 x 310, Tate
In the aftermath of the Second World War, some French colonies sought independence. In an effort to suppress this, troops and supplies were sent to the colonies from France. In 1949, dockers near Marseilles refused to load the ships and staged a strike, but armed police attacked them. The violence of this officially authorised assault shocked the nation, particularly so soon after the war. Taslitzky illustrated the event from newspaper reports. Themes such as conflict, confrontation, drama, power, authority or dynamism can be explored in connection with this work.

Jacques-Emile Blanche, *Ludgate Circus: Entrance to the City (November, Midday)* c.1910, oil on board, 104.8 x 81.6, Tate
The French artist Blanche lived in London for six years and painted numerous views of the city while there. He was self-taught and made a living painting portraits.
Key points to note:

- Unusual viewpoint
- Hansom cabs and buses, leading the eye into the picture
- Steam billowing out at dramatic angles
- The bridge divides the work between foreground and distance, without cutting it in half
- Buildings frame either side of the work
- The sky gives a 'breathing space' in the action-packed composition
- Themes that could be explored with this work: space, cities, viewpoints, progress, commotion and identity.

atmospheric perspective, or you could consider art that explores spiritual or religious perspectives. Alternatively, look back at *To the Studios* 1990–1 by Auerbach on page 21, or consider the fragmented painting *In the Hold* c.1913–14 by David Bomberg on page 115, or, conversely, *Fall* 1963 by Bridget Riley on page 114. Each painting distorts reality and our perspectives. You could look at Cézanne's distortions of objects, painted from several different viewpoints, and the many ideas and experiments he inspired that questioned the traditional methods of perspective. Look at Léger's *Still Life with a Beer Mug* 1921–2 on page 80. It's portrayed from several viewpoints, with flattened and altered perspectives. Or consider *The Uncertainty of the Poet* 1913 by Giorgio de Chirico on page 114, with its distorted perspective and shadows that undermine the conventions of pictorial space and time.

Whatever theme you are investigating, use any of the questioning formats suggested so far.

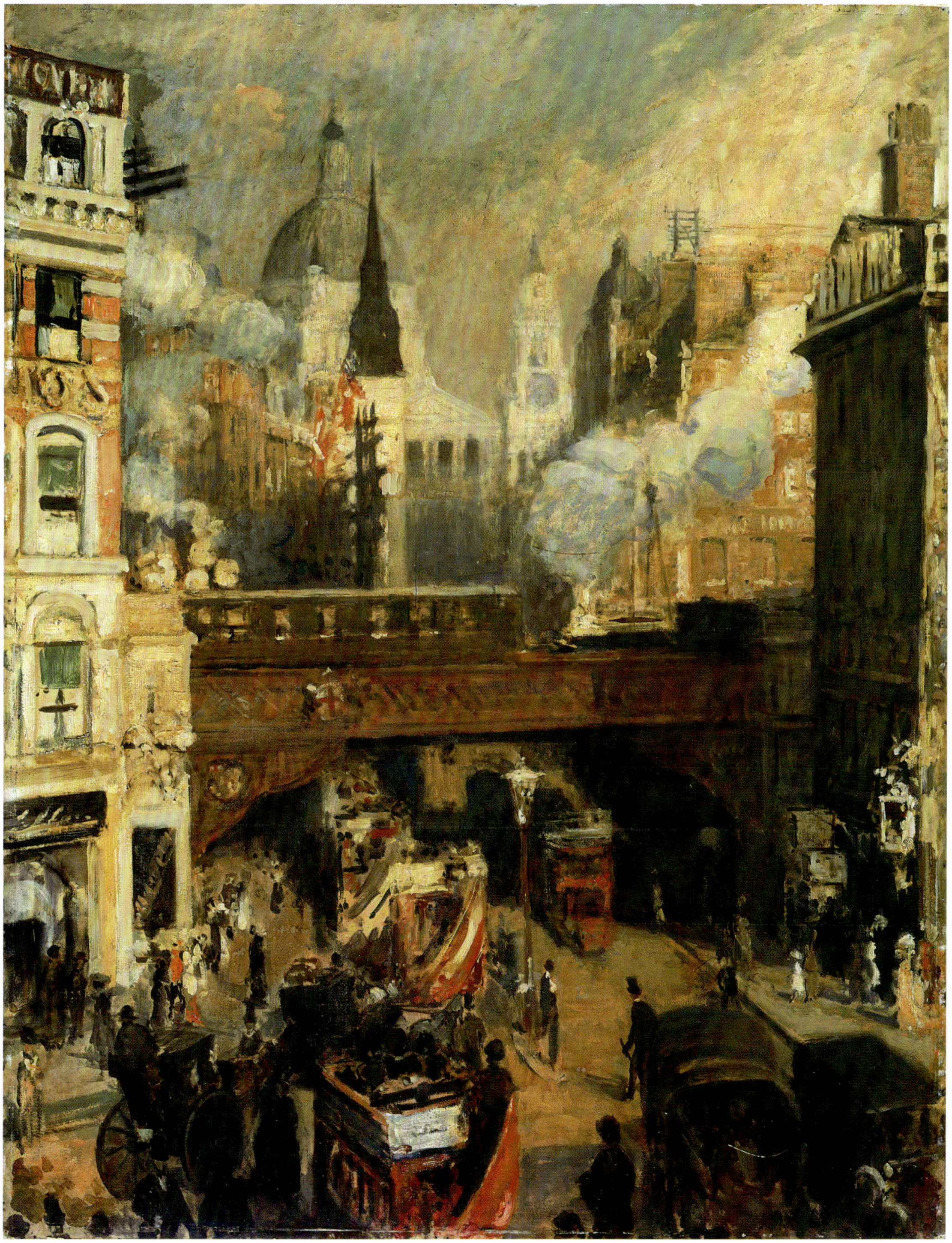

Finding clues

Themes might not be obvious at first, but once you start looking for them, you'll find them everywhere! If you're not sure how to identify them, always begin by looking in a dictionary or thesaurus for alternative words. Once you've found different words, further possibilities should open up in your mind. Always try to think of the theme from other angles, from a different starting point, giving yourself more opportunities to investigate and more works of art to consider. If you find a work and you're not sure whether or not it is really connected to a particular theme, think of the corresponding words to see if you can justify the connections. Here are some questions to help you find and establish different themes:

- What's happening in the work? Does this fit with your theme?
- Do you think the artist explored the theme deliberately or unconsciously?
- What do you think was uppermost in the artist's mind when creating this work? What makes you say that?
- What aspects of this work show explorations of your theme?
- Does this work change your opinion of your theme? In what ways?
- What title would you give the work? Is that the same as, or similar to, its actual title?
- Does the title refer to the theme in any way?
- Do the materials used enhance the theme at all? In what ways?

Find two or three artworks that explore the same or similar themes and look at them together. Compare ways in which each artist has responded to the theme. Make a list of similarities and differences. In what ways have the artists drawn on tradition or reacted against it? How have the events of the day and place affected the ways the artists have worked, and were the themes considered in each work deliberately or unintentionally?

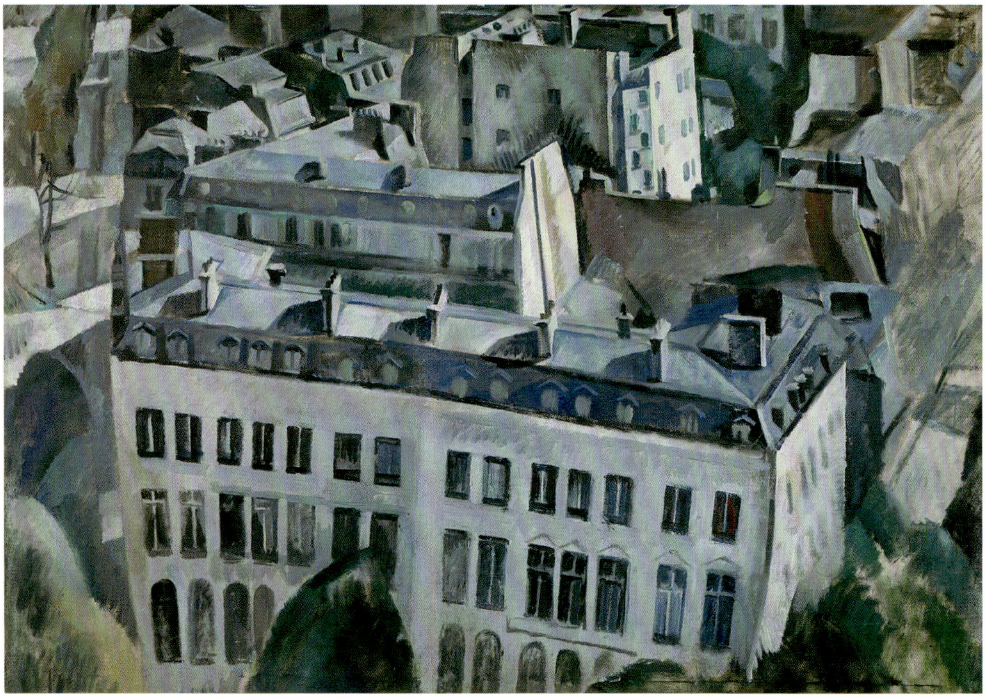

Robert Delaunay, *Study for the City* 1909–10, oil on canvas, 88.3 x 124.5, Tate
Inspired by a postcard of the rooftops of Paris, Delaunay created this study for a finished painting. He worked from an original photograph taken from the top of the Arc de Triomphe, looking towards the Eiffel Tower. Delaunay was inspired by Cézanne, music, colour and Parisian architecture. The angles are distorted and the tonal contrasts are dramatic.

Themes that can be explored in this work include structure, viewpoints, the city, contrasts or rhythm.

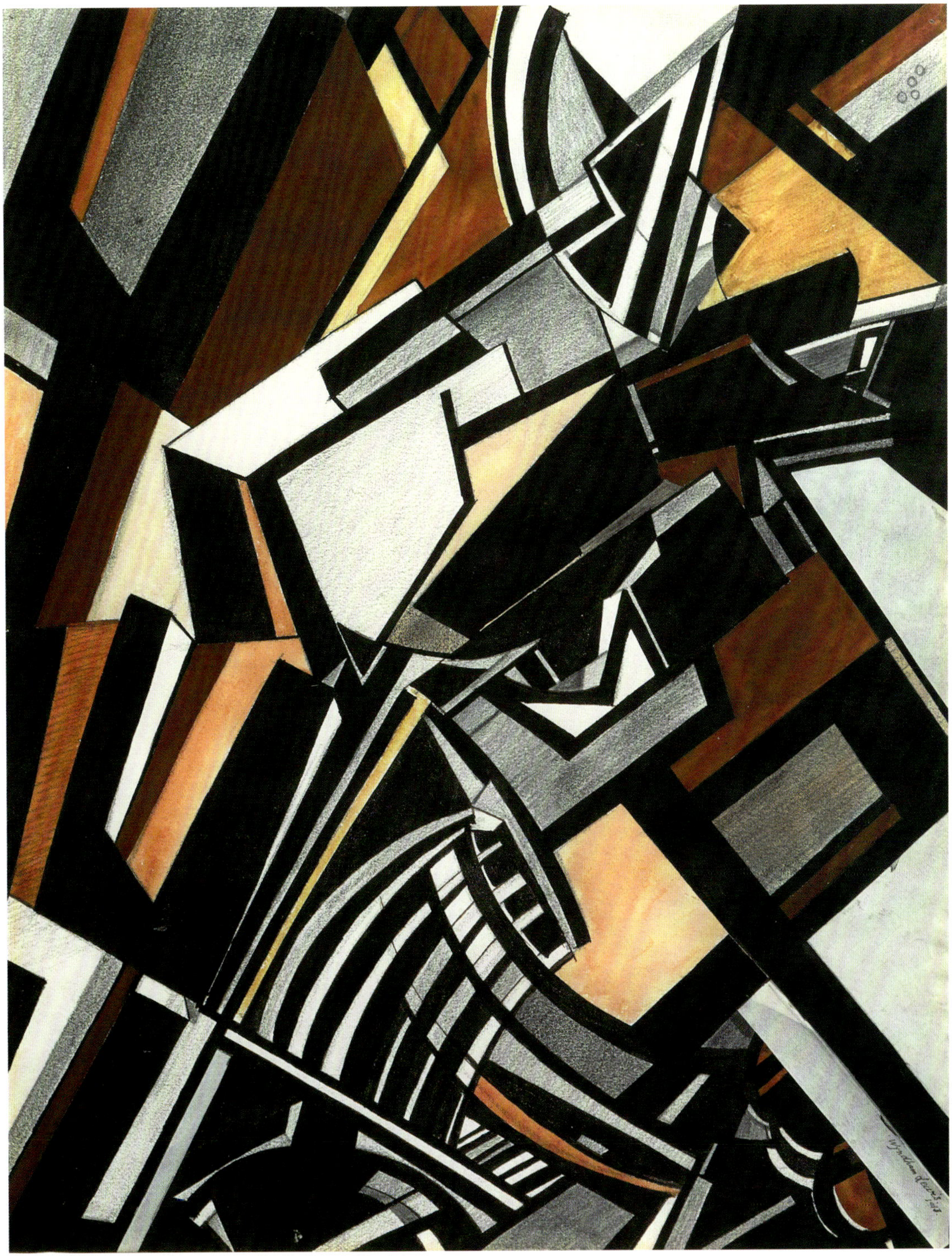

Wyndham Lewis, *Composition* 1913, ink, watercolour and graphite on paper, 34.3 x 26.7, Tate
In 1914 the British artist and writer Wyndham Lewis co-founded the art movement Vorticism with the American poet and critic Ezra Pound (1885–1972). The Vorticists were inspired by Cubist and Futurist painting, the machine and architectural forms. They worked in a geometric style of abstraction that to them celebrated modernity. From July 1914, Lewis published the Vorticists' magazine *Blast*, which he used to pour scorn on the tastes of polite society. This angular composition suggests the structure and mechanisms of urban life. What themes would you say emerge from this work?

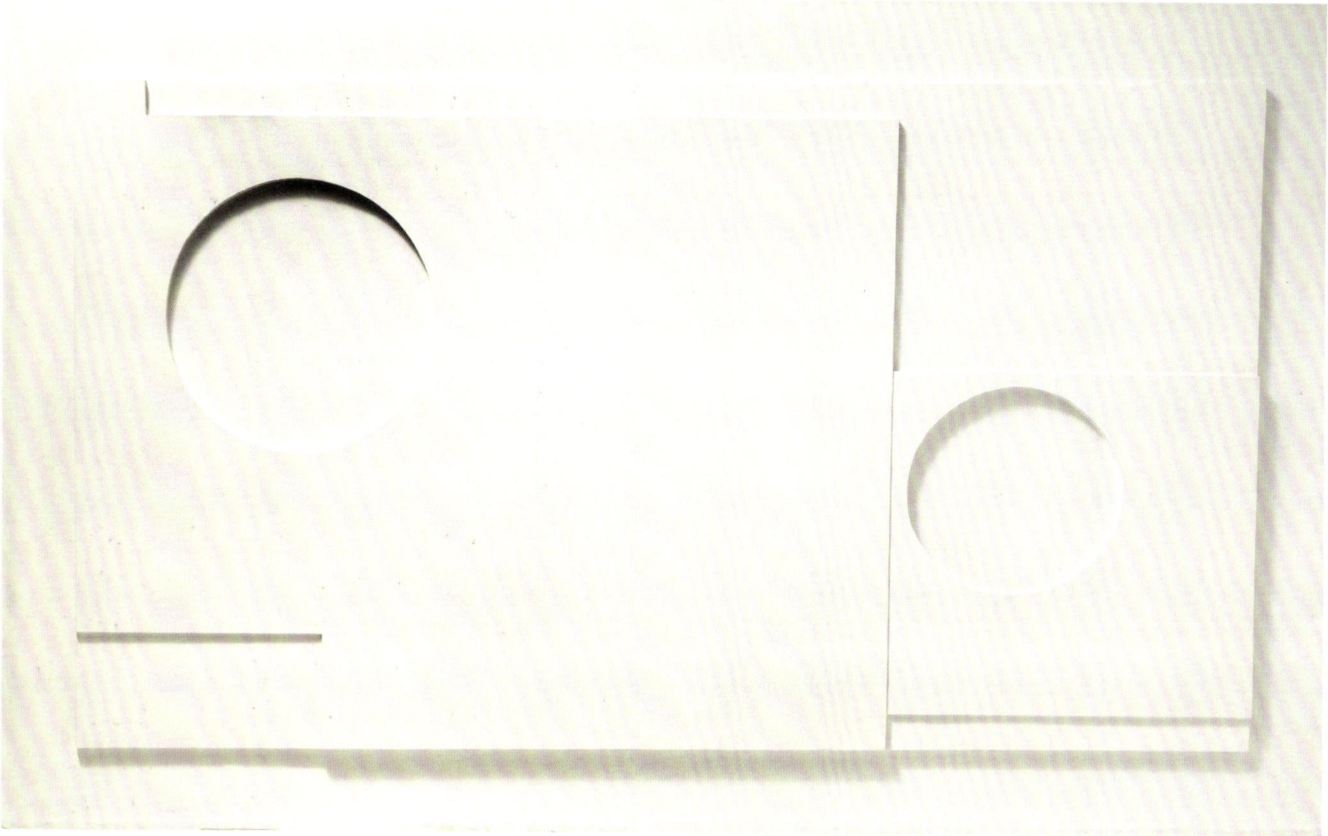

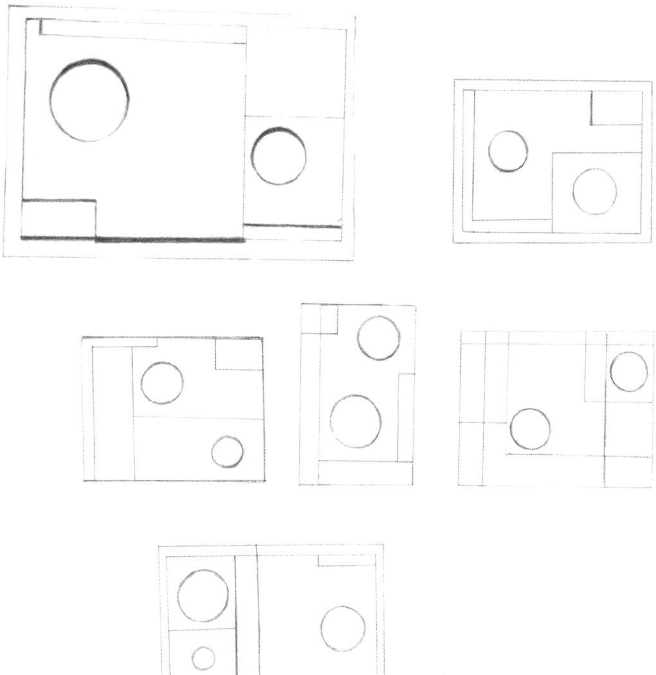

Ben Nicholson, *1935 (white relief)* 1935, painted wood, 101.6 x 166.4, Tate
Nicholson's first relief painting was made on a trip to Paris in 1933. Nicholson (1894–1982) was working on a painting when some thick white paint chipped off, leaving two distinct layers on his canvas. Influenced by the purity of Mondrian's paintings whose studio he had visited that year, he was inspired to develop several white abstract reliefs, to symbolise notions of purity and order, and of ideal universal beauty. This work signifies his attention to detail, dismissing nothing in his determination to develop new ideas. Try working from his geometric shapes (as I have done, right), move them around, experimenting with different arrangements or colours. Are your designs as interesting or as satisfying as his? Use a variety of materials to explore the theme – maybe even create a relief of a Mondrian-style work or translate this work into a sculpture.

MOTIVATION AND INSPIRATION

'The aim of art is to represent not the outward appearance of things, but their inward significance.'
Aristotle

So now you have the tools to delve deeper into any work of art and to understand more about artists' thoughts and processes and how you can respond to them. Remain curious and keep asking questions. Use your sketchbook to gather, explore and develop ideas. Research, annotate, make mind maps, experiment. Look closely. Dismiss nothing! Things you may think are irrelevant rarely are. For example, you might think the small red paint marks in Constable's *Flatford Mill* (page 63) are insignificant. They're not. There were no bright coloured synthetic paints in Constable's day. So he deliberately applied blobs of red paint in the grass and foliage to brighten up the dull greens that he could only make from yellow ochre mixed with Prussian or cobalt blue. Or you may have noticed that the printing of Warhol's *Black Bean Soup* (page 83) is slightly mis-registered. This too was intentional. Warhol created imperfections to make his images seem more individual. What about the tiny shape in lilac on *The Snail* (page 92)? Matisse had the shape of a snail cut out there to compare the size and shape of a real snail against his huge, colourful abstraction.

Drawing in the dark

Almost every suggestion in this book will adapt to any art, any material. Just as the artists have thought 'outside the box', so can you when analysing or responding to their work. Be flexible, change your focus if necessary, explore ideas, use your intuition, and try to approach everything without prejudice. For instance, here's a way of analysing a video:

- Even if you're in a darkened gallery, draw images while you're watching the video. Keep your pen or pencil on the page and sketch lines and shapes as you're looking at the film. Draw without looking down, keeping your eyes on the film.
- Note the name of the artist, title of the work and the date it was made.
- Make notes of any sounds, music or speech. Does this add anything to the work or your experience of it?
- Take notice of the atmosphere and when you're back in the light remember what it felt like. Then jot down adjectives to describe it.
- What do you notice about movement, rhythm and pace in the film?
- What is the work communicating? Does it relate to anything you've seen or are familiar with? Do you think the artist did this purposely? What evidence can you find for this?
- Does the work relate to or compare with any other works you have seen or studied? Which works and in what ways?
- When you're in a well-lit environment, make fresh notes and drawings based on your memories and using your drawings from the dark to prompt you.
- With any new or unusual media, follow a similar pattern of working and questioning: that is, try to respond to the media and process appropriately and immediately, and always note the artist's name, the title and the date of the work. Look out for shapes, nuances, sounds, textures – anything that makes the work unique.

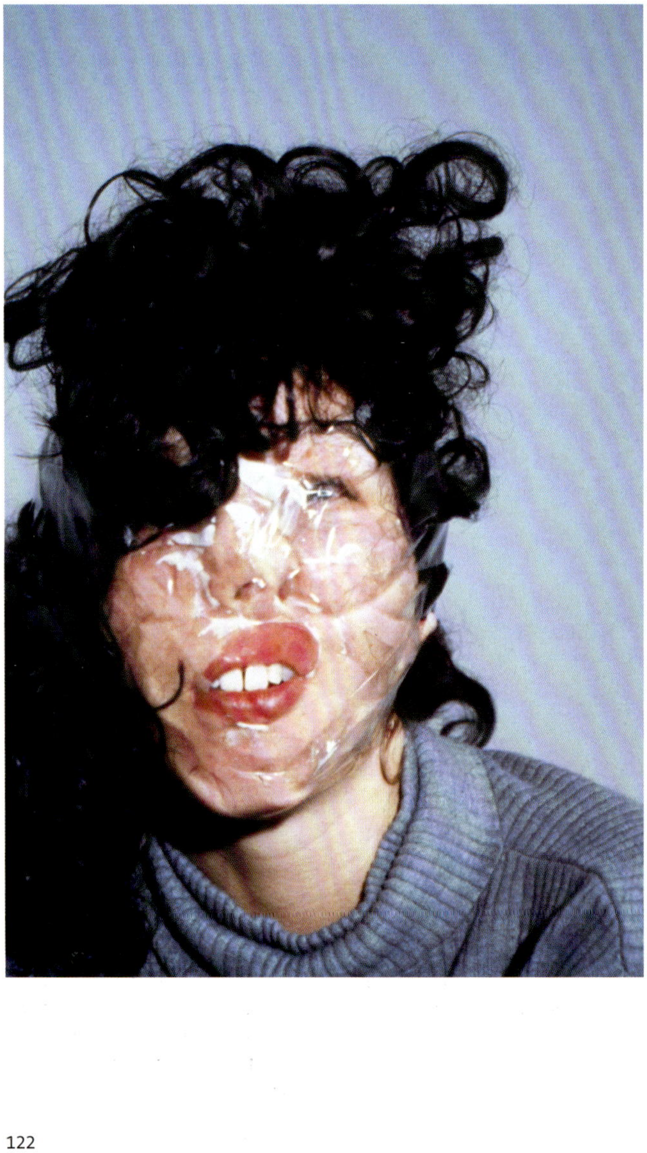

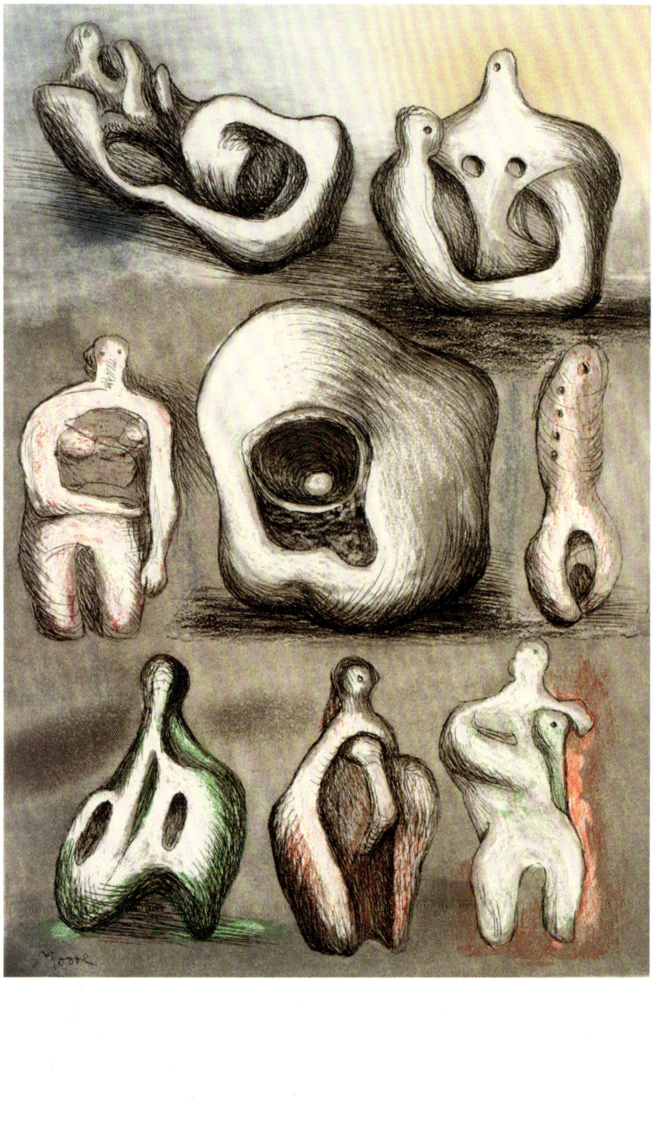

Generating your ideas

All the processes discussed so far will help you to generate your own ideas, as long as you keep questioning and remain positive. Focus by asking yourself:

- What am I trying to achieve?
- What am I trying to say?
- What exactly is the problem I am trying to solve?
- How can I exploit the artists' ideas in my own work?
- Where could this idea take me – what could I make of it?

Even if you feel uninspired, don't give up. Continue to make notes, mind maps, lists, drawings and annotations. Vary your style and approach and keep trying to understand why artists have worked as they have. If an idea comes to you, then build on it.

If, on the other hand, you don't feel inspired, then simply go back a step or two: look again at your mind maps, study another work of art by another artist in a relevant theme or subject, draw more. Explore new materials, take two unrelated ideas and put them together to create a new one. Then relax and give your subconscious time to work.

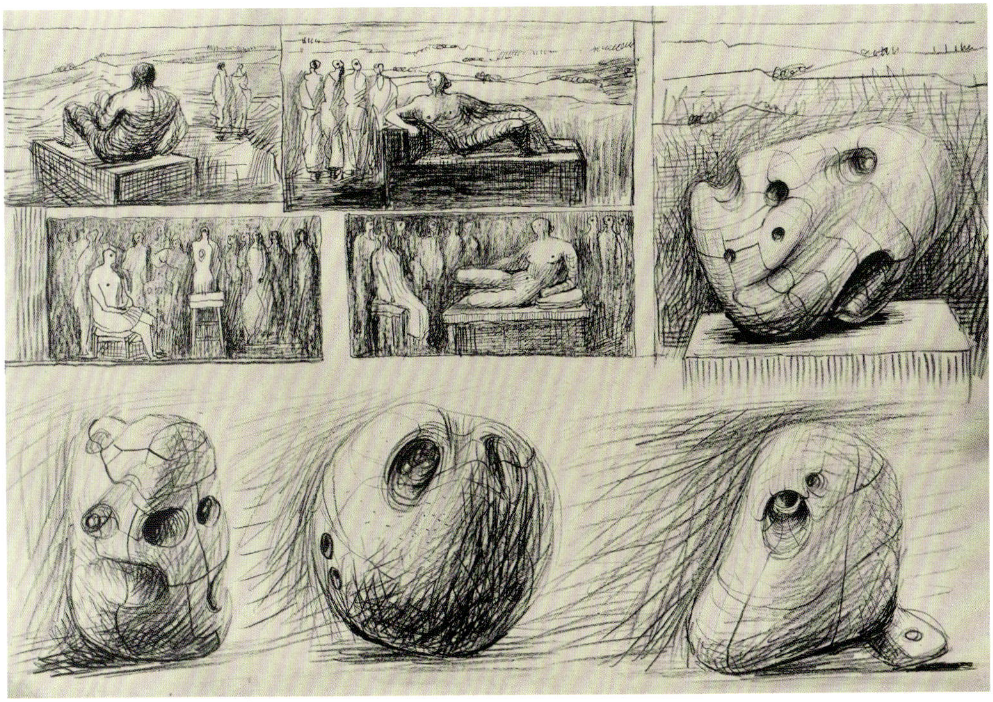

Gillian Wearing, *Confess All On Video. Don't Worry, You Will Be In Disguise. Intrigued? Call Gillian Version II* 1994, colour video for monitor with sound, 30 minutes, Tate
Responding to an advertisement in the London magazine *Time Out*, several people took up an offer by Wearing (born 1963) to make confessions on camera. She had been inspired to create this after seeing 'fly-on-the-wall' documentaries and confessional TV chat shows, but this video also seems like the religious ritual of confession or the medical process of psychoanalysis. The artist disguised her participants so that they felt anonymous and able to confess to things that they might never normally have admitted. Alternatively, they might have felt compelled to exaggerate or lie. Videos should be watched, like paintings or sculpture for example, for their content and the artist's ideas, processes and methods.

Henry Moore, *Eight Sculpture Ideas* 1980–1, etching on paper, 38 x 26, Tate
Looking at other artists' sketchbooks can be helpful in seeing idea-generation, especially when complete works can be seen to have emerged from the sketches. Here, Moore has drawn several almost complete forms, showing his working process.

Henry Moore, *Figures in Settings & Sculptural Ideas* 1949, lithograph on paper, 26 x 36.8, Tate
Compare any of these prints made by Moore in 1949 with his sculpture on page 9. Although that work was completed before these sketches were made, you can still see his thinking and planning methods. Moore made hundreds of sketches of ideas before producing his final works, keeping them all for the benefits the ideas gave him.

ART VOCABULARY

A

abstract art: art with no recognisable subject matter
Abstract Expressionism: abstract art movement of the 1940s and 1950s, in which paint was applied expressively
abstraction: distortion of things from the real world
aerial or atmospheric perspective: when colours and shapes blur and become bluish in the distance
aerial view: seen from above, a bird's eye view
allegory: a work of art with symbolic meanings
assemblage: a sculpture made of numerous elements
automatism: free association, a method first used by Sigmund Freud (1856–1939) to explore the subconscious mind
avant-garde: artists who pioneer new approaches and methods

B

Baroque: dramatic, dynamic style associated with the Catholic Counter-Reformation of the 17th century
Bauhaus: influential German school of art, architecture and design, operating from 1919 to 1933

C

chiaroscuro: dramatic contrasts of light and dark tones
Classical: form of cultural expression that reflects artistic styles of ancient Greece and Rome
collage: technique in which materials are glued to a surface
commission: fee paid to an artist to produce a work of art
complementary colours: opposites on the colour wheel, e.g. red and green, when placed together, appear to make each other brighter
composition: arrangement or layout of a work of art
concept: an idea or plan
Constructivism: early 20th-century Russian art movement based on the ideas that art should be constructed from geometric elements and modern materials
consumerism: shared social attitudes that place emphasis on buying things
contemporary: at that time, current
contrast: the amount of darkness or brightness between colours/tones
crop: to trim or cut something down to size (usually a picture)
cross-hatching: criss-cross lines to build up the look of texture and/or tone
Cubism: art movement started by Picasso and Braque, dismantling traditional methods of perspective in painting

D

Dada: movement founded in Zurich in 1915, opposing the political and cultural establishment
distorted: twisted or altered out of normal or original shape or proportion
Divisionism: the same as Pointillism (below)
dynamic: an appearance of movement

E

***en plein air*:** painting in the open air rather than in the studio
Expressionism: early 20th-century German art movement, emphasising the artists' emotions

F

Fauvism: from the nickname meaning 'wild beasts', a group of artists who produced vividly coloured and distorted paintings from 1905 to c.1908
figurative art: art concerned with representing figures and objects from life
focal point: where viewers' eyes are led first in a work of art; centre of interest
foreground: part of a picture that appears closest to viewers
foreshortening: distorting of objects in close-up because of perspective; usually dramatically shortened or enlarged
fresco: a method of painting directly onto a wall covered in damp, fresh plaster
Futurism: Italian art movement founded by Filippo Tommaso Marinetti (1876–1944) that glorified machines, speed and war

G

genre: this word has two meanings: a scene of everyday life (a genre painting); a type of painting (for example, portraiture)
gestural: expressive, loose style in painting or drawing
ground: surface on which the artist paints, usually coated with a primer

H

hatching: parallel lines to build up the look of tone or texture
highlight: brightest areas in paintings
hue: colour

I

icon: object of worship
impasto: thickly applied paint
Impressionism: a French art movement from c.1874 that aimed to capture natural effects of light, fleeting moments and modern life
installation: art created or assembled for a particular location, usually temporary and often huge
intensity: the brightness or strength of a colour

J

juxtaposition: objects or colours placed side by side

L

limited palette: restricted number of colours used by an artist
linear perspective: method of making 2D images look 3D
local colour: the actual colour of an object (for example, an orange is orange)

M

Mannerism: style of art from 1520s to early 1600s, often exaggerated or distorted
materialism: wanting wealth and material possessions, with little thought for moral or spiritual matters
matt: dull, not shiny
middle ground: area between the background and the foreground
Minimalism: art and design movement of the 1950s to 1980s, characterised by simplicity
mixed media: combination of materials in an artwork
Modernism: broad term for tendencies in 20th-century art and culture that broke with previous conventions
mural: usually large paintings on walls

N

narrative: a story told in detail; a representation of an event or story
negative space: the space around and between objects rather than the objects themselves
Neoclassicism: art of the 18th and early 19th centuries reflecting a

renewed interest in ancient Greek and Roman culture

O

opaque: not transparent
Orphism: deriving from Cubism, Fauvism and colour theory, this art movement focused on pure abstraction and bright colours

P

Palaeolithic: earliest known traces of human activity
patron: a wealthy or influential supporter of an artist
pigment: colours in paint
Pointillism: also known as Divisionism, a form of art created by Georges Seurat (1859–91), using only pure coloured dots
Pop art: art featuring objects from modern popular culture and mass media to draw attention to prevailing attitudes
Pre-Raphaelite Brotherhood: group of English painters, poets and critics, founded in 1848, who aimed to return to the 'honesty' of art styles before Raphael

R

readymade: the name given by Marcel Duchamp to a man-made object chosen by an artist to be exhibited as a work of art in its own right
Realism: mid-19th-century art movement that represented realities of life. Can also refer to lifelike art
recede: in art, to appear smaller in the distance
reflected colour: colour bouncing off another surface
relief: an image with a raised surface
Renaissance: 'rebirth', referring to the flowering of arts and intellectual culture from the 14th to the 16th centuries
representational art: the same as figurative art
Rococo: style of art, design and architecture that developed in the early 18th century as a reaction against the grandeur and strict regulations of the Baroque and featured ornate curves, soft colours, gold and asymmetry

S

screenprint: printing technique using a woven mesh, stencil, ink or paint and squeegee
scumble: thin layer of paint over the top of earlier paint to soften the effect
stable composition: still or balanced, also called static composition
stippling: building up colour or tone with dots
Suprematism: movement in Russian art, started in 1915, based on non-representational geometric forms
Surrealism: a movement that was started in the 1920s by a group of writers and artists in France seeking to release the creative potential of the unconscious mind, inspired by dreams, fantasies and irrationality
symbol: something that represents something else

T

tempera: any liquid or semi-liquid mixed with powdered pigment to bind it together to make paint; usually refers to egg tempera, which is egg mixed with powdered pigment
theosophy: a late-19th-century spiritual theory. Artists involved attempted to create art that had a higher purpose than merely representing nature
tint: colour with white added to it
translucent: semi-transparent
triptych: painting or relief on three panels

V

Vorticism: brief British art movement characterised by an angular, machine-inspired style

W

woodblock: type of print made by cutting away areas from a block of wood

CHECKLIST

Here's a reminder of some different methods of questioning you can use that will help you to understand art better and lead you into more critical and creative ways of thinking. The questions are just suggestions of the types of questions you should ask yourself. You might want to try them all, or you might prefer one approach over another, depending on the type of art you are looking at and your focus.

What you know already

- What is your first reaction to the work?
- What did you notice first? Do you recognise any elements?
- Does the work remind you of anything? What and why? Have you seen or experienced anything like this before? What, where and when?
- Does the work influence your mood? Describe why and how.
- Do you like or dislike the work? Why?
- Do you recognise the style? Have you seen other works that look similar? How does this compare?
- List distinctive characteristics of this work.
- Has the artist exploited new ideas or concepts? What are they and how has the artist done this?

Setting, size, subject, substance

Setting: where is the work displayed and what's around it?
Size: how big or small is it?
Subject: what is it about? What is its 'mood'?
Substance: what is it made of? Traditional materials or not? Is this relevant?

Formal / contextual questions

Formal questions:
What can you see?

- What is the work: a painting, sculpture, building or something else?
- Does it represent something from the real world or is it abstract?
- What is being portrayed?
- What is it made of? Why do you think the artist chose these materials?
- Describe some of the artist's processes and skills.
- Has the artist used colour and has it been used descriptively or emotionally? What effects does this create?
- How big is the work? Is this relevant?
- Describe the composition or structure.
- Has light been shown? Is it natural or artificial, and where is it coming from?
- Are different textures present, or are they illusions?
- How has the artist used space? Is perspective used accurately or not? What effect does this have?
- Has movement been portrayed, or does the work actually move? How have these effects been achieved?

Contextual questions:
What can you see?

- Who made the work? Find out about the background of the artist.
- For whom was the work made? Does this make a difference to the work? In what ways?
- When was the work made and where? Is it part of an art movement? If so, which one, and does it correspond with that movement's ideals?
- Was it made for a particular location? What difference does this make?
- How does the work link to other areas of life when it was made?
- What was the artist trying to say? Does the work convey a story or a message? Are there any underlying meanings? How has the artist portrayed this?
- How do people view the work today – is this different from how it was perceived when it was made?
- Does the work evoke a mood or atmosphere? What is this and why has it been conveyed? What evidence supports your interpretation?
- How original or innovative is the work for the time it was made? Why do you feel this?
- Was the artist deliberately trying to provoke viewers' responses and, if so, why and how?

Content, form, process, mood

Content
What is the work about? Did the artist observe the subject matter directly or is it imagined or remembered? Is the style realistic or not? What effect does this have? Are there any symbols in the work?

Form
How has the work been arranged? Are there combinations of shapes or patterns – what are these? Are colours used objectively or subjectively? What textures are in the work? Does it seem balanced?

Process
What materials and techniques has the artist used? Was this made in a studio or outside? Do you think the work was planned, made quickly or over time? Describe why you think this.

Mood
Does the work arouse your emotions? What's your impression of the work's 'mood'?

Who, what, where, when, why?

- Who produced the work / who commissioned it / who or what is the work about?
- What's happening / what is it made of / what does the title mean?
- When was it made?
- Where was it made?
- Why was it made?

General questioning

As well as all the above methods, you could simply list the following questions, which are an abbreviated version of some of the ideas put together:

- Personal responses – what do you bring to the artwork?
- Subject and meaning – what can you see? What is it about?
- Art in context – who made it? Why? When? Where? How? What with?

INDEX

Numbers in *italic* type refer to pages on which reproductions appear

A

Aboriginal art 91
Abstract Expressionism 102, 108, 115
abstraction 17, 20, 31, 98–109
Adams, Norman
  Christ's Cross and Adam's Tree 55
African art 92, 104
Alberti, Leon Battista
  Della Pittura 49, 56, 66, 67
allegory 30, 49, 81, 94, 114
anatomy 47, 53, 56–7, 58, 90, 95
Andre, Carl
  Steel Zinc Plain 5
animals 90–7
  bestiaries 94
  symbolism 92–3
Appel, Karel
  Questioning Children 15
Art Deco 22
Arte Povera 72, 80
Art Nouveau 22
assemblage 13, 26, 80, 89
Auerbach, Frank
  To the Studios 20, 117
automatism 114

B

Bacon, Francis
  Seated Figure 34, 44
Balla, Giacomo 105
  Abstract Speed, the Car has Passed 105
Barbizon School 65
Bauhaus 107, 115
bestiaries 94
Bierstadt, Albert 66
Blake, Peter
  Self-portrait with Badges 36
Blake, William 59
  Pity 7
  The Tyger 93
Blanche, Jacques-Emile 115
  Ludgate Circus 117
Blast magazine 119
Bloomsbury Group 79
Boccioni, Umberto 105
bodegón 76–7
Bomberg, David 20
  In the Hold 115, 117
Bonington, Richard Parkes
  View of the Piazzetta... 68
Botticelli, Sandro 38
Bramley, Frank
  A Hopeless Dawn 6
Braques, Georges 43, 79, 80, 88, 107
  Glass on a Table 81
Brown, Ford Madox
  Mauvais Sujet (*The Writing Lesson*) *11*
Brunelleschi, Filippo 66
Buzan, Tony 26

C

Calder, Alexander 111
camera obscura 67
Canaletto 63, 115
  A View of Greenwich from the River 61
Caravaggio 38
Carracci, Annibale 58
cave and rock art 48, 91
Celtic art 91, 104
Cézanne, Paul 75, 78, 79, 80, 88, 107, 117, 118
  Still Life with Water Jug 77
Chagall, Marc 101
Chardin, Jean-Baptiste-Siméon 88
Chermayeff, Serge 9
Chinese painting 30, 62
Chirico, Giorgio de
  The Uncertainty of the Poet 114, 117
Church, Frederic Edwin 66
Clatworthy, Robert
  Bull 96
Claude Lorrain 69
Cole, Thomas 66
collage 26, 80, 92
Collier, Edward
  Still Life 74
Collins, Charles Allston
  May, in the Regent's Park 69
colour 10, 14, 42, 44
  abstract art 109
  aerial (atmospheric) perspective 67
Colour Field abstraction 108
Conceptualism 80
Constable, John 64, 70, 121
  Flatford Mill (*Scene on a Navigable River*) *63*
  The Hay Wain 64
  Sketch for Hadleigh Castle 62
Constructivism 101, 105, 107, 115
contextualism 13, 16–17
  compositional 51
Copley, John Singleton
  The Death of Major Peirson... 46
Cornell, Joseph 89
Cragg, Tony
  Britain Seen from the North 26
Cubism 6, *8*, 31, 38, 43, 78, 102, 105, 119
  Cubist constructions 89
  still life 79, 80

D

Dada 115
Dalí, Salvador
  Metamorphosis of Narcissus 112, 115
Dante Alighieri
  Divine Comedy 57
De Bono, Edward 25
Degas, Edgar 29, 58
  Horse Clearing an Obstacle 97
  Little Dancer Aged Fourteen 56
  Woman in a Tub 24
de Kooning, Willem 108
  Women Singing II 108
Delacroix, Eugène 63
Delaunay, Robert 80, 105, 115
  Study for the City 118
  Windows Open Simultaneously 106
Derain, André 101
  The Pool of London 13
De Stijl 80, 106, 107, 115
De Wint, Peter
  River Scene at Sunset 67
Dickens, Charles 47
Doesburg, Theo van 106
  Countercomposition 107
Duchamp, Marcel 89
  Fountain 80, 102, *103*, 115
Durand-Ruel, Paul 79
Dürer, Albrecht 40, 67
  landscape sketches 62
Dutch School 4, 30, 62, 63, 67, 73
  still life painting 74, 75, 76–7

E

Earth art 72
Eastlake, Charles Locke
  Christ Lamenting over Jerusalem 54
Egyptian art 48, 91, 92, 95, 104
Eliasson, Olafur
  The Weather Project 69, *71*
Environmental art 65, 72
Epstein, Jacob
  Torso in Metal from the Rock Drill 58, 59
Expressionism 59, 115

F

Fantin-Latour, Henri
  A Still Life with Apples 75
Farquharson, Joseph
  The Joyless Winter Day 95
Fauvism 13, 102
fête galante 63
figurative art 53, 99
figures 46–59
  anatomy 47, 53, 56–7, 58
  history painting 30, 46–50
  ideal proportions 56
  narrative works 46–51
  nudes 50, 52–3, 56
  realism 55, 58
  religious imagery 47, 48, 49, 54–5
film, analysing 122
First World War 58, 65, 80, 103, 105
Fluxus 80
Ford, Laura
  Moose 97
formalism 13–15
found objects 80, 89, 95, 103
Franco, General Francisco 42
Friedrich, Caspar David 63
Frith, William Powell
  The Derby Day 48
Futurism 65, 78, 105, 115, 119

G

Gabo, Naum 101, 107
  Head No 2 104
Gauguin, Paul 19, 59, 101
  Harvest, Le Pouldu 102
genre painting 30
Gestural abstraction 108
Ghiberti, Lorenzo
  I Commentarii 56
Giacometti, Alberto 58
Giotto 62
Goldsworthy, Andy 72
Gonzalez, Julio
  Maternity 12
Grand Tour 63
Granges, David des
  The Saltonstall Family 45
Grant, Duncan 88
  Still Life with Carrots 79
Greek art 30, 48, 52, 62
Gris, Juan 80
Guernica 42

H

Hardaker, Charles
  Still Life: Vertical Structures... 87
Highmore, Joseph
  ... Anatomical Studies 53
Hilliard, Nicholas
  Queen Elizabeth I (attributed) *32*
Hirst, Damien 91
  Life without You 89
history painting 30, 46–50, 78
Hockney, David
  My Parents 44
Hoyland, John
  North Sound 16
Hudson River School 66
Hunt, William Holman
  Our English Coasts (*The Strayed Sheep*) *94*

I

Impressionism 6, 65, 69, 73, 76, 79, 100, 102, 115

J

Japanese art 72, 92
John, Augustus 29
John, Gwen
  Nude Girl 52

K

Kahlo, Frida 40
  The Broken Column 59
Kahnweiler, Daniel-Henry 79
Kandinsky, Wassily 99, 100, 101, 104, 107
  Cossacks 98
  Swinging 99
Kossoff, Leon 20
kouros 52

L

Land art 72
landscapes 30, 60–73, 78
  Barbizon School 65
  Dutch School 63, 73
  effects of light 63, 69
  fête galante 63
  mood and atmosphere 69, 71
  perspective 66–7
  plein air 63, 64–5, 67, 69, 95
  skies 70
  trompe-l'oeil 81
  urban 73
  water 70
Landseer, Sir Edwin 95
  Dignity and Impudence 91
  Trafalgar Square lions 95

INDEX

Léger, Fernand 80, 105
Still Life with a Beer Mug *80*, 117
Leighton, Frederic, Lord 52
The Bath of Psyche *50*
Leonardo da Vinci 27, 53, 57, 67
landscape sketches 62
Mona Lisa 30
Vitruvian Man 56
Leverett, David
Lost Messages *110*, 114
Lewis, Wyndham 115
Composition *119*
life drawing 52–3
Lipchitz, Jacques
Sculpture *31*
Lissitzky, El 107
Long, Richard 72
A Hundred Mile Walk *65*, 116
Loutherbourg, Philip de 17
Lowry, L.S.
Industrial Landscape *64*, 115
Lucas, Sarah
Self-portrait with Fried Eggs *33*, 56
Luini, Bernadino 38

M
Maar, Dora 42
McEvoy, Ambrose
The Ear-Ring *28*
Mackintosh, Charles Rennie
Fetges *22*
Malevich, Kazimir 100, 107
Dynamic Suprematism *101*, 115
Manet, Edouard 88
Le Déjeuner sur l'Herbe 53
Olympia 53
Marc, Franz 91
Marini, Marino
Horseman *96*
Martin, John
The Great Day of His Wrath *112*, 114
The Last Judgement 114
The Plains of Heaven 114
Matisse, Henri 47, 79, 88, 101
Draped Nude *52*
The Snail *92*, 121
Michelangelo Buonarroti 53, 58
Millais, John Everett
Christ in the House of His Parents *46*
mind maps 23, 25–7
Minimalism 72
Miró, Joan
Message from a Friend *110*, 114
Moholy-Nagy, László 107
Mondrian, Piet 100, 106, 120
Composition with Yellow, Blue and Red *100*
Monet, Claude 13, 69, 70, 78, 79
Moore, Henry
Figures in Settings and Sculptural Ideas *123*
Recumbent Figure *9*
Sculptural Ideas *122*
Morandi, Giorgio 82, 88
Still Life *78*
Munch, Edvard 59, 101

Muybridge, Eadweard 97

N
narrative paintings 46–51, 99
Nash, Paul 88
Totes Meer 71, *73*, 115
Native American totem poles 91
Neoplasticism 106
Newlyn School 6
Nicholson, Ben
1935 (white relief) *120*
nudes 52–3, 56
acceptability 50

O
odalisques 52
Ofili, Chris 56
Op art 115
Orpen, William 29
Orphism 107

P
papiers découpés 92
Pasmore, Victor 88
perspective 15, 18, 20, 31, 66–7
aerial (atmospheric) 66, 67
linear 66–7
photography 44, 48, 100, 104
Physiologus 94
Picasso, Pablo 33, 79, 80, 110
Baboon and Young 95
Guernica 42
Seated Nude *8*
Still Life *88*
Still Life with Chair Caning 80
Weeping Woman 42–3, *43*, 59, 115
Pissarro, Camille
Self-portrait *40*
Plato 86, 100
plein air 63, 64–5, 67, 69, 95
Pollaiuolo, Antonio 56–7
Pollock, Jackson 108
Yellow Islands *109*
Pop art 36, 80, 82–5, 115
Porphyry of Tyros 26
portraiture 30, 32–45
and identity 36–7
animal 90–1
comparing 38–9, 40
expanding creativity through 44
family 44–5
self-portraits 33–41
symbolism 33, 36, 42, 44
Post-Impressionism 65, 79, 80
Pound, Ezra 119
Pre-Raphaelites 54, 69, 94
Purism 80

R
Raphael 6, 58
readymades 80, 103
realism 42, 55, 58, 77
Pre-Raphaelites 94
Rego, Paula
The Dance *51*, 116
religious imagery 47, 48, 49, 54–5
Adam and Eve 52
symbolism 54, 92–3

Rembrandt van Rijn 38, 40
Renaissance 48, 68
Renoir, Pierre-Auguste 78, 79, 91
Peaches and Almonds *76*
Riley, Bridget 61
Fall *114*, 117
Rococo 48
Rodin, Auguste 58
The Kiss *57*
Roman art 30, *30*, 48, 67, 75
Romanticism 30, 63, 66, 70
Rossetti, Dante Gabriel 54
Rothko, Mark 108
Light Red over Black *10*
Rousseau, Henri 95
Rubens, Peter Paul 52
Ruskin, John 54
Russian Revolution 101, 105, 107

S
Schiele, Egon 52
School of London 20
Schwitters, Kurt 89
screenprinting 83, 84, 110
Second World War 73, 85, 96
self-portraits 33–41
Severini, Gino
Suburban Train Arriving in Paris *65*
Shakespeare, William
Macbeth 6
Sherman, Cindy 56
Untitled, Bus Riders *59*
Siberechts, Jan
Landscape with Rainbow, Henley-on-Thames *60*
Sickert, Walter 29
Signac, Paul 101
Smithson, Robert 72
Soutine, Chaim 88
space 15
negative and positive 15, 42, 68
spatial depth 69
see also perspective
Spain 76
Spanish Civil War 42
Spencer, Stanley
Self-Portrait (1914) *38*
Self-Portrait (1959) *39*
Still, Clyfford 108
still life 30, 74–89
bodegón 76–7
content, style and context 86
memento mori 76
realism 77
symbolism 74, 81, 86, 88
trompe-l'oeil 81
vanitas 76–7, 81, 114
Stokes, Adrian
Still Life *86*
Stubbs, George
The Anatomy of the Horse 90
Mares and Foals in a River Landscape *90*
Suprematism 101, 115
Swan, John Macallan
Head and Forepart of a Tiger *93*
symbolism 16, 51, 54, 120
animals in art 92–3
portraiture 33, 36, 42, 44

religious 54, 92–3
still life 74, 81, 86, 88
synaesthesia 104

T
Taslitzky, Boris
Riposte 115, *116*
Theosophy 101, 104
Thoreau, David Henry 9
Titian 52
trompe-l'oeil 81
Turner, Joseph Mallord William 64, 69, 70, 86
Fishermen at Sea *17*
influence 4
Moonlight, a Study at Millbank *4*, 116
Norham Castle, Sunrise *66*
The Shipwreck *70*
Snow Storm – Steam-Boat off a Harbour's Mouth... *18*, 19

V
van Gogh, Vincent 40, 59
vanitas 76–7, 81, 114
Vasari, Giorgio
Lives... 56–7
Velázquez, Diego
The Rokeby Venus 20
verdaccio 55
video, analysing 122, 123
viewfinder 22, 24
visual thinking 19–26
Vitruvius
De Architectura 56
Vorticism 105, 115, 119

W
Warhol, Andy 82, 89, 121
Black Bean Soup *83*
Brillo Boxes 82, *84*
watercolour 22, 54, 64
Waterford, Louisa Anne, Marchioness of
Christ Raising the Dead *54*
Watteau, Jean-Antoine
fête galante *63*
Watts, George Frederic
Self-portrait *41*
Wearing, Gillian
Confess All On Video *122*
Weschke, Karl
Tiger, Tiger *93*
Whistler, James McNeill 29, 104
Nocturne: Blue and Silver – Chelsea 71, *72*
Wright of Derby, Joseph
An Iron Forge *49*
Wyn Evans, Cerith
Inverse Reverse Perverse *113*, 114–15

Y
Yanagi, Yukinori
Pacific *14*